Penguin Books

IDENTITY LESSONS

Maria Mazziotti Gillan is the founder and director of the Poetry Center at Passaic County Community College in Paterson, New Jersey, editor of the *Paterson Literary Review*, and co-editor of the acclaimed anthology *Unsettling America: An Anthology of Contemporary Multicultural Poetry* (Penguin, 1994). She has won numerous awards for her work, including the May Sarton Award, the 1998 National Public Radio *Poet and the Poem* Award for Literary Excellence, and two New Jersey State Council on the Arts fellowships, and was a finalist in the PEN Syndicated Fiction competition. She is also the author of seven books of poetry, including *The Weather of Old Seasons*, *Where I Come From: Selected and New Poems*, and her latest book, *Things My Mother Told Me*. She has had several poems published in the *New York Times*, the *Christian Science Monitor*, and *Poetry Ireland*. She has appeared on National Public Radio's *All Things Considered*, Leonard Lopate's *Books and Co.*, and Garrison Keillor's *Writer's Almanac*.

Jennifer Gillan is an assistant professor at Bentley College in the Boston area. With Maria Mazziotti Gillan, she edited *Unsettling America: An Anthology of Contemporary Multicultural Poetry*. She has authored several book reviews and academic articles, including "Reservation Home Movies: Sherman Alexie's Poetry," which appeared in *American Literature*, and "The Hazards of Osage Fortunes," published in *Arizona Quarterly*. She is at work on a book, *Ambivalent Ancestries: Critical Perspectives on Chivalry, Rescue, and the Wild West*.

D0047148

IDENTITY LESSONS

Contemporary Writing
About Learning to Be American

EDITED BY MARIA MAZZIOTTI GILLAN

AND JENNIFER GILLAN

Penguin Books

PENGUIN BOOKS
Published by the Penguin Group
Penguin Putnam Inc., 375 Hudson Street,
New York, New York 10014, U.S.A.
Penguin Books Ltd, 27 Wrights Lane, London W8 5TZ, England
Penguin Books Australia Ltd, Ringwood, Victoria Australia
Penguin Books Canada Ltd, 10 Alcorn Avenue
Toronto, Ontario, Canada M4V 3B2
Penguin Books (N.Z.) Ltd, 182–190 Wairau Road,
Auckland 10, New Zealand

Penguin Books Ltd, Registered Offices:
Harmondsworth, Middlesex, England

First published in Penguin Books 1999

3   5   7   9   10   8   6   4   2

LIBRARY OF CONGRESS CATALOGING IN PUBLICATION DATA
Identity lessons : contemporary writing about learning to be American
/ edited by Maria Mazziotti Gillan and Jennifer Gillan.
p.   cm.
ISBN 0 14 02.7167 8
1. American literature—minority authors.   2. National
characteristics, American—Literary collections.   3. Ethnic groups—
United States—Literary collections.   4. Group identity—United
States—Literary collections.   5. Immigrants—United States—
Literary collections.   6. American literature—20th century.
I. Gillan, Maria M.   II. Gillan, Jennifer.
PS508.M54I24   1999
810.8'0920693—dc21   98-28816

Printed in the United States of America
Set in Granjon
Designed by Betty Lew

Dedicated to
Alfred Weiss, Eastside High School
Joan Ozark Holmer, Georgetown University
Susan Lanser, Georgetown University
Richard Adinaro, Seton Hall University

Teachers who taught us to believe in ourselves

Contents ∿

III. CALLING ROLL

IV. PLEDGING ALLEGIANCE

V. SCHOOL DAZE

VI. LEARNING BY ROTE

VII. OUR BODIES, OURSELVES

VIII. BEYOND DICK AND JANE

Introduction ∿

From early childhood, we learn to measure our own lives against a battery of models provided by friends, schools, advertisements, movies, and television shows. These comparisons are often painful because they encourage us to see ourselves as different; they can even affect the way we look at our bodies, our families, our cultures, and our future roles as adults. What we take from these identity lessons may be the desire for a common name or a television family. More generally, however, these lessons encourage new allegiances—allegiances that teach us to value the Hollywood version of America over our own unique families and cultures.

Despite the rich diversity of the United States, the American educational system has often taught conformity and assimilation along with history and geography. Toni Morrison was one of the first novelists to illustrate the conformity implied by the limiting family tableaus depicted in the *Dick and Jane* grade school primers. It is access to this middle-class Dick-and-Jane world that Maria Mazziotti Gillian's speaker in "Daddy, We Called You" craves, as represented by a *Father Knows Best* father and a house filled with space and silence. Many of the other writers included in this collection reveal similar agonizing attempts at transforming their own awkward families and bodies into typically American ones. At the same time, the poems and stories included in *Identity Lessons* are a testament to the way that we can create art out of our differences. Filled with characters who display a tenacity for holding on to their own cultural practices despite the ever-encroaching assembly-line culture of frozen dinners and TV sitcoms, this anthology is about learning to see difference as a positive and enriching aspect of American life.

The creative work in *Identity Lessons* reflects the increasing diversity of American styles, American families, and American cultures. By including both new and familiar voices that represent a spectrum of American identities, *Identity Lessons* attempts to expand the definition of America itself. We have tried to choose work that is immediate and accessible and that deals with topics and concerns about identity that many Americans have confronted.

This anthology began as a collection of school experiences, but we soon realized that those experiences are framed by the early education we receive in the family and by the lessons we learn in the boardrooms, living rooms, and movie houses of the United States. The book opens, therefore, with the issue of origins in "Family Primer I" and turns, more specifically, to parent-child relationships in "Family Primer II." Part three, "Calling Roll," considers the ways people are categorized by the genetic and cultural traces inscribed on their bodies. Whereas the selections in part three are about the categorizing of others by appearances and assumptions, those in part four, "Pledging Allegiance," are about the ways we feel pressured into choosing sides. "School Daze" emphasizes how education can open our minds to new experiences and new ways of thinking, and introduce us to lifelong friends and inspiring role models. "Learning by Rote," on the other hand, considers the way education is sometimes limiting, by asking us to subscribe to generic formulas and, often, punishing nonconformity. Part seven, "Our Bodies, Ourselves," considers the lessons we learn about our expected gender roles. Finally, the poems and stories in part eight, "Beyond Dick and Jane," attempt to unsettle restrictive conceptions of personal and national identity. This section returns us to the first one because it suggests that understanding one's place in American culture comes only after a careful reading of one's "family primer."

Most basic to our identities is our sense of origins. From the beginnings of the United States, Americans have been honing their skill for inventing origins and for shedding the past. At the same time, other Americans such as Nathaniel Hawthorne and Abraham Lincoln have cautioned their fellow citizens about the necessity of coming to terms with the past. Tension between the desire to forget the past and the need to remember surfaces in personal and national identity crises. As Walt Whitman claimed, "What is any nation after all—and what is a human being—but a struggle between conflicting, paradoxical, opposing elements."

That personal and national histories are intimately linked is evidenced by T. H. S. Wallace's "Magnalia Christi Americana," a poem about the continuing impact of his Puritan predecessors four generations after their deaths. Trying to come to terms with the deep-seated fictions stemming from his Puritan ancestry, the speaker declares,

We are his people.
We pleasure in industry,

are diligent even in leisure.
Vigilant at rest, we work
even as we dream

The Puritan patriarch in the poem is the prototype of the American ancestor, the figure of the hardworking American man against which future generations have measured themselves. Struggling with the potency of The Father as American icon and grappling with the legacy of his own father's secretiveness and reticence, the narrator of Stephen Dunn's "Legacy" confesses,

I carry silence with me
the way others carry snapshots
of loved ones. I offer it
and wait for a response.

It is against the fetish of the posed family photograph that the speaker in Vivian Shipley's "The Word You Did Not Speak" measures her family. After trying ineffectually to contain her relationship with her mother in a conventional frame, she recognizes the futility of this whitewashing of the past:

Praise you didn't give me wasn't in you
like helium that seeped from birthday balloons
No amount of searching will fill
pages of the past, the space inside me
where the word love should have been

The woman bravely breaks the code of family silence and speaks about the carefully positioned poses families offer to the world as evidence of their harmony. The conspicuous display of these nostalgic family tableaus can be part of an attempt to contain family discord and escape one's chaotic history. This tendency to validate the present by creating idealized images of a stable, nuclear family past has been the source of psychological damage for those whose families could not measure up to the ideal. In "Those Were the Days," Philip Levine fantasizes about the perfect family history:

The sun came up before breakfast,
perfectly round and yellow, and we
dressed in the soft light and shook out
our long blond curls and waited

*for Maid to brush them flat and place
the part just where it belonged.*

Levine portrays a typical childhood fantasy of trading in an ordinary life for one of fabulous privilege. Because of the popularity of this desire for storybook origins, many family primers have remained closed books. Braving the musty vaults of buried family histories, the speaker in Sharon Olds's "I Go Back to May 1937" imagines going back in time to stop her parents from marrying in order to spare them all from the aftershocks of that choice. Because this would mean the erasure of her existence, she cannot go through with it. Instead, she envisions clutching her parents as if they were "paper dolls," banging them together "at the hips like chips of flint as if to / strike sparks from them," and admonishing them, "Do what you are going to do, and I will tell about it."

Comprehending the meaning of these familial "Alliances so deep and dark and sore," as Hayden Carruth phrases it, is never easy. But for those writers who hold on to intergenerational connections like lifelines, family relationships prove to be the foundation upon which they build their adult lives. The speaker in Sonia Sanchez's "Dear Mama" describes the Saturday afternoons of her childhood spent listening to the women gathered in her mother's living room as they teased out the frayed ends of their lives. She recalls feeling the intensity of each breath and tasting the deliciousness of their laughter, learning all the while how to be a black woman in America: "And history began once again. I received it and let it circulate in my blood. I learned on those Saturday afternoons about women rooted in themselves, raising themselves in dark America, discharging their pain without ever stopping."

Like Sanchez, Lucille Clifton and Ruth Stone do not simply replace the patriarchal icon with a matriarchal one; they envision their female ancestors not as omnipotent matriarchs but rather as supportive sisters from a long line of dazzling strong women. Strength is the focus of "Shelling Shrimp," Lê Thi Diem Thúy's poem about how seemingly ordinary acts can serve as life lessons about patience and love. Yet, it may be only in adulthood that we come to appreciate what our parents and grandparents teach us. It is not until long after college graduation that the speaker in Leroy V. Quintana's "Sangre 24" realizes that his grandfather's explanation of planting corn and praying to the four directions was the most meaningful schooling of his life. Quintana recognizes that it is only by dusting off those family scrapbooks and reading the lessons inscribed within that we can start to build foundations for the future.

Although tracing family lineage can broaden an individual's understanding of himself or herself, strangers often base their judgments about who we are on appearances—reading the traces of race, culture, or religion they see written upon us and affixing an appropriate label. As Maxine Kumin claims, "the names that we go by are nothing / compared to the names we are called." Kumin writes in "The Riddle of Noah" about a boy named Noah who wishes that he could have a more ordinary name like all the Justins and Carolines in his first-grade class. Exploring the issue of naming and its effects on our sense of identity, she guesses that Noah's quest for "suitability" originated in the comments of teachers or images from television. The idea that taking on new names will give us new identities is also considered in Joseph Bruchac's "Baptism." Referring to the Native American rituals of naming and renaming people during the different stages of their lives, Bruchac comments on the process of trying to embody the names we are given:

> *Believing that people*
> *were or became*
> *what they were named,*
> *they rose with the Sun,*
> *called themselves Eagle,*
> *Fox, Otter, Hawk, Wolf,*

The poem suggests the excitement and possibility of taking new names with each rising of the sun, "names which we have not yet heard, / names about to be spoken."

Of course, the ways in which we choose to name ourselves often do not correspond with the names and categories under which others try to group us. Even more confusing is the often necessary process of shuttling between identities in order to maintain one's multiple cultural allegiances. In "Mestizo," Alfred Encarnacion describes how the "fierce dichotomy" of the mestizo identity can feel like a severing of the self into two. Feeling the pull of both his white and Filipino heritage, the narrator sees himself as simultaneously "defeater and invader." With his description of his "flags sovereign and imperiled," Encarnacion broadens his analysis of personal identity to include national identity. These references to the pressure of choosing sides are echoed in Abraham Rodriguez Jr.'s "The Boy Without a Flag," a story about a Puerto Rican boy who is suspended for refusing to salute the American flag. The boy assumes his father, who talks revolution in their apartment kitchen, will support him, but the father, torn by his own multiple allegiances, chastises the boy for jeopardizing his education. Needless to say, the boy is very confused by the mixed messages he receives. The story uncovers the ambivalence that accompanies taking sides. On the one hand, we crave acceptance by the larger American community represented by the school or the flag; on the other, we feel loyal to our homes and families. We are caught in the classic American dilemma—do we leave our baggage on the other side, cross over, and never look back, or do we take it with us, and try to negotiate the difficult passage weighed down as much with the burdens as with the riches that we brought with us from our previous lives?

This straddling of two worlds is not always negative, especially when it is part of the panoramic world-traveling we can undertake in the process of our formal educations. Education can be a scary, painful, enlightening, or enriching process. For one thing, it introduces us to worlds beyond our own insular neighborhoods and family circles. It allows us to experience constellations of knowledge to which we would have no other access. This education can open our minds to how others think and feel. In addition to these lessons in empathy, schooling can also introduce us to people who would otherwise be outside our line of vision. These people can teach us to think beyond the often stifling confines of normalcy and to value eccentricity. Head, the hero in Sean Thomas Dougherty's poem, wears his Afro in defiance of changing styles, his hair "a graceful dance / Of follicles in the face / Of every hair-weave, plait, / Or braid the decades have to offer." He revels in the freedom of his otherness

A dangerous freedom can also result from agreeing to take our places in the class roster of roles: a freedom like that of Dona Luongo Stein's teenage narrator, who finds herself living up to her bad reputation; or that of Sterling Williams, the subject of David Chin's poem, who is so good at being the bad kid that he becomes "condemned to act out for the class." Embodying these roles can become second nature, as Stephen Dunn suggests in his poem "The Substitute," in which a young girl who puts on a new identity for a substitute teacher becomes trapped by the part she plays. Also concerned with these alternate identities, Tobias Wolff's "The Liar" is about a boy who makes up exaggerated stories about his family, claiming that they were missionaries captured by Communists or that his mother is a tragic heroine dying of consumption.

The story demonstrates our imaginative attempts to bridge the gap between our actual heritage and the more exciting one that we learn to desire as we travel through the romantic worlds of the books we read.

The personas that Wolff's boy adopts separate him from the person he actually is at home. This phenomenon has been written about by Richard Rodriguez in another context. In his memoir, *The Achievement of Desire*, Rodriguez explained how going to school was like crossing over the border into another country. Separated from the world of his immigrant parents, he began to see their lifestyle as "starkly opposed to that of the classroom." At first he balanced "allegiance," but soon discerned that he had to let go of his emotional attachment to his family and their intuitive ways of understanding the world if he wanted to succeed in academic terms. Rodriguez quickly comprehended that his success would be measured by the number of books he could consume, by the praise he would receive from teachers as he successfully parrots what they teach him.

Familiar with the process of rote learning, most children learn to memorize rules without questioning them, often even absorbing information without actually understanding it. They learn from what Peter Cooley calls the "priestesses of wisdom" lessons of "obedience, / silence and devotion to their measured tones." Obedience and atonement are the lessons the nuns teach the children in Len Roberts's poem, "The Way of the Cross." Enacting the lesson that all people must learn to bear life's crosses, Roberts describes

> twenty-two eleven-year-olds lifting heavy crosses
> of air onto our shoulders
> balancing them there as we staggered around
> the empty seats . . .

Roberts's poem details how we sometimes stagger under the burden of our teachers' assumptions about us. Literary critics such as Fred Gardaphe have theorized that ethnic Americans often carry an additional burden because their experiences and communities are often not represented in typical school curricula. Gardaphe recalls in the introduction to his critical study, *Italian Signs / American Streets*, how his instructors viewed his attempts to insert American writers of Italian heritage into his course papers as "breaking and entering" that deserved reprimand. In contrast, Gary Soto describes in his poem "Teaching English from an Old Composition Book" a teacher who tries to dismantle this learning model and interact with his students, guiding them and encouraging them to see their education as a process of discovering more about themselves.

While classrooms are focused on the process of intellectual discovery, students are often engaged outside the classroom in other kinds of experimentation. School hallways and locker rooms are often the sites of an adolescent's introduction to sex education. As Margie Norris claims, "sex was on the sneak in 1964." Encouraged to think about our bodies in secretive and shrouded ways (or, more often, to not think about them at all), many of us left school completely uneducated about the most intimate aspects of our lives. Thus it is not surprising that those whisperings in the school hallways have been the source of much of the misinformation that we carry into our adulthood. The title and refrain of Allen Ginsberg's poem " 'You know what I'm saying?' " illustrates the veiled ways in which sexuality is often discussed. The lack of information leads to misunderstanding, pain, and often entrenchment of negative body stereotypes.

Exemplifying how our bodies bear the brunt of our painful relationships, the acupuncturist in Len Roberts's poem "Acupuncture and Cleansing at Forty-eight" claims, "the body is nothing but a map of the heart." His diagnosis is that all of his disappointments in life are lodged in different parts of his body; he recommends, therefore, that his patient needs to cleanse himself of all of these disappointments and setbacks. Roberts suggests that in order to release the tensions brought on by our attempt to live up to ideals, we need to find those pressure points—all the negative energy generated by storybooks, family scrapbooks, grade school primers, novels, films, and TV shows, the toxic energy that we keep stored in our bodies. The act of writing the poem, Roberts implies, is his way of cleansing himself.

Building on this image of the healing power of poetry, Joe E. Weil calls for "language to leech" the soul-poisoning monotony of dead-end jobs "from the blood." Celebrating such curative poetry, Diane di Prima is pleased that writers and revolutionaries have always found solace at City Lights, the bookshop that is the subject of her poem of the same name. She expresses her thanks that there is still a place for those who are straining to hear those rhythms barely audible over the canned music at the Megabookshop, that there is still a refuge for those who are "hunting for voices from all quarters / of the globe." Listening to the strains of her own ancestral music, the girl in Edwidge Danticat's *Krick? Krack!* tells the story of the women in her family who kept their heads down: "They were singing, searching for meaning in the dust." They were waiting for a girl to be born who would tell their stories: "These women, they asked for your voice so they could tell your mother in your place that yes, women like you do speak, even if they speak in a tongue that is hard to understand. Even if it's patois, dialect, Creole."

It is only by learning all of the vernaculars that are the offshoots of the language of American identity that we can move beyond the limited vision and vocabulary of the *Dick and Jane* primers. By creating characters who reclaim their own difference and speakers who try to articulate the impact of American identity lessons on their lives, the writers in this anthology envision other educational possibilities and explore the potential for different kinds of inter- as well as intra-cultural communication in the United States. In the process, they help their readers understand what the narrator of Gary Soto's story "Like Mexicans" means when he meets a friend's family and marvels, "Her people were like Mexicans, only different."

Jennifer Gillan
Cambridge, Massachusetts

I. ~

FAMILY PRIMER I

In fourteen hundred and ninety-two,

Columbus sailed the ocean blue

Names

My grandmother's name was Nora Swan.
Old Aden Swan was her father. But who was her mother?
I don't know my great-grandmother's name.
I don't know how many children she bore.
Like rings of a tree the years of woman's fertility.
Who were my great-aunt Swans?
For every year a child; diphtheria, dropsy, typhoid.
Who can bother naming all those women churning butter,
leaning on scrub boards, holding to iron bedposts,
sweating in labor? My grandmother knew the names
of all the plants on the mountain. Those were the names
she spoke of to me. Sorrel, lamb's ear, spleenwort, heal-all;
never go hungry, she said, when you can gather a pot of greens.
She had a finely drawn head under a smooth cap of hair
pulled back to a bun. Her deep-set eyes were quick to notice
in love and anger. Who are the women who nurtured her for me?
Who handed her in swaddling flannel to my great-grandmother's
   breast?
Who are the women who brought my great-grandmother tea
and straightened her bed? As anemone in midsummer, the air
cannot find them and grandmother's been at rest for forty years.
In me are all the names I can remember—pennyroyal, boneset,
bedstraw, toadflax—from whom I did descend in perpetuity.

RUTH STONE

Pokeberries

I started out in the Virginia mountains
with my grandma's pansy bed
and my Aunt Maud's dandelion wine.
We lived on greens and back-fat and biscuits.
My Aunt Maud scrubbed right through the linoleum.
My daddy was a northerner who played drums
and chewed tobacco and gambled.
He married my mama on the rebound.
Who would want an ignorant hill girl with red hair?
They took a Pullman up to Indianapolis
and someone stole my daddy's wallet.

My whole life has been stained with pokeberries.
No man seemed right for me. I was awkward
until I found a good wood-burning stove.
There is no use asking what it means.
With my first piece of ready cash I bought my own
place in Vermont; kerosene lamps, dirt road.
I'm sticking here like a porcupine up a tree.
Like the one our neighbor shot. Its bones and skin
hung there for three years in the orchard.
No amount of knowledge can shake my grandma out of me;
or my Aunt Maud; or my mama, who didn't just bite an apple
with her big white teeth. She split it in two.

RUTH STONE

Beets

In fourth-grade history class I learned that the Plains Indians weren't cut out to be farmers; the government tried to get them to plant corn and stuff, but it was one of those no-win situations, meaning that no matter how hard the Indians fought against progress, Manifest Destiny and the American Dream, they'd never win.

This history lesson occurred around the same time the United States began its hyper-ecological awareness, which soon seeped into the media. Theories and speculations developed, assertions that the Earth was heading towards another ice age; whereas today scientists tell us that the Earth is getting hotter. It was during this time that my father's convictions regarding the demise of the twentieth century began tipping toward fanaticism. *The Whole Earth Catalogue* took up residence in our home and my father began reciting from it as if it were Scripture. He wanted us to get back to nature. I think he would have sold the house and moved us all into the mountains to raise goats and chickens, but my mother, who didn't have much of a say in most of the family decisions, must have threatened to leave him for good if he took his plans to fruition. So he settled for gardening. Gardening is too light a word for the blueprints he drew up that would transform our backyard into a small farming community.

One day I returned home from school and discovered my father shoveling manure from a pile tall as a two-story building. I couldn't help but wonder where he ever purchased such a magnificent pile of shit, and impressive though it was, I doubt the neighbors shared in my father's enthusiasm. I wouldn't have been surprised if they were circulating a petition to have it removed.

"Good, you're home!" my father said. "Grab a rake."

Knowing I didn't stand a chance arguing, I did just as he ordered. I spent the rest of the day raking manure, thinking the Plains Indians opted not to farm because they knew enough not to. I think my father would have kept us out there shoveling and raking until midnight if my mother hadn't insisted I come in the house and do my homework. The next day I had blisters on my hands and couldn't hold a pencil.

"Hard work builds character," my father preached. "Children have it too easy today. All you want to do is sit around and pick lint out of your bellybuttons."

I was saved from hard labor for the next week because the blisters on my hands burst open and spilled oozy blood all over the music sheets in singing class. The teacher sent me home, back to the plow.

"No pain, no gain," Father said. "Next time, wear gloves."

The following weekend our suburban nuclear unit had transformed into the spitting image of the Sunshine Family Dolls. I began calling my sister Dewdrop, myself Starshine. I renamed my mother Corn Woman and my father Reverend Buck. Reverend Buck considered it his mission in life to convert us from our heathen Bisquick, Pop-Tart, and Hungry-Man TV dinner existence.

"Do you realize that with all these preservatives, after you're dead and buried, your body will take several extra years to completely decompose?" Father preached.

"I don't care," my sister said. "I plan on being cremated."

As the good reverend's wife and children, we must have represented some deprived tribe of soulless, bereft Indians, and he designated himself to take us, the godless parish, under his wing.

Mother resigned herself to his plans and we trudged along behind her. When she was growing up on the reservation, her family had cultivated and planted every season, so gardening wasn't a completely foreign activity. The difference was, her family planted only what they could use. Their gardens were conservative. But my father's plans resembled a large midwestern crop, minus the tractors. He even drew up sketches of an irrigation system that he borrowed from *The Whole Earth Catalogue*. It was a nice dream. His heart was in the right place. I'm sure the government back in the days of treaties, relocation and designation of reservation land thought their intentions were noble, too. I kind of admired my father for his big ideas, but sided with my mother on this one. Father was always more interested in the idea of something rather than the actuality; to him, bigger meant better. My father liked large things—generous mass, quantity, weight. To him, they represented progress, ambition, trust. Try as he might to be a true renegade, adopt Indian beliefs and philosophies, and even go so far as to marry an Indian woman, he still could never avoid the obvious truth. He was a white man. He liked to build large things.

"What do you plan to do with all these vegetables?" my mother asked him.

"Freeze and can 'em," he replied. Mother was about to say something, but then looked as if she'd better not. I knew what she was thinking. She was thinking that our father expected *her* to freeze and can them. She didn't looked thrilled at the prospect. Father may have accused her of being an *apple* from time to time, even went so far as to refer to her as "apple pie"—what he thought to be a term of endearment—but Mother must have retained much of that Plains Indian stoic refusal to derive pleasure from farming large acreage.

Father assigned each of us a row. Mother was busily stooped over, issuing corn into the soil, as if offering gems of sacrifice to the earth goddess. I was in charge of the radishes and turnips, which up until that day I'd had no previous experience with, other than what I could recall from tales of Peter Rabbit stealing from Mr. McGregor's garden. I bent down over my chore, all the while on keen lookout for small white rabbits accessorized in gabardine trousers.

My sister was diligently poking holes in the soil for her onions when our adopted collie began nosing around the corn rows looking for a place to pee. "Get out of the corn, Charlie!" I ordered him.

Father chuckled and said, "Hey look, a scorned corndog!"

Mother rolled her eyes and quipped, "What a corny joke!"

My sister feigned fainting and said, "You punish me!"

Yeah, we were an image right out of a Rockwell classic with the caption reading, *Squawman and family, an American portrait of hope.*

In school we learned that the Indians were the impetus behind the Thanksgiving holiday that we practice today. This legend depicts that the eastern tribes were more reverent and accepting of the white colonists than any fierce and proud Plains Indians ever was. My father challenged this theory by suggesting that I take armfuls of our sown vegetables to school. "It'll be like helping out the pilgrims," he told me. I brought grocery sacks of turnips to class one day and offered them as novelties for our class show and tell. Everyone was left with the assumption that it was the Sioux Indians who were farmers and who had guided and helped the pilgrims in their time of need. Mrs. Morton didn't discourage this faux pas; but rather, rattled on about how noble, how Christian, of the Indians to assist the poor colonists in the unsettling and overwhelming wilderness they'd arrived in. My classmates collected my offering of turnips and, at recess, we rounded up a game of turnip baseball. Lisa Parker got hit in the face with a turnip and went bawling to the school nurse. Mrs. Morton ignored me the rest of the day and sent me home with a note to my parents, which said, *Please do not allow this to happen again.*

At Father's suggestion, my sister engineered a baking factory. Every evening after dinner she would bake loaves of zucchini bread. These baked goods went to the neighbors, co-workers and the public just happening by. My father also had suggested she sell them at school, but Mother firmly reminded him that the teachers weren't supportive of free enterprise in the elementary schools. "Well, she could organize a bake sale and the proceeds could go to charity," my father offered. So the following week Helen Keller Elementary School had a bake sale in the school gymnasium. Tables were loaded up with flour-and-sugar concoctions of every creed and color. Cookies, cupcakes, strudel, fudge, brownies and whole cakes. My sister's table was the most impressive and I swelled up with pride at her arrangement. She had a banner struck across the wall behind the table that read *zucchini's R R friends.* Along with her stacks of loaves she also had our season's bounty of zucchini. I even snuck in a few turnips for color. The teachers milled around her table praising her for her fine ingenuity.

Mrs. Morton asked me, "How did your family ever come into so many zucchinis?" As if zucchini was old money we had inherited.

"Oh, zucchini is a fast-growing vegetable," I told her. "My father says that it breeds in the garden like rabbits—really, really horny rabbits that multiply exponentially."

Mrs. Morton ignored me for the rest of the day and sent a note home to my parents that read, *Please do not allow this to happen again.*

In school we learned about the fur trappers and traders who migrated all over the frontier trading with the Indians. We learned about the Hudson Bay Company and how the Plains Indians bartered with them for the glass beads and shells that modernized and increased the value of their traditional regalia. We learned that before money, folks just traded stuff, bartered their wares. But then gold was discovered throughout the West and bartering furs and beads took a back seat. The Indians weren't gold diggers.

Aside from the Trouble with Tribbles zucchini problem in our garden, we had another problem to contend with. The beets. Some evening I would discover my father stooped down over the beet rows, shaking his head and muttering, "Borscht . . . borscht."

My sister was encouraged to invent a recipe for beet bread, as she had done with the zucchini, but it kept coming out of the oven soggy and oozing red juice, as if it were hunks of animal flesh trickling trails of blood all over the kitchen counters. Not a very appetizing sight. Father had a bit more success with his beet experimentation, inventing such delicacies as beetloaf, Sunday morning succotash surprise and beet omelets. He'd counteracted the red by adding blue food coloring, so we ended up with purple tongues after eating. My all-time favorite was beet Jell-O. And Mother packed our lunches to include bologna-beet sandwiches. We took sacks of beets to our grandparents' house and my German grandmother was delighted with our offering. "Oh, I just love beets!" she exclaimed. "I shall make borscht and pickles."

The beets were beginning to get on everyone's nerves. But there were other cauldrons bubbling in our household; my father's overstimulated dread of waste. He'd been raised by a tough and hearty Montana farm girl, who in turn had been bred from a stock of immigrant Germans from Russia who had escaped the banks of the Volga River after the reign of Catherine the Great. As if injected straight through the bloodline, my grandmother Gertrude instilled a heavy dose of "Waste not, want not" medication to my father. My grandfather also ladled out his own brand of practical conservationism, but more out of his penny-pinching and obsessive attention to dollars and cents, than out of some necessity imprinted from childhood to "Save today, you'll not starve tomorrow." The examination of water and electric bills was one of my grandfather's favorite hobbies. Either wattage fascinated him or he was always expecting to get stiffed—the latter being more true, because he was one of *the* great complainers.

It didn't come as much of a surprise when my father promoted his newest scheme: bartering our surplus beets door to door. The catch was, we were the ones doing the soliciting, he was going to stay home and watch the World Series. He furthered his cause by explaining to us that the Indians traded long ago and this would be our own personal tribute to an old way of life.

"Yeah, but they didn't sell beets door to door like encyclopedia salesmen," my sister said. "I'll feel so stupid!"

"Nonsense!" my father said. "It's a fine idea. Whatever money you make, I'll just deduct it from your allowance, and if you make more than your allowance you can keep the difference. Save up for a bike or a mitt or something."

I couldn't help thinking that if only my mother had stopped my father when he'd decided to become Reverend Buck and toil and sweat in the garden, none of this would be happening. This was a bad episode from *Attack of the Killer Tomatoes,* and my father's insistence on doing things only on a large scale didn't seem to justify the embarrassment that resulted when we were coaxed to distribute the fruits of our labor. However, his latest plan I was for the most part agreeable to, but only because it would elevate me in his eyes as angelic and perfect and because, secretly, I enjoyed witnessing my sister's discomfort.

We filled up the grocery sacks with surplus. Father had suggested we fill up the wheelbarrow, but Julie wouldn't hear of it. "For cripe's sake, with that wheelbarrow filled with beets we'd look pathetic!" she argued. "We'd look like Okies from *The Grapes of Wrath!*" My father was a fanatic about Steinbeck. He taught my sister to read "The Red Pony" before she entered the second grade. I, on the other hand, was considered the "slow" one.

We set out: Our own personal tribute to Indians of long ago. We weren't very conspicuous. Nothing out of the ordinary, just a couple of brown-skinned kids in braids walking grocery sacks down the suburban streets. Indians weren't a common sight in residential neighborhoods, and my sister and I had experienced our share of racial prejudice. When my mother wrote out checks at the grocery store, the store manager was always called by the clerk to verify her driver's license. This occurring immediately after a white woman wrote a check to the same clerk, but no verification was needed. Once riding my bike, I heard some kids call me "nigger." I don't know what hurt more, the fact that they had called me an ugly name or misinterpreted my race. My sister during a football game at Hecht Ed Stadium was insulted by a black man when she was buying hot dogs. "Must eat a lot of hot dogs on the reservation, huh?" he told her. Later, when we told Father, he responded with, "Did you ask him if he ate a lot of watermelon?"

We had walked most of a mile to a neighborhood outside the confines of our own, so as not to be further embarrassed by people we actually knew. When we had come to a point where we felt we were at a safe enough distance, my sister told me to go up to the house with the pink flamingos balanced in the flower bed. "Only if you come too," I told her. So together we marched up to the door and rang the bell.

A woman with frizzy red hair answered the door. "Hello?" she asked. "What can I do for you girls?"

My sister nudged me with her elbow. "Would you like to buy some beets?" I asked.

The woman's brows knitted together. "What's that? What's that you asked?"

"BEETS!" I shouted. "WOULD YOU LIKE TO BUY SOME BEETS!?"

I yelled so loudly that some kids stopped what they were doing and looked toward the house.

The woman was having a great deal of difficulty disguising her perplexity. Her brow was so busy knitting together she could have made up an afghan. Finally, some expression resembling resolution passed over her face. "No, not today," she said, and very curtly closed the door in our faces.

I wasn't going to let her go that easily. "BORSCHT, LADY!" I yelled. "YOU KNOW HOW TO MAKE BORSCHT!?"

My sister threw me a horrified look, shoved me aside and ran down the street. "HEY JULIE!" I called after her. "YOU SHOULD SEE YOUR FACE, IT'S BEET RED!"

We didn't sell any beets that day. Our personal tribute had failed. After I caught up with my sister, I found her sitting on the pavement at the top of a steep hill, with her face in her hands. I didn't say anything because there wasn't anything to say. I knew that she was crying and I knew that it was partly my fault. I wanted to make it up to her. Though I wasn't bothered by her pained frustrations, tears were another matter entirely. When she cried, I always felt compelled to cry right along with her. But on this day, I didn't. Instead, I took the grocery sacks filled with beets and turned them upside down. The beets escaped from the bags, and as we watched them begin their descent to the bottom of the hill, I noticed the beginning of a smile on my sister's face. When the plump red vegetables had arrived at the bottom of the hill, leaving a bloody pink trail behind, we were both chuckling. And when a Volkswagen bus slammed on its brakes to avoid colliding with our surplus beets, we were laughing. And by the time the beets reached the next block and didn't stop rolling, but continued down the asphalt street heading into the day after tomorrow, my sister and I were displaying pure and uncensored hysterics—laughing uncontrollably, holding our bellies as tears ran down our cheeks, pressing our faces against the pavement and rejoicing in the spectacle that we viewed from the top of that concrete hill.

TIFFANY MIDGE

Magnalia Christi Americana*

The Reverend Samuel John Wallace

We stop, show our identification,
drive slowly off, knowing he will be
there again somewhere up ahead,
for we are his sons and daughters
down to the fourth generation

I sit at moral attention at five
already shout-shaken and awake
in church by his arm-slicing, fist-
banging, finger-jabbing style,
hard charging the congregation.

I was too young to comprehend
what his farmers had long known, that—
though the land stretched like a garden—
hell grew silently, like weeds among
soybeans, sprouting up everywhere,

except for his quick eye,
his hoe's sharp slice.
Even his terrier, with all
of a dog's wild enthusiasm,
would chase rabbits only to the curb,

---

* *Magnalia Christi Americana*, or *The Great Work of Christ in America*, was the earliest religious history written in the Massachusetts Bay Colony.

then stop still and eye the house.
It violated that rule once
years after our grandfather died
and dragged its hindquarters home
dark hours later.

The boy will do it whether he
likes it or not! He's old enough
to learn a hard day's work,
he warns off his wife,
and I, his seven-year-old helper,

lay concrete and resentment against
the future on a hot July
afternoon. I pour. He trowels.
Nothing is smoothed over,
but the form holds; the mixture hardens.

In college I meet him again,
a decade after his death, two
hundred and fifty years younger
and alive on every page from
Plymouth through Massachusetts Bay.

He shoulders the Mathers aside
to stride across New England and
the Burned Over District headed West,
where, he believed, we were yet to be God's
people in the devil's wilderness.

The farmers, surmising nature's
theocracy, sacrificed bushels
of corn and whole flocks of chickens
which died in staccato succession
under his axe.

We buried him thirty years ago.
He needed no stone.
Each of us carried one under
our tongues against hungry days,
for we are his people.

We are his people.
We pleasure in industry,
are diligent even in leisure.
Vigilant at rest, we work
even as we dream

T. H. S. WALLACE

daughters

woman who shines at the head
of my grandmother's bed,
brilliant woman, i like to think
you whispered into her ear
instructions. i like to think
you are the oddness in us,
you are the arrow
that pierced our plain skin
and made us fancy women;
my wild witch gran, my magic mama,
and even these gaudy girls.
i like to think you gave us
extraordinary power and to
protect us, you became the name
we were cautioned to forget.
it is enough,
you must have murmured,
to remember that i was
and that you are. woman, i am
lucille, which stands for light,
daughter of thelma, daughter
of georgia, daughter of
dazzling you.

LUCILLE CLIFTON

fury

for mama

remember this.
she is standing by

the furnace.
the coals
glisten like rubies.
her hand is crying.
her hand is clutching
a sheaf of papers.
poems.
she gives them up.
they burn
jewels into jewels.
her eyes are animals.
each hank of her hair
is a serpent's obedient
wife.
she will never recover.
remember, there is nothing
you will not bear
for this woman's sake.

LUCILLE CLIFTON

Dear Mama,

It is Christmas eve and the year is passing away with calloused feet.
My father, your son and I decorate the night with words. Sit cer-
emoniously in human song. Watch our blue sapphire words eclipse
the night. We have come to this simplicity from afar.

He stirs, pulls from his pocket a faded picture of you. Blackwoman.
Sitting in frigid peace. All of your biography preserved in your
face. And my eyes draw up short as he says, "her name was Elizabeth but we used to call her Lizzie." And I hold your picture in
my hands. But I know your name by heart. It's Mama. I hold
you in my hands and let time pass over my face: "Let my baby be.
She ain't like the others. She rough. She'll stumble on gentleness
later on."

Ah Mama. Gentleness ain't never been no stranger to my genes.
But I did like the roughness of running and swallowing the wind,
diving in rivers I could barely swim, jumping from second story
windows into a saving backyard bush. I did love you for loving me

so hard until I slid inside your veins and sailed your blood to an uncrucified shore.

And I remember Saturday afternoons at our house. The old sister deaconesses sitting in sacred pain. Black cadavers burning with lost aromas. And I crawled behind the couch and listened to breaths I had never breathed. Tasted their enormous martyrdom. Lives spent on so many things. Heard their laughter at Sister Smith's latest performance in church—her purse sailing toward Brother Thomas's head again. And I hugged the laughter round my knees. Draped it round my shoulder like a Spanish shawl.

And history began once again. I received it and let it circulate in my blood. I learned on those Saturday afternoons about women rooted in themselves, raising themselves in dark America, discharging their pain without ever stopping. I learned about women fighting men back when they hit them: "Don't never let no mens hit you mo than once girl." I learned about "womens waking up they mens" in the nite with pans of hot grease and the compromises reached after the smell of hot grease had penetrated their sleepy brains. I learned about loose women walking their abandoned walk down front in church, crossing their legs instead of their hands to God. And I crept into my eyes. Alone with my daydreams of being woman. Adult. Powerful. Loving. Like them. Allowing nobody to rule me if I didn't want to be.

And when they left. When those old bodies had gathered up their sovereign smells. After they had kissed and packed up beans snapped and cakes cooked and laughter bagged. After they had called out their last goodbyes, I crawled out of my place. Surveyed the room. Then walked over to the couch where some had sat for hours and bent my head and smelled their evening smells. I screamed out loud, "ooweeee! Ain't that stinky!" and I laughed laughter from a thousand corridors. And you turned Mama, closed the door, chased me round the room until I crawled into a corner where your large body could not reach me. But your laughter pierced the little alcove where I sat laughing at the night. And your humming sprinkled my small space. Your humming about your Jesus and how one day he was gonna take you home . . .

Because you died when I was six Mama, I never laughed like that again. Because you died without warning Mama, my sister and I moved from family to stepmother to friend of the family. I never felt your warmth again.

But I knew corners and alcoves and closets where I was pushed when some mad woman went out of control. Where I sat for days while some woman raved in rhymes about unwanted children. And work. And not enough money. Or love. And I sat out my childhood with stutters and poems gathered in my head like some winter storm. And the poems erased the stutters and pain. And the words loved me and I loved them in return.

My first real poem was about you Mama and death. My first real poem recited an alphabet of spit splattering a white bus driver's face after he tried to push cousin Lucille off a bus and she left Birmingham under the cover of darkness. Forever. My first real poem was about your Charleswhite arms holding me up against death.

My life flows from you Mama. My style comes from a long line of Louises who picked me up in the nite to keep me from wetting the bed. A long line of Sarahs who fed me and my sister and fourteen other children from watery soups and beans and a lot of imagination. A long line of Lizzies who made me understand love. Sharing. Holding a child up to the stars. Holding your tribe in a grip of love. A long line of Black people holding each other up against silence.

I still hear your humming, Mama. The color of your song calls me home. The color of your words saying, "Let her be. She got a right to be different. She gonna stumble on herself one of these days. Just let the child be."

And I be Mama.

SONIA SANCHEZ

Linked

My American grandmother said, I don't know,
oh I don't know, and my grandfather said, You'd better.
She took a little bow backwards: whatever you say.
Luckily I had two others across the sea who were mysteries.

My mother wrote her own early story down
in a red book which I found.
Saw movie. New dress.
When I was ten, I wanted her to complete the sentence.

We lived in the grayest city on earth
with a broom and a frazzled mop.
My daddy kept his passport in his pocket.
My daddy had a long eye and a manner of speaking.

Where are you from? people asked him.
He liked to tease. *I am from the land of stones.*
I fell down from the tallest, oldest tree.
In school, we were all from our own families.

I wanted a common name—Debbie, or Karen.
But the rest of it was good for me.
We had hummos, pine nuts.
We had olive oil tipped from a shiny can.

Who wanted to go to the Methodist Church
or the neighborhood fish fry? We tried it all.
We didn't have to belong. Our parents took us seriously.
They took us everywhere they went.

Our days were studded with attention,
shadowed by twin cherry trees, thick.
We had umbrellas and boots.
We used good sense.

Our teachers said, Excuse me, how do you
pronounce this? Our teachers said, Welcome.
I don't know much about it, but tell me.
Do they still ride camels over there?

Whenever I think about the small white house,
our father is pitching sticks into a flaming barrel
in the backyard. It's as tall as I am. He sings as he stirs it.
His old country smelled like smoke.

What day can ever feel more real?
I'm linked to the jingling sound of keys

in someone else's pocket. I'm following behind.
I'll come in when they tell me to.

NAOMI SHIHAB NYE

I Go Back to May 1937

I see them standing at the formal gates of their colleges,
I see my father strolling out
under the ochre sandstone arch, the
red tiles glinting like bent
plates of blood behind his head, I
see my mother with a few light books at her hip
standing at the pillar made of tiny bricks with the
wrought-iron gate still open behind her, its
sword-tips black in the May air,
they are about to graduate, they are about to get married,
they are kids, they are dumb, all they know is they are
innocent, they would never hurt anybody.
I want to go up to them and say Stop,
don't do it—she's the wrong woman,
he's the wrong man, you are going to do things
you cannot imagine you would ever do,
you are going to do bad things to children,
you are going to suffer in ways you never heard of,
you are going to want to die. I want to go
up to them there in the late May sunlight and say it,
her hungry pretty blank face turning to me,
her pitiful beautiful untouched body,
his arrogant handsome blind face turning to me,
his pitiful beautiful untouched body,
but I don't do it. I want to live. I
take them up like the male and female
paper dolls and bang them together
at the hips like chips of flint as if to
strike sparks from them, I say
Do what you are going to do, and I will tell about it.

SHARON OLDS

The Portrait

My mother never forgave my father
for killing himself,
especially at such an awkward time
and in a public park,
that spring
when I was waiting to be born.
She locked his name
in her deepest cabinet
and would not let him out,
though I could hear him thumping.
When I came down from the attic
with the pastel portrait in my hand
of a long-lipped stranger
with a brave moustache
and deep brown level eyes,
she ripped it into shreds
without a single word
and slapped me hard.
In my sixty-fourth year
I can feel my cheek
still burning.

STANLEY KUNITZ

Cracked Portraits

(for Agha Zafar Ali)

My grandfather's painted grandfather,
son of Ali, a strange physician
in embroidered robes, a white turban,
the Koran lying open on a table beside him.

I look for prayers
in his eyes, for inscriptions
in Arabic.
I find his will:
He's left us plots
in the family graveyard.

Great-grandfather? A sahib in breeches.
He simply disappoints me,
his hands missing in the drawing-room photo
but firm as he whipped the horses
or the servants.

He wound the gramophone to a fury,
the needles grazing Malika Pukhraj's songs
as he, drunk, tore his shirts
and wept at the refrain,
"I still am young."

Grandfather, a handsome boy,
sauntered toward madness
into Srinagar's interior.
In a dim-lit shop he smoked hashish,
reciting verses of Sufi mystics.
My father went to bring him home.

As he grew older, he moved toward Plato,
mumbling "philosopher-king,"
Napoleon on his lips.
Sitting in the bedroom corner,
smoking his hookah, he told me
the Siberian snows
froze the French bones.

In his cup,
Socrates swirled.

I turn the pages,
see my father holding a tennis racquet,
ready to score with women,
brilliance clinging to his shirt.

He brings me closer to myself
as he quotes Lenin's love of Beethoven,
but loses me as he turns to Gandhi.

Silverfish have eaten his boyhood face.

Cobwebs cling
to the soundless
words of my ancestors.

No one now comes from Kandahar,
dear Ali, to pitch tents by the Jhelum,
under autumn maples,
and claim descent from the holy prophet.

Your portrait is desolate
in a creaking corridor.

AGHA SHAHID ALI

Those Were the Days

The sun came up before breakfast,
perfectly round and yellow, and we
dressed in the soft light and shook out
our long blond curls and waited
for Maid to brush them flat and place
the part just where it belonged.
We came down the carpeted stairs
one step at a time, in single file,
gleaming in our sailor suits, two
four year olds with unscratched knees
and scrubbed teeth. Breakfast came
on silver dishes with silver covers
and was set in table center, and Mother
handed out the portions of eggs
and bacon, toast and juice. We could
hear the ocean, not far off, and boats
firing up their engines, and the shouts
of couples in white on the tennis courts.

I thought, Yes, this is the beginning
of another summer, and it will go on
until the sun tires of us or the moon
rises in its place on a silvered dawn
and no one wakens. My brother flung
his fork on the polished wooden floor
and cried out, "My eggs are cold, cold!"
and turned his plate over. I laughed
out loud, and Mother slapped my face,
and when I cleared my eyes the table
was bare of even a simple white cloth,
and the steaming plates had vanished.
My brother said, "It's time," and we
struggled into our galoshes and snapped
them up, slumped into our pea coats,
one year older now and on our way
to the top through the freezing rains
of the end of November, lunch boxes
under our arms, tight fists pocketed,
out the door and down the front stoop,
heads bent low, tacking into the wind.

PHILIP LEVINE

The Substitute

When the substitute asked my eighth-grade daughter
    to read out loud,
she read in Cockney, an accent she'd mastered

listening to rock music. Her classmates laughed
    of course, and she kept on,
straightfaced, until the merciful bell.

Thus began the week my daughter learned
    it takes more than style
to be successfully disobedient.

Next day her regular teacher didn't return;
    she had to do it again.
She was from Liverpool, her parents worked

in a mill, had sent her to America to live
    with relatives.
At night she read about England, looked at her map

to place and remember exactly where she lived.
    Soon her classmates
became used to it—just a titter from Robert

who'd laugh at anything. Friday morning,
    exhausted from learning
the manners and industry of modern England,

she had a stomachache, her ears hurt, there were
    pains, she said,
all over. We pointed her toward the door.

She left bent over like a charwoman, but near
    the end of the driveway
we saw her right herself, become the girl
who had to be another girl, a substitute
    of sorts,
in it now for the duration.

STEPHEN DUNN

The Liar

My mother read everything except books. Advertisements on buses,
entire menus as we ate, billboards; if it had no cover it interested
her. So when she found a letter in my drawer that was not ad-
dressed to her she read it. "What difference does it make if James
has nothing to hide?"—that was her thought. She stuffed the letter
in the drawer when she finished it and walked from room to room
in the big empty house, talking to herself. She took the letter out
and read it again to get the facts straight. Then, without putting
on her coat or locking the door, she went down the steps and
headed for the church at the end of the street. No matter how
angry and confused she might be, she always went to four o'clock
Mass and now it was four o'clock.

It was a fine day, blue and cold and still, but Mother walked as though into a strong wind, bent forward at the waist with her feet hurrying behind in short, busy steps. My brother and sisters and I considered this walk of hers funny and we smirked at one another when she crossed in front of us to stir the fire, or water a plant. We didn't let her catch us at it. It would have puzzled her to think that there might be anything amusing about her. Her one concession to the fact of humor was an insincere, startling laugh. Strangers often stared at her.

While Mother waited for the priest, who was late, she prayed. She prayed in a familiar, orderly, firm way: first for her late husband, my father, then for her parents—also dead. She said a quick prayer for my father's parents (just touching base; she had disliked them) and finally for her children in order of their ages, ending with me. Mother did not consider originality a virtue and until my name came up her prayers were exactly the same as on any other day.

But when she came to me she spoke up boldly. "I thought he wasn't going to do it anymore. Murphy said he was cured. What am I supposed to do now?" There was reproach in her tone. Mother put great hope in her notion that I was cured. She regarded my cure as an answer to her prayers and by way of thanksgiving sent a lot of money to the Thomasite Indian Mission, money she had been saving for a trip to Rome. She felt cheated and she let her feelings be known. When the priest came in Mother slid back on the seat and followed the Mass with concentration. After communion she began to worry again and went straight home without stopping to talk to Frances, the woman who always cornered Mother after Mass to tell about the awful things done to her by Communists, devil-worshipers, and Rosicrucians. Frances watched her go with narrowed eyes.

Once in the house, Mother took the letter from my drawer and brought it into the kitchen. She held it over the stove with her fingernails, looking away so that she would not be drawn into it again, and set it on fire. When it began to burn her fingers she dropped it in the sink and watched it blacken and flutter and close upon itself like a fist. Then she washed it down the drain and called Dr. Murphy.

The letter was to my friend Ralphy in Arizona. He used to live across the street from us but he had moved. Most of the letter was about a tour we, the junior class, had taken of Alcatraz. That was all right. What got Mother was the last paragraph where I said that she had been coughing up blood and the doctors weren't sure what was wrong with her, but that we were hoping for the best.

This wasn't true. Mother took pride in her physical condition, considered herself a horse: "I'm a regular horse," she would reply when people asked about her health. For several years now I had been saying unpleasant things that weren't true and this habit of mine irked Mother greatly, enough to persuade her to send me to Dr. Murphy, in whose office I was sitting when she burned the letter. Dr. Murphy was our family physician and had no training in psychoanalysis but he took an interest in "things of the mind," as he put it. He had treated me for appendicitis and tonsillitis and Mother thought that he could put the truth into me as easily as he took things out of me, a hope Dr. Murphy did not share. He was basically interested in getting me to understand what I did, and lately he had been moving toward the conclusion that I understood what I did as well as I ever would.

Dr. Murphy listened to Mother's account of the letter, and what she had done with it. He was curious about the wording I had used and became irritated when Mother told him she had burned it. "The point is," she said, "he was supposed to be cured and he's not."

"Margaret, I never said he was cured."

"You certainly did. Why else would I have sent over a thousand dollars to the Thomasite Mission?"

"I said that he was responsible. That means that James knows what he's doing, not that he's going to stop doing it."

"I'm sure you said he was cured."

"Never. To say that someone is cured you have to know what health is. With this kind of thing that's impossible. What do you mean by curing James, anyway?"

"You know."

"Tell me anyway."

"Getting him back to reality, what else?"

"Whose reality? Mine or yours?"

"Murphy, what are you talking about? James isn't crazy, he's a liar."

"Well, you have a point there."

"What am I going to do with him?"

"I don't think there's much you can do. Be patient."

"I've been patient."

"If I were you, Margaret, I wouldn't make too much of this. James doesn't steal, does he?"

"Of course not."

"Or beat people up or talk back."

"No."

"Then you have a lot to be thankful for."

"I don't think I can take any more of it. That business about leukemia last summer. And now this."

"Eventually he'll outgrow it, I think."

"Murphy, he's sixteen years old. What if he doesn't outgrow it? What if he just gets better at it?"

Finally Mother saw that she wasn't going to get any satisfaction from Dr. Murphy, who kept reminding her of her blessings. She said something cutting to him and he said something pompous back and she hung up. Dr. Murphy stared at the receiver. "Hello," he said, then replaced it on the cradle. He ran his hand over his head, a habit remaining from a time when he had hair. To show that he was a good sport he often joked about his baldness, but I had the feeling that he regretted it deeply. Looking at me across the desk, he must have wished that he hadn't taken me on. Treating a friend's child was like investing a friend's money.

"I don't have to tell you who that was."

I nodded.

Dr. Murphy pushed his chair back and swiveled it around so he could look out the window behind him, which took up most of the wall. There were still a few sailboats out on the Bay, but they were all making for shore. A woolly gray fog had covered the bridge and was moving in fast. The water seemed calm from this far up, but when I looked closely I could see white flecks everywhere, so it must have been pretty choppy.

"I'm surprised at you," he said. "Leaving something like that lying around for her to find. If you really have to do these things you could at least be kind and do them discreetly. It's not easy for your mother, what with your father dead and all the others somewhere else."

"I know. I didn't mean for her to find it."

"Well." He tapped his pencil against his teeth. He was not convinced professionally, but personally he may have been. "I think you ought to go home now and straighten things out."

"I guess I'd better."

"Tell your mother I might stop by, either tonight or tomorrow. And James—don't underestimate her."

While my father was alive we usually went to Yosemite for three or four days during the summer. My mother would drive and Father would point out places of interest, meadows where boom towns once stood, hanging trees, rivers that were said to flow upstream at certain times. Or he read to us; he had that grown-ups' idea that children love Dickens and Sir Walter Scott. The four of us sat in the back seat with our faces composed, attentive, while our hands and feet pushed, pinched, stomped, goosed, prodded, dug, and kicked.

One night a bear came into our camp just after dinner. Mother had made a tuna casserole and it must have smelled to him like something worth dying for. He came into the camp while we were sitting around the fire and stood swaying back and forth. My brother Michael saw him first and elbowed me, then my sisters saw him and screamed. Mother and Father had their backs to him but Mother must have guessed what it was because she immediately said, "Don't scream like that. You might frighten him and there's no telling what he'll do. We'll just sing and he'll go away."

We sang "Row Row Row Your Boat" but the bear stayed. He circled us several times, rearing up now and then on his hind legs to stick his nose into the air. By the light of the fire I could see his doglike face and watch the muscles roll under his loose skin like rocks in a sack. We sang harder as he circled us, coming closer and closer. "All right," Mother said, "enough's enough." She stood abruptly. The bear stopped moving and watched her. "Beat it," Mother said. The bear sat down and looked from side to side. "Beat it," she said again, and leaned over and picked up a rock.

"Margaret, don't," my father said.

She threw the rock hard and hit the bear in the stomach. Even in the dim light I could see the dust rising from his fur. He grunted and stood to his full height. "See that?" Mother shouted: "He's filthy. Filthy!" One of my sisters giggled. Mother picked up another rock. "Please, Margaret," my father said. Just then the bear turned and shambled away. Mother pitched the rock after him. For the rest of the night he loitered around the camp until he found the tree where we had hung our food. He ate it all. The next day we drove back to the city. We could have bought more supplies in the valley, but Father wanted to go and would not give in to any argument. On the way home he tried to jolly everyone up by making jokes, but Michael and my sisters ignored him and looked stonily out the windows.

Things were never easy between my mother and me, but I didn't underestimate her. She underestimated me. When I was little she suspected me of delicacy, because I didn't like being thrown into the air, and because when I saw her and the others working themselves up for a roughhouse I found somewhere else to be. When they did drag me in I got hurt, a knee in the lip, a bent finger, a bloody nose, and this too Mother seemed to hold against me, as if I arranged my hurts to get out of playing.

Even things I did well got on her nerves. We all loved puns except Mother, who didn't get them, and next to my father I was the best in the family. My specialty was the Swifty—" 'You can bring the prisoner down,' said Tom condescendingly." Father encouraged me to perform at dinner, which must have been a trial for outsiders. Mother wasn't sure what was going on, but she didn't like it.

She suspected me in other ways. I couldn't go to the movies without her examining my pockets to make sure I had enough money to pay for the ticket. When I went away to camp she tore my pack apart in front of all the boys who were waiting in the bus outside the house. I would rather have gone without my sleeping bag and a few changes of underwear, which I had forgotten, than be made such a fool of. Her distrust was the thing that made me forgetful.

And she thought I was cold-hearted because of what happened the day my father died and later at his funeral. I didn't cry at my father's funeral, and showed signs of boredom during the eulogy, fiddling around with the hymnals. Mother put my hands into my lap and I left them there without moving them as though they were things I was holding for someone else. The effect was ironical and she resented it. We had a sort of reconciliation a few days later after I closed my eyes at school and refused to open them. When several teachers and then the principal failed to persuade me to look at them, or at some reward they claimed to be holding, I was handed over to the school nurse, who tried to pry the lids open and scratched one of them badly. My eye swelled up and I went rigid. The principal panicked and called Mother, who fetched me home. I wouldn't talk to her, or open my eyes, or bend, and they had to lay me on the back seat and when we reached the house Mother had to lift me up the steps one at a time. Then she put me on the couch and played the piano to me all afternoon. Finally I opened my eyes. We hugged each other and I wept. Mother did not really believe my tears, but she was willing to accept them because I had staged them for her benefit.

My lying separated us, too, and the fact that my promises not to lie anymore seemed to mean nothing to me. Often my lies came back to her in embarrassing ways, people stopping her in the street and saying how sorry they were to hear that ———. No one in the neighborhood enjoyed embarrassing Mother, and these situations stopped occurring once everybody got wise to me. There was no saving her from strangers, though. The summer after Father died I visited my uncle in Redding and when I got back I found to my surprise that Mother had come to meet my bus. I tried to slip away from the gentleman who had sat next to me but I couldn't shake him. When he saw Mother embrace me he came up and presented her with a card and told her to get in touch with him if things got any worse. She gave him his card back and told him to mind his own business. Later, on the way home, she made me repeat what I had said to the man. She shook her head. "It's not fair to people," she said, "telling them things like that. It confuses them." It seemed to me that Mother had confused the man, not I, but I didn't say so. I agreed with her that I shouldn't say such things and promised not to do it again, a promise I broke three hours later in conversation with a woman in the park.

It wasn't only the lies that disturbed Mother; it was their morbidity. This was the real issue between us, as it had been between her and my father. Mother did volunteer work at Children's Hospital and St. Anthony's Dining Hall, collected things for the St. Vincent de Paul Society. She was a lighter of candles. My brother and sisters took after her in this way. My father was a curser of the dark. And he loved to curse the dark. He was never more alive than when he was indignant about something. For this reason the most important act of the day for him was the reading of the evening paper.

Ours was a terrible paper, indifferent to the city that bought it, indifferent to medical discoveries—except for new kinds of gases that made your hands fall off when you sneezed—and indifferent to politics and art. Its business was outrage, horror, gruesome coincidence. When my father sat down in the living room with the paper Mother stayed in the kitchen and kept the children busy, all except me, because I was quiet and could be trusted to amuse myself. I amused myself by watching my father.

He sat with his knees spread, leaning forward, his eyes only inches from the print. As he read he nodded to himself. Sometimes he swore and threw the paper down and paced the room, then picked it up and began again. Over a period of time he developed the habit of reading aloud to me. He always started with the society section, which he called the parasite page. This column began to take on the character of a comic strip or a serial, with the same people showing up from one day to the next, blinking in chiffon, awkwardly holding their drinks for the sake of Peninsula orphans, grinning under sunglasses on the deck of a ski hut in the Sierras. The skiers really got his goat, probably because he couldn't understand them. The activity itself was inconceivable to him. When my sisters went to Lake Tahoe one winter weekend with some friends and came back excited about the beauty of the place, Father calmed them right down. "Snow," he said, "is overrated."

Then the news, or what passed in the paper for news: bodies unearthed in Scotland, former Nazis winning elections, rare animals slaughtered, misers expiring naked in freezing houses upon mattresses stuffed with thousands, millions; marrying priests, divorcing actresses, high-rolling oilmen building fantastic mausoleums in honor of a favorite horse, cannibalism. Through all this my father waded with a fixed and weary smile.

Mother encouraged him to take up causes, to join groups, but he would not. He was uncomfortable with people outside the family. He and my mother rarely went out, and rarely had people in, except on feast days and national holidays. Their guests were always the same, Dr. Murphy and his wife and several others whom they had known since childhood. Most of these people never saw each other outside our house and they didn't have much fun together. Father discharged his obligations as host by teasing everyone about stupid things they had said or done in the past and forcing them to laugh at themselves.

Though Father did not drink, he insisted on mixing cocktails for the guests. He would not serve straight drinks like rum-and-Coke or even Scotch-on-the-rocks, only drinks of his own devising. He gave them lawyerly names like "The Advocate," "The Hanging Judge," "The Ambulance Chaser," "The Mouthpiece," and described their concoction in detail. He told long, complicated stories in a near-whisper, making everyone lean in his direction, and repeated important lines; he also repeated the important lines in the stories my mother told, and corrected her when she got something wrong. When the guests came to the ends of their own stories he would point out the morals.

Dr. Murphy had several theories about Father, which he used to test on me in the course of our meetings. Dr. Murphy had by this time given up his glasses for contact lenses, and lost weight in the course of fasts which he undertook regularly. Even with his baldness he looked years younger than when he had come to the parties at our house. Certainly he did not look like my father's contemporary, which he was.

One of Dr. Murphy's theories was that Father had exhibited a classic trait of people who had been gifted children by taking an undemanding position in an uninteresting firm. "He was afraid of finding his limits," Dr. Murphy told me: "As long as he kept stamping papers and making out wills he could go on believing that he didn't *have* limits." Dr. Murphy's fascination with Father made me uneasy, and I felt traitorous listening to him. While he lived, my father would never have submitted himself for analysis; it seemed a betrayal to put him on the couch now that he was dead.

I did enjoy Dr. Murphy's recollections of Father as a child. He told me about something that happened when they were in the Boy Scouts. Their troop had been on a long hike and Father had fallen behind. Dr. Murphy and the others decided to ambush him as he came down the trail. They hid in the woods on each side and waited. But when Father walked into the trap none of them moved or made a sound and he strolled on without even knowing they were there. "He had the sweetest look on his face," Dr. Murphy said, "listening to the birds, smelling the flowers, just like Ferdinand the Bull." He also told me that my father's drinks tasted like medicine.

While I rode my bicycle home from Dr. Murphy's office Mother fretted. She felt terribly alone but she didn't call anyone because she also felt like a failure. My lying had that effect on her. She took it personally. At such times she did not think of my sisters, one happily married, the other doing brilliantly at Fordham. She did not think of my brother Michael, who had given up college to work with runaway children in Los Angeles. She thought of me. She thought that she had made a mess of her family.

Actually she managed the family well. While my father was dying upstairs she pulled us together. She made lists of chores and gave each of us a fair allowance. Bedtimes were adjusted and she stuck by them. She set regular hours for homework. Each child was made responsible for the next eldest, and I was given a dog. She told us frequently, predictably, that she loved us. At dinner we were each expected to contribute something, and after dinner she played the piano and tried to teach us to sing in harmony, which I could not do. Mother, who was an admirer of the Trapp family, considered this a character defect.

Our life together was more orderly, healthy, while Father was dying than it had been before. He had set us rules to follow, not much different really than the ones Mother gave us after he got sick, but he had administered them in a fickle way. Though we were supposed to get an allowance we always had to ask him for it and then he would give us too much because he enjoyed seeming magnanimous. Sometimes he punished us for no reason, because he was in a bad mood. He was apt to decide, as one of my sisters was going out to a dance, that she had better stay home and do something to improve herself. Or he would sweep us all up on a Wednesday night and take us ice-skating.

He changed after he learned about the cancer, and became more calm as the disease spread. He relaxed his teasing way with us, and from time to time it was possible to have a conversation with him which was not about the last thing that had made him angry. He stopped reading the paper and spent time at the window.

He and I became close. He taught me to play poker and sometimes helped me with my homework. But it wasn't his illness that drew us together. The reserve between us had begun to break down after the incident with the bear, during the drive home. Michael and my sisters were furious with him for making us leave early and wouldn't talk to him or look at him. He joked: though it had been a grisly experience we should grin and bear it—and so on. His joking seemed perverse to the others, but not to me. I had seen how terrified he was when the bear came into the camp. He had held himself so still that he had begun to tremble. When Mother started pitching rocks I thought he was going to bolt, really. I understood—I had been frightened too. The others took it as a lark after they got used to having the bear around, but for Father and me it got worse through the night. I was glad to be out of there, grateful to Father for getting me out. I saw that his jokes were how he held himself together. So I reached out to him with a joke: " 'There's a bear outside, said Tom intently.' " The others turned cold looks on me. They thought I was sucking up. But Father smiled.

When I thought of other boys being close to their fathers I thought of them hunting together, tossing a ball back and forth, making birdhouses in the basement, and having long talks about girls, war, careers. Maybe the reason it took us so long to get close was that I had this idea. It kept getting in the way of what we really had, which was a shared fear.

Toward the end Father slept most of the time and I watched him. From below, sometimes, faintly, I heard Mother playing the piano. Occasionally he nodded off in his chair while I was reading to him; his bathrobe would fall open then, and I would see the long new scar on his stomach, red as blood against his white skin. His ribs all showed and his legs were like cables.

I once read in a biography of a great man that he "died well." I assume the writer meant that he kept his pain to himself, did not set off false alarms, and did not too much inconvenience those who were to stay behind. My father died well. His irritability gave way to something else, something like serenity. In the last days he became tender. It was as though he had been rehearsing the scene, that the anger of his life had been a kind of stage fright. He managed his audience—us—with an old trouper's sense of when to clown and when to stand on his dignity. We were all moved, and admired his courage, as he intended we should. He died downstairs in a shaft of late afternoon sunlight on New Year's Day, while I was reading to him. I was alone in the house and didn't know what to do. His body did not frighten me but immediately and sharply I missed my father. It seemed wrong to leave him sitting up and I tried to carry him upstairs to the bedroom but it was too hard, alone. So I called up my friend Ralphy across the street. When he came over and saw what I wanted him for he started crying but I made him help me anyway. A couple of hours later Mother got home and when I told her that Father was dead she ran upstairs, calling his name. A few minutes later she came back down. "Thank God," she said, "at least he died in bed." This seemed important to her and I didn't tell her otherwise. But that night Ralphy's parents called. They were, they said, shocked at what I had done and so was Mother when she heard the story, shocked and furious. Why? Because I had not told her the truth? Or because she had learned the truth, and could not go on believing that Father had died in bed? I really don't know.

"Mother," I said, coming into the living room, "I'm sorry about the letter. I really am."

She was arranging wood in the fireplace and did not look at me or speak for a moment. Finally she finished and straightened up and brushed her hands. She stepped back and looked at the fire she had laid. "That's all right," she said. "Not bad for a consumptive."

"Mother, I'm sorry."

"Sorry? Sorry you wrote it or sorry I found it?"

"I wasn't going to mail it. It was a sort of joke."

"Ha ha." She took up the whisk broom and swept bits of bark into the fireplace, then closed the drapes and settled on the couch. "Sit down," she said. She crossed her legs. "Listen, do I give you advice all the time?"

"Yes."

"I do?"

I nodded.

"Well, that doesn't make any difference. I'm supposed to. I'm your mother. I'm going to give you some more advice, for your own good. You don't have to make all these things up, James. They'll happen anyway." She picked at the hem of her skirt. "Do you understand what I'm saying?"

"I think so."

"You're cheating yourself, that's what I'm trying to tell you. When you get to be my age you won't know anything at all about life. All you'll know is what you've made up."

I thought about that. It seemed logical.

She went on. "I think maybe you need to get out of yourself more. Think more about other people."

The doorbell rang.

"Go see who it is," Mother said. "We'll talk about this later."

It was Dr. Murphy. He and Mother made their apologies and she insisted that he stay for dinner. I went to the kitchen to fetch ice for their drinks, and when I returned they were talking about me. I sat on the sofa and listened. Dr. Murphy was telling Mother not to worry. "James is a good boy," he said. "I've been thinking about my oldest, Terry. He's not really dishonest, you know, but he's not really honest either. I can't seem to reach him. At least James isn't furtive."

"No," Mother said, "he's never been furtive."

Dr. Murphy clasped his hands between his knees and stared at them. "Well, that's Terry. Furtive."

Before we sat down to dinner Mother said grace; Dr. Murphy bowed his head and closed his eyes and crossed himself at the end, though he had lost his faith in college. When he told me that, during one of our meetings, in just those words, I had the picture of a raincoat hanging by itself outside a dining hall. He drank a good deal of wine and persistently turned the conversation to the subject of his relationship with Terry. He admitted that he had come to dislike the boy. Then he mentioned several patients of his by name, some of them known to Mother and me, and said that he disliked them too. He used the word "dislike" with relish, like someone on a diet permitting himself a single potato chip. "I don't know what I've done wrong," he said abruptly, and with reference to no particular thing. "Then again maybe I haven't done anything wrong. I don't know what to think anymore. Nobody does."

"I know what to think," Mother said.

"So does the solipsist. How can you prove to a solipsist that he's not creating the rest of us?"

This was one of Dr. Murphy's favorite riddles, and almost any pretext was sufficient for him to trot it out. He was a child with a card trick.

"Send him to bed without dinner," Mother said. "Let him create that."

Dr. Murphy suddenly turned to me. "Why do you do it?" he asked. It was a pure question, it had no object beyond the satisfaction of his curiosity. Mother looked at me and there was the same curiosity in her face.

"I don't know," I said, and that was the truth.

Dr. Murphy nodded, not because he had anticipated my answer but because he accepted it. "Is it fun?"

"No, it's not fun. I can't explain."

"Why is it all so sad?" Mother asked. "Why all the diseases?"

"Maybe," Dr. Murphy said, "sad things are more interesting."

"Not to me," Mother said.

"Not to me, either," I said. "It just comes out that way."

After dinner Dr. Murphy asked Mother to play the piano. He particularly wanted to sing "Come Home Abbie, the Light's on the Stair."

"That old thing," Mother said. She stood and folded her napkin deliberately and we followed her into the living room. Dr. Murphy stood behind her as she warmed up. Then they sang "Come Home Abbie, the Light's on the Stair," and I watched him stare down at Mother intently, as if he were trying to remember something. Her own eyes were closed. After that they sang "O Magnum Mysterium." They sang it in parts and I regretted that I had no voice, it sounded so good.

"Come on, James," Dr. Murphy said as Mother played the last chords. "These old tunes not good enough for you?"

"He just can't sing," Mother said.

When Dr. Murphy left, Mother lit the fire and made more coffee. She slouched down in the big chair, sticking her legs straight out and moving her feet back and forth. "That was fun," she said.

"Did you and Father ever do things like that?"

"A few times, when we were first going out. I don't think he really enjoyed it. He was like you."

I wondered if Mother and Father had had a good marriage. He admired her and liked to look at her; every night at dinner he had us move the candlesticks slightly to right and left of center so he could see her down the length of the table. And every evening when she set the table she put them in the center again. She didn't seem to miss him very much. But I wouldn't really have known if she did, and anyway I didn't miss him all that much myself, not the way I had. Most of the time I thought about other things.

"James?"

I waited.

"I've been thinking that you might like to go down and stay with Michael for a couple of weeks or so."

"What about school?"

"I'll talk to Father McSorley. He won't mind. Maybe this problem will take care of itself if you start thinking about other people."

"I do."

"I mean helping them, like Michael does. You don't have to go if you don't want to."

"It's fine with me. Really. I'd like to see Michael."

"I'm not trying to get rid of you."

"I know."

Mother stretched, then tucked her feet under her. She sipped noisily at her coffee. "What did that word mean that Murphy used? You know the one?"

"Paranoid? That's where somebody thinks everyone is out to get him. Like that woman who always grabs you after Mass—Frances."

"Not paranoid. Everyone knows what that means. Sol-some-thing."

"Oh. Solipsist. A solipsist is someone who thinks he creates everything around him."

Mother nodded and blew on her coffee, then put it down without drinking from it. "I'd rather be paranoid. Do you really think Frances is?"

"Of course. No question about it."

"I mean really *sick*?"

"That's what paranoid *is,* is being sick. What do you think, Mother?"

"What are you so angry about?"

"I'm not angry." I lowered my voice. "I'm not angry. But you don't believe those stories of hers, do you?"

"Well, no, not exactly. I don't think she knows what she's saying, she just wants someone to listen. She probably lives all by herself in some little room. So she's paranoid. Think of that. And I had no idea. James, we should pray for her. Will you remember to do that?"

I nodded. I thought of Mother singing "O Magnum Mysterium," saying grace, praying with easy confidence, and it came to me that her imagination was superior to mine. She could imagine things as coming together, not falling apart. She looked at me and I shrank; I knew exactly what she was going to say. "Son," she said, "do you know how much I love you?"

The next afternoon I took the bus to Los Angeles. I looked forward to the trip, to the monotony of the road and the empty fields by the roadside. Mother walked with me down the long concourse. The station was crowded and oppressive. "Are you sure this is the right bus?" she asked at the loading platform.

"Yes."

"It looks so old."

"Mother—"

"All right." She pulled me against her and kissed me, then held me an extra second to show that her embrace was sincere, not just like everyone else's, never having realized that everyone else does the same thing. I boarded the bus and we waved at each other until it became embarrassing. Then Mother began checking through her handbag for something. When she had finished I stood and adjusted the luggage over my seat. I sat and we smiled at each other, waved when the driver gunned the engine, shrugged when he got up suddenly to count the passengers, waved again when he resumed his seat. As the bus pulled out my mother and I were looking at each other with plain relief.

I had boarded the wrong bus. This one was bound for Los Angeles but not by the express route. We stopped in San Mateo, Palo Alto, San Jose, Castroville. When we left Castroville it began to rain, hard; my window would not close all the way, and a thin stream of water ran down the wall onto my seat. To keep dry I had to stay away from the wall and lean forward. The rain fell harder. The engine of the bus sounded as though it were coming apart.

In Salinas the man sleeping beside me jumped up but before I had a chance to change seats his place was taken by an enormous woman in a print dress, carrying a shopping bag. She took possession of her seat and spilled over onto half of mine, backing me up to the wall. "That's a storm," she said loudly, then turned and looked at me. "Hungry?" Without waiting for an answer she dipped into her bag and pulled out a piece of chicken and thrust it at me. "Hey, by God," she hooted, "look at him go to town on that drumstick!" A few people turned and smiled. I smiled back around the bone and kept at it. I finished that piece and she handed me another, and then another. Then she started handing out chicken to the people in the seats near us.

Outside of San Luis Obispo the noise from the engine grew suddenly louder and just as suddenly there was no noise at all. The driver pulled off to the side of the road and got out, then got on again dripping wet. A few moments later he announced that the bus had broken down and they were sending another bus to pick us up. Someone asked how long that might take and the driver said he had no idea. "Keep your pants on!" shouted the woman next to me. "Anybody in a hurry to get to L.A. ought to have his head examined."

The wind was blowing hard around the bus, driving sheets of rain against the windows on both sides. The bus swayed gently. Outside the light was brown and thick. The woman next to me pumped all the people around us for their itineraries and said whether or not she had ever been where they were from or where they were going. "How about you?" She slapped my knee. "Parents own a chicken ranch? I hope so!" She laughed. I told her I was from San Francisco. "San Francisco, that's where my husband was stationed." She asked me what I did there and I told her I worked with refugees from Tibet.

"Is that right? What do you do with a bunch of Tibetans?"

"Seems like there's plenty of other places they could've gone," said a man in front of us. "Coming across the border like that. We don't go there."

"What do you do with a bunch of Tibetans?" the woman repeated.

"Try to find them jobs, locate housing, listen to their problems."

"You understand that kind of talk?"

"Yes."

"Speak it?"

"Pretty well. I was born and raised in Tibet. My parents were missionaries over there."

Everyone waited.

"They were killed when the Communists took over."

The big woman patted my arm.

"It's all right," I said.

"Why don't you say some of that Tibetan?"

"What would you like to hear?"

"Say 'The cow jumped over the moon.'" She watched me, smiling, and when I finished she looked at the others and shook her head. "That was pretty. Like music. Say some more."

"What?"

"Anything."

They bent toward me. The windows suddenly went blind with rain. The driver had fallen asleep and was snoring gently to the swaying of the bus. Outside the muddy light flickered to pale yellow, and far off there was thunder. The woman next to me leaned back and closed her eyes and then so did all the others as I sang to them in what was surely an ancient and holy tongue.

TOBIAS WOLFF

Daddy, We Called You

"Daddy" we called you, "Daddy"
when we talked to each other in the street,
pulling on our American faces,
shaping our lives in Paterson slang.

Inside our house, we spoke
a southern Italian dialect
mixed with English
and we called you "Papa"

but outside again, you became Daddy
and we spoke of you to our friends

as "my father"
imagining we were speaking
of that *Father Knows Best*
TV character
in his dark business suit,
carrying his briefcase into his house,
retreating to his paneled den,
his big living room and dining room,
his frilly-aproned wife
who greeted him at the door
with a kiss. Such space

and silence in that house.
We lived in one big room—
living room, dining room, kitchen, bedroom,
all in one, dominated by the gray oak dining table
around which we sat, talking and laughing,
listening to your stories,
your political arguments with your friends,

Papa, how you glowed in company light,
happy when the other immigrants
came to you for help with their taxes
or legal papers.

It was only outside that glowing circle
that I denied you, denied your long hours
as night watchman in Royal Machine Shop.
One night, riding home from a date,
my middle-class, American boyfriend
kissed me at the light; I looked up
and met your eyes as you stood at the corner
near Royal Machine. It was nearly midnight.
January. Cold and windy. You were waiting
for the bus, the streetlight illuminating
your face. I pretended I did not see you,
let my boyfriend pull away, leaving you
on the empty corner waiting for the bus
to take you home. You never mentioned it,
never said that you knew
how often I lied about what you did for a living

or that I was ashamed to have my boyfriend see you,
find out about your second shift work, your broken English.

Today, remembering that moment,
still illuminated in my mind
by the streetlamp's gray light,
I think of my own son
and the distance between us,
greater than miles.

Papa,
silk worker,
janitor,
night watchman,
immigrant Italian,
I honor the years you spent in menial work

while your mind, so quick and sharp,
longed to escape,
honor the times you got out of bed
after sleeping only an hour,
to take me to school or pick me up;
the warm bakery rolls you bought for me
on the way home from the night shift,

the letters
you wrote
to the editors
of local newspapers.

Papa,
silk worker,
janitor,
night watchman,
immigrant Italian,
better than any *Father Knows Best* father,
bland as white rice,
with your wine press in the cellar,
with the newspapers you collected
out of garbage piles to turn into money
you banked for us,

with your mousetraps,
with your cracked and calloused hands,
with your yellowed teeth.

Papa,
dragging your dead leg
through the factories of Paterson,
I am outside the house now,
shouting your name.

MARIA MAZZIOTTI GILLAN

Sangre 24
A Legacy

Grandfather never went to school
spoke only a few words of English,
a quiet man; when he talked
talked about simple things

planting corn or about the weather
sometimes about herding sheep as a child.
One day pointed to the four directions
taught me their names

El Norte

Poniente   Oriente

El Sur

He spoke their names as if they were
one of only a handful of things
a man needed to know

Now I look back
only two generations removed
realize I am nothing but a poor fool
who went to college

trying to find my way back
to the center of the world

where Grandfather stood
that day

LEROY V. QUINTANA

Working Class

(for Angela Jackson)

The blues dig rows
in sun-hot
fields.
A girl hands her daddy's
history to the woman
looping tobacco.
A boy slaps his mama's
clues of tobacco blues
beneath his arms
as his footprints
crush yards of hurt.
A man clenches his fist
and walks and walks
round in his troubles,
swallowing words
in his throat,
digesting
vowels of Motherland's
culture.
A woman recites
what her mother's
mother told of whips
cracking and
snapping strong backs.
Blues
haunt wherever they slow-walk
down
long rows sprinkled
and sprinkled
with dusty tears.

LENARD D. MOORE

from attic

the stairs sag with
                  the bannister
thin
    with fingernails

air grey-green and

spare parts of grandma's wheelchair
the high button shoe that's her rod
my old maid aunts' trousseaux
grandpa's Sunday suit and spats
the tophat he wears to jail
piles of his Daily Worker
(brittle as the walls) and
the law degree my father waves
to bail him out

the lead pipes my uncles cherish
the gutters they ascend
a civic award for Italian Baptists
and some *lire* big as kerchiefs
we can't change on Ellis Island

grooveless records of the Great Caruso
the china set he shatters
the speaker that is his trumpet
and in the console
stogey ashes

the iron stove where my Jewish mother
learns to cook Neapolitan style
an egg-beater full of cobwebs

like an abandoned beehive
and the gyroscope, too subtle for me to spin,
my father produces after months away

JUSTIN VITIELLO

Always Running

All night vigil.
My two-and-a-half-year-old boy
and his 10-month-old sister
lay on the same bed,
facing opposite ends;
their feet touching.
They looked soft, peaceful,
bundled there in strands of blankets.
I brushed away roaches that meandered
across their faces,
but not even that could wake them.
Outside, the dark cover of night tore
as daybreak bloomed like a rose
on a stem of thorns.
I sat down on the backsteps,
gazing across the yellowed yard.
A 1954 Chevy Bel-Air stared back.
It was my favorite possession.
I hated it just then.
It didn't start when I tried to get it going
earlier that night. It had a bad solenoid.
I held a 12-gauge shotgun across my lap.
I expected trouble from the Paragons gang
of the west Lynwood *barrio*.
Somebody said I drove the car
that dudes from *Colonia Watts* used
to shoot up the Paragons' neighborhood.
But I got more than trouble that night.
My wife had left around 10 p.m.
to take a friend of mine home.
She didn't come back.
I wanted to kill somebody.
At moments, it had nothing to do
with the Paragons.
It had to do with a woman I loved.
But who to kill? Not her—
sweet allure wrapped in a black skirt.
I'd kill myself first.
Kill me first?

But she was the one who quit!
Kill her? No, think man! I was hurt, angry . . .
but to kill her? To kill a Paragon?
To kill anybody?
I went into the house
and put the gun away.

Later that morning, my wife came for her things:
some clothes, the babies . . . their toys.
A radio, broken TV, and some dishes remained.
I didn't stop her.
There was nothing to say that my face
didn't explain already.
Nothing to do . . . but run.

So I drove the long haul to Downey
and parked near an enclosed area
alongside the Los Angeles River.
I got out of the car,
climbed over the fence
and stumbled down the slopes.
A small line of water rippled in the middle.
On rainy days this place flooded and flowed,
but most of the time it was dry
with dumped garbage and dismembered furniture.
Since a child, the river and its veins of canals
were places for me to think. Places to heal.
Once on the river's bed, I began to cleanse.
I ran.

I ran into the mist of morning,
carrying the heat of emotion
through sun's rays;
I ran past the factories
that lay smack in the middle
of somebody's backyard.
I ran past alleys with overturned trashcans
and mounds of tires.
Debris lay underfoot. Overgrown weeds
scraped my leg as I streamed past;
recalling the song of bullets
that whirred in the wind.

I ran across bridges, beneath overhead passes,
and then back alongside the infested walls
of the concrete river;
splashing rainwater as I threaded,
my heels colliding against the pavement.
So much energy propelled my legs
and, just like the river,
it went on for miles.

When all was gone,
the concrete river
was always there
and me, always running.

LUIS J. RODRÍGUEZ

Company Outing

There we are in bathing suits
my sister and I
at the company outing
Father had every year
for his milk plant
workers and their families.

There I am, about eleven
next to the wives of the non-
Armenians, slender women

with triangles of air
showing between their thighs

while the Armenian
women look sturdy, if not stout,
no such spaces under
their sensibly skirted
bathing suits. When we grow up,
I whispered to my sister,
let's be sure to have space
showing between our legs.
And air between our ears?
she laughed pushing me.

Imagine our luck having
a father with an ice cream
plant and all the heavy
cream and ice cream
we wanted. Right there—a good
start toward fat thighs.

There they are the Armenian
survivors at the beach
picnic who ate, ate and
never satisfied the hunger
for the missing.

But my sister and I who did
not know what was eating them
would have no trouble staying slim.

DIANA DER-HOVANESSIAN

Tending

In the pull-out bed with my brother
    in my grandfather's Riverton apartment
my knees and ankles throbbed from growing,
    pulsing so hard they kept me awake—
or was it the Metro North train cars
    flying past the apartment, rocking the walls,
or was it the sound of apartment front doors
    as heavy as prison doors clanging shut?
Was the Black Nation whispering to me
    from the Jet magazines stacked on the floor, or
was it my brother's unfamiliar ions
    vibrating, humming in his easeful sleep?
Tomorrow, as always, Grandfather will rise
    to the Spanish-Town cock's crow deep in his head
and perform his usual ablutions,
    and prepare the apartment for the day,
and peel fruit for us, and prepare a hot meal
    that can take us anywhere, and onward.
Did sleep elude me because I could feel
    the heft of unuttered love in his tending

our small bodies, love a silent, mammoth thing
  that overwhelmed me, that kept me awake
as my growing bones did, growing larger
  than anything else I would know?

ELIZABETH ALEXANDER

I cannot write a poem to bless all the givers of pain

for T.D.

I cannot write a poem to bless all the givers of pain a poem to
forgive those that should not be forgiven a poem to go on forever
that starts with my grandmother who gave birth to my father
through pain into pain my grandmother who loved and hated my
father my grandmother who gave away her only child my grandmother who told my father she wished he didn't have nappy hair
so he wouldn't be a nigger my grandmother who ignored my sisters
and me my grandmother who kept pictures of my dark sister and
me in her photo album my grandmother who kept pictures of my
fair sister up on her mantle my grandmother who called me three
times in twenty-four years my grandmother who called me dear
my grandmother who died without telling me she needed me my
grandmother who gave birth to my father who married my mother
whose mother gave birth to her through pain into pain my grandmother who hated and loved my mother my grandmother who
called my mother black and ugly my grandmother who called me
pretty and brown my grandmother who was ashamed of my
mother my grandmother who was proud of me my grandmother
who would not believe my mother my grandmother who is crazy
and will not recognize my mother anymore my grandmother who
gave birth to my mother who gave birth to me through pain into
pain my mother who gave me her milk in exchange for my silence
my mother who would not believe me or herself my mother whose
words I hold in my mouth my mother who loved me who loved
me who loved my father who loved my mother who hated my
father who hated my mother who married my father who loved
and hated me my father who gave me his poems through his seed
my father whose face is worn by every man who raped me my
father who claims me as his child when I am no longer his child

my father who frightens me when I don't have to be afraid of him my father who hit me with his hands my father who held me to his heart that deserved to explode in the pieces that I keep in my fingers to write this poem for the givers of pain whom I hated whom I loved who made me ugly who made me beautiful

HONORÉE JEFFERS

II. ～

FAMILY PRIMER II

See Mother. Mother is very nice.

See Father. Father is very strong.

Family

My father was brilliant   embarrassed   funny   handsome
my mother was plain   serious   principled   kind
my grandmother was intelligent   lonesome for her
                            other life   her dead children   silent
my aunt was beautiful   bitter   angry   loving

I fell among these adjectives in earliest childhood
and was nearly buried with opportunity
some of them stuck to me   others
finding me American and smooth slipped away

GRACE PALEY

Why the Violin Is Better

I don't know why you want to play
the drums, Mother said. They won't prepare
you for anything in life, except how to be
a garbage man, & bang cans around. But if
you keep studying the violin you could be
in an orchestra. It'll teach you how
to dress. You'll have to wear a suit
or a tuxedo. And you'll learn how
to play in harmony with other instruments,
like the trombone, which will help you
get along better with me. Because
quite frankly you've been living
in this house like you're the soloist,
making a lot of noise, but never stopping
for a moment to see if I wanted to blow my horn.

HAL SIROWITZ

My Aunts

On Sundays my mother's father Giovanni sat in his cane chair in
a white shirt, white pants and white shoes and listened to the opera
records that became his legacy. I marched toward him through
mountains of snow. "Hut-two-three-four, hut, hut!" my father

called out so I would keep up. It was difficult to reconcile Giovanni's affectionate gesture of lowering his cheek for me to kiss with the deadness of his face. His neck was red and scabbed from picking it with his fingernails, and rivulets of blood vessels had surfaced on his giant mushroom nose—all this frightened me so I made it my business to sit directly at his left during dinner, thinking that by my being on the periphery his cold, faraway look would miss me as it purveyed the dishes of food, was captured by Aunt Matilda's incessant activity of fetching the food from the kitchen.

Giovanni was a master tailor. While my father was courting my mother, Giovanni made him a beautiful cashmere coat. I have the coat now and no matter how shabby it makes me look, how inappropriate it is against the bright new colors on Fourteenth Street, I wear it with pride. The cloth is soothing to my skin. The coat itself has inspired stories. After Giovanni suffered his first heart attack, he booked passage on the SS *Constitution*. He would climb to the top of *Monte Royale* and sing *La Traviata*. In the shrine of *Santa Rosalia,* he would place his gold beside the gold of his ancestors and pray. My father and I went to the boat and stood beside Giovanni's bosses, two brothers. My father showed them his new coat. The brothers agreed that Giovanni was a fine tailor but said he had better enjoy his trip because he would not have a job when he returned.

"Why?" my father asks to this day.

"The man is sick," the brothers said. "We can't use him."

My father punched them and knocked them into the water. I got lost in the boat's corridors and so was able to appreciate its grandeur, it was a palace befitting men of great stature and wealth. I came upon a staircase and looked at it for a long time. No one ascended or descended, it was set apart from its function by its beauty, by the brilliance of its light, the steps and bannisters radiated with pure white light and swirled to the upper decks.

After her mother dies, Matilda will continue to care for the house and after Matilda dies, her daughter will care for it. Antonia's pilgrimage to Connecticut with her husband Flaherty is temporary. For twenty years she stood beside our grandmother at the stove and learned how to cook and to speak Sicilian. The house on Bay Ridge Parkway will be the only house we can return to, for after my parents die their house will be blown to smithereens, the bricks will go flying over the el as far away as the Eighty-sixth Street station, will smash the neighbors' windows, cause the pigeons to fly away. It was not so much the trains that awoke my father and me but the crazy woman who every morning at daybreak threw open her window and screamed, "John-nee! John-nee!" I'd ask after this Johnny, had he died, been lost at war, and was told there was no such person—the woman longed to have a son and name him Johnny. When she could not, she imagined she had him and every morning called him in from his play.

Sometimes I'd hear the woman's screams in my sleep and would tell my father to go and fetch the stick I had left in Matilda's backyard among the thorny roses and old paint cans. Since then, Matilda has transformed the yard into a thing of beauty. On her own she has planted flowers and when the flowers die, she replants the seeds. I have dreamed of sitting among her roses and watching her till the soil with her tongue out, a skimpy housedress allowing a full view of her knotty bowlegs. We conjure up the voice of Licia Albanese; her voice was that of an angel. Grandpa had the original 78s with her singing *La Bohème* with Beniamino Gigli. That's music! Where are the records now? Who will take care of them after we die? Flaherty likes Italian food more than the opera . . . their children will be Irish . . . that's life, what can you do . . . there's always John McCormack, a fine Irish tenor.

When my grandmother really began to die, I brought her a cat because a cat had been part of her house when it was flourishing. She did not have sufficient energy to search her mind for a name for the cat, her mind had fixed on the past, so she named him Pussy. "Pussy! Pussy!" she calls, and he comes and sits on the arm of her chair. Thanks to Matilda's generous feedings, he has grown big and fat. Black stripes course his face like an executioner's mask. He likes to roam around in Matilda's garden and sniff the flowers, take in some fresh air, bathe in the warmth of the sun, savor the smells of my grandmother's cooking escaping the window facing the garden. Matilda ties a rope around his neck so he will not wander to another garden, the gardens being adjacent to one another, separated by fences. If it were not for these fences, there would be one beautiful garden extending from one avenue to the next. When it is time for the cat to come in, Matilda gently takes off his collar and carries him inside. As a rule he is satisfied, his rope is long enough to permit traveling the length and breadth of the garden, but one evening he wanted to stay outside. As Matilda was taking off his collar, he attacked her, viciously clawing and biting her arm. She punched him, punched and punched him. Teethmarks remained on her skin for months, but she kept the incident to herself, knowing how much her husband loves her. If she had told him, he would have gotten rid of the cat, might even have killed him. Matilda knows nothing about circuits or motors, nothing about Newton or Doppler, yet her husband enjoys her body. Her lack of scientific knowledge is the underpinning of the family. There are times when Frank's mind gets out of hand, threatening the solidarity of the family. Like the time he invented a staircase that he said one could ascend but could not descend. Matilda called me: "Please hurry over, Anthony!"

Frank tends to act like a freak because the family treats him like one. Instead of asking him to fix our bells and toasters, we should listen to his theories on time and space, on the future of the planet. "The material world is a load of shit, that's my philosophy," Frank has said. "Einstein was a prankster . . . Italians have a future on Jupiter . . . " When Maryanne left the nunnery and became a physical therapist, Frank said, "I'd rather have a nice-lookin' nurse take care of me than a male homosexual." And when he says, "Rebirth is possible in the predeath stage," I believe he is saying that he misses his mother, is holding out hope that he may see her again. And if we examine his racism, we will see that it is directed toward a single native on an island in the Pacific and not toward the entire black race. This native was out of cigarettes and asked Frank for one. Frank gave and gave his cigarettes to the native and soon was out himself. He asked for one back, the native agreed but quoted a price.

Frank's ultimate sacrifice occurred early in his marriage to Matilda. He had an opportunity in Columbus, Ohio. Computers had not spread to Columbus as yet and Frank was called on to establish them there, but Matilda would not leave her family. Frank understood this, he repeats over and over how much he understands. He could have carried the family banner to Ohio. Many an Italian man has sacrificed his future to his wife's family. Adequate compensation for such a man is that he becomes part of his wife's family, but this is impossible; his blood and theirs are not the same. He tries to achieve equality through communion with his wife's body and then at the age of sixty his prostate and testicles go bad and his sacrifice comes back to haunt him. If not for this insanity, we might have had prominent Italians on the moon, maybe even a few in Ohio.

Frank showed me his staircase. He was laughing, having a grand time. Every now and then he places himself outside the family's comprehension so Matilda will continue making love to him. Pussy has not attacked her since that day. She lets him stay out for longer periods. She waits until he scratches at the kitchen door before letting him in.

In-laws cannot become Head of the Family. At the same time they are capable of fracturing the family, those upon whom abuse has been heaped for years by the blue bloods and who then transmit their hatred to their children. The children flee the family, liberating the mother. One such in-law is Freddie's wife, Mary Hermann, a German. The abuse she suffers is slow, dissimulated, delivered by inappropriate glances and tones of voice, overfriendliness; she is made to feel like one of the family. Mary Hermann is a beautiful, sensitive woman. On rainy days her son and I played with our toy soldiers in her bedroom and I'd watch her come out of the bathroom with her hair wet and long, a robe draped over her body, camouflaging its mountains and valleys. On my first day home after being born, I stopped in at Mary's and peed on her lap. There is some significance to this. I loved her from the beginning and she loved me. When we meet now, if I see her shoveling the snow around her brick fortress and go over to her and take the shovel from her hands, she says, "Oh, you're getting fat! Oh, you're getting thin!" She knows every inch of my body. She would like to hold it again and press it close to her.

Once, her daughter told me to go upstairs where I belonged. I slapped her. She tried to kick me in the groin, I held her legs. Mary rushed over from her position behind the stove and began pounding me with her fists. I took her arms in my hands and holding them still at her side, I looked into her eyes and discovered her womanliness. I felt the strength of her body. For a fleeting moment I was a man and she was the woman in my arms.

Late in Aunt Anna's life, after she buried her daughters' husbands, her parents and her husband, she made an attempt to look desirable by propping up her hair and spraying it with silver. Her body wilted, yet her hair stands on her head like a proud silver peacock in defiance of the succession of hardships. The mountain of silver hair stands in testament to the bright future of her children's children. After her daughters' husbands died, Anna wanted to look pretty for any suitors. One who kept coming around the house was a handsome builder who lived nearby with his mother. Picking between Alice and Frances, he chose Frances and asked her to marry him. Frances agreed to marry the builder out of spite directed to the man she really wanted to marry, a bartender who was already married but whom Frances was trying to coax into a divorce. The newlyweds spent their wedding night in a splendid hotel in Manhattan. Frances immediately shed her wedding gown, climbed into bed and waited. Her husband was undressing in the bathroom. He turned out to be a virgin. Frances placed his hands on her breasts. He defecated on the sheet, crying, "Don't be angry with me, mommy!"

Frances put on her gown and ran through the lobby and onto Broadway. "Help! Help!" she screamed, running against the traffic.

Anna introduced me to my first friends, a pair of blind twins who lived across the road. We played ball on the road. If a car approached, I'd lead them to the roadside. They wore white shirts, black pants and had black, short-cropped hair. They were pleasant, kind, quiet. The twittering of the birds in the nearby forest filled our ears. The twins taught me not to underestimate the blind, so years later when I heard people marveling at the blind twins who ran a dairy farm in Sag Harbor, at how they got around acre upon acre of rolling green hills collecting the eggs and milk, I smiled to myself with satisfaction. I believed that all one's friends are cripples and that it is natural and good to be nice. I was nice to my next friend, Brian, a polio victim. He was already in the station wagon when it arrived to transport me to my school adjacent to the ocean. By the time I was torn from the bannister leading to my mother and father, it was eight-fifteen. The children in the wagon were growing restless. I climbed in among them and went directly to Brian, who as soon as I was within striking distance raised his iron legs and hit me.

ANTHONY VALERIO

My Son Is Worried About Me

My son is worried about me
He worries that I'll grow to have no money
& then no place to rent without money
& then no food without money (reinforcing his image
      of me starving & gaunt)
& then with no food—
a homeless mother—
a few shopping bags (probably ancient
      ones from Annie Sez and Bloomingdales)
her smelling of urine—

her with dirty orange streaked hair—
her a worse embarrassment to him than ever
And so, he declares to her on the 'phone, he's going to help
her get a CONDOMINIUM—going to erase the possibility of a
homeless, reeking of urine, shopping bagcart mother for
all his friends to see—
for his conscience to wrestle with—
And also after I die, I will
will it to him, he tells me—
& if he dies first—I can barely write that—he
will leave his half to me but meantime he'll pay half
the mortgage—but I should mail him my check early so
his credit won't be ruined by my careless ways

And if he gets married—it's understood
this imagined wife will never be able to get
his half—or would I then if they get divorced
have to live here with her—the two of us—
divorced women—living as divorced women do—
& me thinking if he doesn't like her
& can't live with her
then how will I ever be able
to live with this unknown woman
whom he will divorce and give his half
of this condominium to—Is she worth
my living in this condominium my son
wants me to have—
& I hear him silently saying
remember never to embarrass me after
the mortgage goes through—

Oh, darling son, I promise you,
my son, not ever to embarrass
you, except perhaps in my poems

LAURA BOSS

The Word You Did Not Speak

Mother, reaching back, I could touch you
kneeling with a Comet can by your bathtub
or dropping wads of paper towels

like a flower girl at a wedding as you stretch
your arm around bedroom windows to windex them.

Do you remember when I won the poetry recitation?
Coming home, my head stuck up proud as a moccasin
swimming on top of the creek, you stopped
only long enough to look up from pruning grapevines
for wreaths you twisted and sold at Berea College.

Even if we were only two feet apart, our love
was not simple, not clear
like the glass you cleaned every day.
Even now, I picture you backing into the screen door
with your left hip or rubbing your forehead
with the heel of a hand, greasy from supper dishes.
If we played Hearts, I held up a fan of cards
to hide my eyes, to mask my need for approval.
You never tilted your cards to let me win.

I keep Christmas pictures of us, of the mother
I want to create, a past I need to settle
like place holders that seat guests at dinner.
Washing won't erase splotches on my hands, oil
colored stains etched by acid from suckering
tomatoes or the memory of failing you when
I was elected Kentucky's homecoming queen.
The runner-up was crowned but the mistake was
corrected on the sidelines. You said the rhinestones,
the roses I handed to you were second hand;
my name did not blast through stadium speakers.

Mother, I reach back to touch you
the one night you came to my softball game.
Summer, playing under lights, running from smell
of sewage, I caught my breath like a grounder
when you sat down in the front bleachers.
No applause. Nothing can help me find what
wasn't there any more than I can understand why
you made your knees bleed from carpet burn
as you climbed risers one by one to wipe dust
from backs and corners. I substitute poems

for experience but I cannot fool myself as you
did leaving lights on all night in the coop to trick
nesting hens into behaving as if it were day.
What I needed was withheld, was not there.

Praise you didn't give me wasn't in you
like helium that seeped from birthday balloons.
No amount of searching will fill
pages of the past, the space inside me
where the word love should have been.

VIVIAN SHIPLEY

Words for My Daughter from the Asylum

Alas, that earth's mere measure strains our blood
And makes more airy still this parentage.
The bond is all pretending, and you sleep
When my affections leap
And gasp at old hope vainly in my night's cage.

Dear marvelous alien snippet, yes, you move
Like a down-raining cloud in my mind, a bird
Askim on low planes under lightning thought,
An alter-image caught
In gossamer seed, my most elusive word.

There must be some connection, more than mood,
The yearning wit of loneliness, and more
Than meets the law on that certificate.
Strangers do not create
Alliances so deep and dark and sore.

Yet we are strangers. I remember you
When you began, a subtle soft machine;
And you remember me, no, not at all,
Or maybe you recall
A vacancy where someone once was seen.

I can address you only in my mind
Or, what's the same, in this untouching poem.

We are the faceless persons who exist
Airily, as a gist
Of love to twist the staid old loves of home.

Strangers we are, a father and a daughter,
This Hayden and this Martha. And this song,
Which turns so dark when I had meant it light,
Speaks not at all of right
And not at all, since they are dim, of wrong.

Distance that leaves me powerless to know you
Preserves you from my love, my hurt. You fare
Far from this room hidden in the cold north;
Nothing of me goes forth
To father you, lost daughter, but a prayer.

That some small wisdom always may endure
Amidst your weariness; that lovers may
Be kind to you; that beauty may arouse
You; that the crazy house
May never, never be your home: I pray.

HAYDEN CARRUTH

My Mad Son Helps Me Into Heaven

He calls again
to say people are talking about him,
want to kill him,
"the Mafia run this hospital,
hit men are trying to get me,
even the nurses whisper about me, I
don't want to live anymore, Dad,
too painful."

I have many times heard
such anxiety and despair
that make living
hell,
shared in this way his torments,
reassured him, reasoned with him,
talked to him till his demons let go.

Today I conjure a sympathizing story,
tell him about my being
a poor public school boy from Brooklyn on scholarship
when Princeton wished to change its preppie WASP image,
how I worked two and three jobs
gardening, cleaning houses, hawking sandwiches and sodas
in the dorms, night-watching the pseudo-Gothic "cathedral,"
doing research for the Philosophy Department's Chairman,
how I saved money by eating suppers of bread, beans, coffee
heated on a hot plate in my room,
how one day in the front row of class
I looked at my outstretched feet and noticed
holes in my socks as well as the tops of my size 13 shoes,
naked toes wriggling embarrassment at me
(where could I hide my big Italian feet?),
how on weekends I watched limousines
drive up to chauffeur other students
and wished I had train fare to escape home,
how my only real friends were other outsiders,
Jews, poor bright students, homely or shy young men,
how I could not afford to import blonde, blue-eyed girls
for football weekends at this all-boys college,
how I was blackballed from the Social Clubs,
how a few weeks from graduation,
I put a razor to my wrists
and bled on my newly completed senior thesis.
I try to tell him what a tempering these experiences were,
how much, not just academically, I learned,
what the joy of coming through is like.
Silence at his end of the phone.

I offer "You have suffered much."
"Yes. I have."
"So you needn't fear death,
if there is a heaven, your sufferings
have earned your way in.
Your suffering helps me, too, to get into heaven."

I want to add, compassion strengthens the heart,
like jogging or swimming,
kindness keeps the razor from the wrist,
both one and the other, consoled and consoler.

I do not speak these last words,
but, innocent sufferer, he understands
in a sense, understands
the silence.

"Dad, you're a great talker,
I always learn something from you.
You've earned your way in, too."

Consoled
for now,
we can hang up.

ARTHUR L. CLEMENTS

The Children

They are not
what we want them to be
don't see
what we tell them
stare past
mass of soft hair
called Mommy
to some black hole
that eats at her
know   unfulfillment
before they are old enough
to know regret

They do not
embrace the tinsel
that is offered
but look
thru transparent ground
at the whirlpool spinning
under their feet
birth/death   hear the cries
of newborn kittens
abt to be drowned

DIANE DI PRIMA

Mother's Voice

In these few years
since her death I hear
mother's voice say
under my own, I won't

want any more of that.
My cheekbones resonate
with her emphasis. Nothing
of not wanting only

but the distance there from
common fact of others
frightens me. I look out
at all this demanding world

and try to put it quietly back,
from me, say, thank you,
I've already had some
though I haven't

and would like to
but I've said no, she has,
it's not my own voice anymore.
It's higher as hers was

and accommodates too simply
its frustrations when
I at least think I want more
and must have it.

ROBERT CREELEY

Singing Lessons

They kept saying
I had to take singing lessons
because all we have is song
and don't *you* want to be
bewitching

They forgot to say
I had to open my mouth first,
hear the notes
not think them

But what if
some ghastly tone emerged?
Please teacher,
move back

Since I was a child
they said something's wrong
with the way you speak,
dragging me
to speech class after speech class

Didn't they realize
trying to force me
only made me fight

Didn't they know
Couldn't they see
Didn't they understand
how much one song would cost?

ROCHELLE RATNER

photo poem

I
super-8 home movies
every time
dad shoots
mama's decapitated

II
washington square north
we take pictures here
opposite the park
posing in front of
trees and flowers
elegant brownstones

not in front of our building
trash cans and concrete
we sent the pictures to italy

III
on dad's dresser
his favorite picture of me
1969
yellow easter coat
hair long
head tilted
smiling an almost mona lisa smile
1969
the year
i pulled a knife on him

IV
on my own
1975
for dad's birthday
a framed photo of me
blue flannel shirt
hair short
playing with a cat
he hides it in the dresser drawer

VITTORIA REPETTO

Saying Farewell to My Father

His voice starts
slurs into language.
With both hands on the wheel
he heads into consciousness,
one coherent word after another.

I lean forward,
put his hand into mine
realize this may be the last time
he'll be back for me.

He's asking for my mother,
when he stops,
recognizes me.
Our relationship the new construction
in his town.

Face-to-face fully,
the bridge we've built
above our years of conflict begins to hold.
With his eyes he lets me know
he's crossed it.

We are spirit to spirit,
father to son
in Biblical awe and silence
unable and unwilling
to say goodbye.

Then it's over.
He turns and goes off into the foothills.
My memory awake now
and in pursuit.

I want to be five again
propped up on pillows
in the front seat of our '48 Ford,
able to see up the road
so I can protect him.

JAMES P. HANDLIN

The Birthday—August 25, 1980

For Bert

all my life I wanted a brother
not the one I had
not the one who lived
in a separate world like I did

I wanted the brother who defended me
against Freddy the *Chango* and Jaime Portillo

against Califas and all those white guys
who called me spic and mule-headed injun

I wanted the brother who loved Roberto Duran
who would come to my lonely apartment
to watch his fights on TV
I wanted the brother I spoke with by glance
by the tones of words that brothers speak

I didn't want the brother of our father's fists
because I cried when he couldn't
in my room next to his   listening
and flinching praying under pillows
for my father's last grunt
for the silence of my brother's flesh

for the day I could carry all of his pain
like he had carried my sins
when he took the blame for wrecking the car
let my father beat him

that was the brother who knew love
has no opinions   who knew how lonely
the truth is   who knew brothers
have no questions about each other

I always wanted a brother
like the brother I wanted to be
but I was too busy being younger
I was too busy being the brother
neither one of us wanted to be

I always wanted to be the brother I had
so that when he came to me
on his 24th birthday   near suicide
I would say what he would say
I would do what he would do
then perhaps both of us
would still be alive

EDGAR GABRIEL SILEX

Late

This late, no one is clean,
not the bus's worn blue seats
which keep themselves company,
or the nurse in her drowsy yellow uniform.
It's February and I haven't spoken
to my mother since she told me
to take my shit and go, her face
bare and serious as a wall.
The driver waves a gloved hand
at a passing bus, slow and half empty
like us. Heads of the riders turned
so that I cannot say how they appear.
I am 25. I was not born in this place,
but it is where I will try to live. The miles
between my mother and here, stretching me
into more of a man than my father,
who'd drive from his out-of-state job
each weekend to let her break his skin.
I am glad I have left her sitting in that house
waiting for her nails to grow.
Once she pulled a gun on me because,
as she'd tell the police, I was too big
for a belt. I called them, but they did not
take her away. Later, my father drove home
and said, *Never put our business in the street.*
So I shouldn't be telling you this:
how we sat in that house like a family
while a small light beat the blinds,
my mother stubborn as a girl
who will not comb her hair.
There is no light beyond the windows
of this bus. I am given my face,
transparent and bare on the glass.
After my father left that night,
the two of us sat apart in the living-room
as the TV lit the walls, the old white gown
trembling on her shoulders like the wings
of a moth. I will say I did not know

she began to cry. I was 18, trying to be
a man. It has taken me too long to say this,
I am the same thing I have always been,
a son. I do not know my mother,
but I want to touch her now, as I did not then.

TERRANCE HAYES

Hotel Nights with My Mother

The hometown flophouse
was what she could afford
the nights he came after us
with a knife. I'd grab my books,
already dreading the next day's
explanations of homework undone
—*I ran out of paper*—the lies
I'd invent standing in front of
the nuns in the clothes I'd lain in
full-bladdered all night, a flimsy
chair-braced door between us
and the hallway's impersonal riot.

Years later, then, in the next
city, standing before my first class,
I scanned the rows of faces,
their cumulative skill in the
brilliant adolescent dances
of self-presentation, of hiding.
New teacher, looking young, seeming
gullible, I know, I let them
give me any excuse and took it.
I was watching them all
for the dark-circled eyes,
yesterday's crumpled costume, the marks
—the sorrowful coloring of marks—
the cuticles flaming and torn.
I made of myself each day a chink
a few might pass through unscathed.

LINDA McCARRISTON

Legacy

for my father, Charles Dunn (1905–1967)

1. THE PHOTOGRAPH
My father is in Captain Starns,
a restaurant in Atlantic City.
It's 1950,
I'm there too, eleven years old.
He sold more Frigidaires

than anyone. That's why we're there,
everything free.
It's before the house started
to whisper, before testimony
was called for and lives got ruined.

My father is smiling. I'm smiling.
There's a bowl of shrimp
in front of us.
We have identical shirts on,
short sleeve with little sailboats.
It's before a difference set in

between corniness and happiness.
Soon I'll get up
and my brother will sit next to him.
Mother will click the shutter.
We believe in fairness,

we still believe America
is a prayer, an anthem.
Though his hair is receding
my father's face says nothing
can stop him.

2. THE SECRET
When mother asked him
where the savings went, he said
"the track" and became lost
in his own house, the wastrel,

my mother and her mother
doling out money to him
the rest of his life.

I was sixteen when he told me
the truth, making me his private son,
making anger the emotion
I still have to think about.
I see now that chivalric code
held like a child's song

in the sanctum of his decency,
the error that led to error,
the eventual blur of it all.
And so many nights in the living room
the pages of a newspaper being turned

and his sound—Scotch over ice
in a large glass—how conspicuous
he must have felt,
his best gesture gone wrong,
history changed, the days going on and on.

3. THE FAMILY
The family I was part of
was always extended, grandfather
and grandmother on my mother's side
living with us, and grandfather
with a mistress only my father

knew about, beautiful supposedly
and poor. When she began to die
and wouldn't die fast,
when money became love's test,
grandfather had no one

to turn to except my father
who gave him everything.
It was a pact between men,
a handshake and a secret,
then the country turned

to war and all other debts
must have seemed just personal.
Every night the two of them
huddled by the radio waiting for news
of the clear, identifiable enemy.

4. THE SILENCE
My father became a salesman
heavy with silence.
When he spoke he was charming,
allowed everyone to enjoy
not knowing him.

Nights he'd come home drunk
mother would cook his food
and there'd be silence.
Thus, for years, I thought
all arguments were silent
and this is why silence
is what I arm myself with
and silence is what I hate.

Sleep for him was broken speech,
exclamations, the day come back.
Sleep was the surprise
he'd wake up from, on the couch,
still in his clothes.

I carry silence with me
the way others carry snapshots
of loved ones. I offer it
and wait for a response.

5. THE VISITATION
At the airport, on my way to Spain,
he shook my hand too hard,
said goodbye too long.

I spent his funeral in a room
in Cádiz, too poor to fly back
and paying for what I couldn't afford.

The night he died, the night before
the telegram arrived,
something thumped all night

on the flat roof.
It was my father, I think,
come to be let in.

I was in another country,
living on savings. It must have seemed
like heaven to him.

STEPHEN DUNN

Apples

No use waiting for it to stop
raining in my face like a wet towel
having to catch a plane.
to pick the apples from her tree
and bring them home.

The safest place to be
is under the branches. She
in her bed and her mouth
dry in the dry room.
Don't go out in the rain.

I stretch my arms for apples
anyway, feel how the ripe ones
slide in my hands like cups
that want to be perfect. Juices
locked up in the skin.

She used to slice them in quarters,
cut through the core,
open the inside out. Fingers
steady on the knife, expert
at stripping things.

Sometimes she split them sideways
into halves to let a star break

from the center with tight seeds,
because I wanted that,
five petals in the flesh.

Flavor of apples inhaled as flowers,
not even biting them.
Apples at lunch or after school
like soup, a fragrance rising
in the stream, eat and be well.

I bring the peeled fruit to her
where she lies, carve it
in narrow sections, celery white,
place them between her fingers,
Mother, eat. And be well.

Sit where her brown eyes
empty out the light, watching
her mind slip backwards
on the pillow, swallowing
apples, swallowing her life.

SHIRLEY KAUFMAN

Day Worker

    . . . and much of her life would be spent on her knees in white
folks kitchens . . . or with her back to the sun with huge windows
across her thighs, feet dangling inside, hands full of damp, wet
newspaper shining the thick glass . . . but she would leave these
"mansions" these "out to the houses" as she called them, she would
leave them with shopping bags full of old clothes, unwanted food
. . . yes, she would leave with this and think how kind these white
people were . . . she would take these "gifts" back with her to her
"third floor home" and teach her sons how to be gentle, how to be
gentle . . .
    . . . momma . . . momma . . . after all those cold winters, after
all those hot summers, after all those years of your life you gave to
those white people for our sake, how can it be that you could teach
us how to be gentle? do you know what that has cost me, momma?
do you know how many city streets i've walked? do you know how
many times i've cried? do you know the madness i've endured?

. . . and when buses weren't running because of snow or strike, she would walk. she would bundle up in old clothes and new clothes . . . she would wear the majority of her meager wardrobe to keep warm . . . she would keep her son home from school so she could wear his boots, keep her daughter from work, so she could wear her overcoat . . . but she would go, she would walk . . . she would freeze but she'd go to do her floors, her dusting, her wall washing . . . she would go . . .

. . . she'd be one of many of this race of Black women, who would walk or limp or shuffle on frostbitten feet, feet full of corns because they never wore shoes meant for them, feet swollen by dampness, cellar dampness, feet wore-out-walked-out, used up feet, feet only kept going by hot salt baths at night and corns trimmed by razor blades . . .

. . . these were the feet of this army of women who were "day workers" to survive . . . the years would pass and the faces would sag, the breasts become limp and rest on bellies, the feet more grotesque and misshapen, the hands gnarled and rough, the hair grayer and grayer, the back more and more painful, the teeth fewer and fewer . . . but still they would go . . . they would go until they died of sunstroke on some hot summer afternoon with the heavy windows across their thighs or their high blood pressure would kill them as they scrubbed some kitchen floor and they fell face first in the soap suds, or they would complain of headaches and backaches for a week or so and then one day go home and die . . . but they would go and do those same windows and same floors year after year . . . this was what they were caught in . . . this vicious trap . . . with every swipe of the mop, one more dream would be forgotten, one more hot-cold-rush-of-youth used up, dried out, dusted off, hung up, put away . . . forever, forever, forever . . .

LAMONT B. STEPTOE

Breakfast

My father brought
fish after silence
in the Bayou
with sun soaked
colors
of quiet jubilation.
Smoothness

of water
like its sky,
like gray emptiness
of a blank TV screen.

I scaled them,
taking pleasure
in the cleansing
with songs soaking
my mouth with
that newness
of rock and roll

and in the morning
we ate fried fish
with hot grits
and sipped cups of coffee
between arguments
and business
of survival

we left kitchen table
going on
to invent the rest
of our lives.

YICTOVE

Shelling Shrimp

heaven
and
earth
and
every
thing
in
between

oh

she says
shelling shrimp.

she says this
removing the thinnest purple of their veins
later
rinsing her hands under the faucet
my mother calls everyone to the table

eat
she says
pushing her hair back with
a wet hand
eat

and we do

LÊ THI DIEM THÚY

The Last Lesson

The last lesson
mother taught
was how to die.

As with so many
other lessons
she made it seem like

such a natural
thing to do.
When first she

took to bed
it hardly seemed as if
she would spend

her remaining days
there; the late summer
sun dropping kerchiefs

of light around her
seemed to promise quick
recovery, but then

the spells grew more
insistent, the visits
to the hospital grew

more frequent
and the blood transfusions
more urgent

until there was nothing
left. She had taken
flight before us

lifting from her linens
with the grace
of a bird,

her transparent hands
closing 'round the air
of her last day.

TONI LIBRO

Poem for My Father

for Quincy T. Trouppe, Sr.

father, it was an honor to be there, in the dugout with you
the glory of great black men swinging their lives as bats
at tiny white balls burning in at unbelievable speeds
riding up & in & out
a curve breaking down wicked, like a ball falling off a high table
moving away, snaking down, screwing its stitched magic
into chitling circuit air, its comma seams spinning
toward breakdown, dipping, like a hipster
bebopping a knee-dip stride in the charlie parker forties
wrist curling, like a swan's neck
behind a slick black back
cupping an invisible ball of dreams

& you there, father, regal as african obeah man
sculpted out of wood, from a sacred tree of no name no place
   origin
thick roots branching down into cherokee & someplace else lost
way back in africa, the sap running dry crossing
from north carolina into georgia, inside grandmother mary's
   womb
who was your mother & had you there in the violence of that red
   soil
ink blotter news gone now into blood & bone graves
of american blues, sponging rococo
truth long gone as dinosaurs
the agent-oranged landscape of former names
absent of african polysyllables, dry husk consonants there now
in their place, names flat as polluted rivers
& that guitar string smile always snaking across
some virulent american redneck's face
scorching, like atomic heat, mushrooming over nagasaki
& hiroshima, the fever-blistered shadows of it all
inked, as body etchings, into sizzled concrete
but you there, father, through it all, a yardbird solo
riffing on bat & ball glory, breaking down all fabricated myths
of white major-league legends, of who was better than who
beating them at their own crap game with killer bats
as bud powell swung his silence into beauty
of a josh gibson home run skittering across piano keys of bleachers
shattering all manufactured legends up there in lights, struck out
white knights on the risky slippery edge of amazement
awe, the miraculous truth slipping through
steeped & disguised in the blues, confluencing
like the point at the cross
when a fastball hides itself up in a shimmying slider
curve breaking down & away in a wicked sly grin
curved & broken-down like the back of an ass-scratching uncle tom
who like old satchel paige delivering his famed hesitation pitch
before coming back with a high hard fast one, rising
is sometimes slicker, slipping & sliding
& quicker than a professional hitman—
the deadliness of it all, the sudden strike
like that of the brown bomber's short crossing right
or the hook of sugar ray robinson's lightning cobra bite

& you there father through it all, catching rhythms of chono
pozo balls, drumming like cuban conga beats into your catcher's
   mitt
hard & fast as cool papa bell jumping into bed
before the lights went out

of the old negro baseball league, a promise you were
father, a harbinger, of shock waves, soon come

QUINCY TROUPE

Sports Heroes, Cops, and Lace

Jackie Robinson was my first real sports hero,
my first real hero period.
My father once took me to see Jersey Joe Walcott
work out for one of his fights.
It was in a summer camp in the North Jersey hills.
We called them mountains back then.
Jersey Joe was already getting old, but he was game
and carried himself like a champ.
I even got introduced to him by my father's friend,
and I remember how nice he was.
In fact I was struck by it, by his openness and
friendliness and unexpected gentleness
when it was obvious he could have easily killed
anybody there with his bare hands
if he felt like it. My father was a sporting man.
He played the ponies every day
and knew everybody at the track and even made a
little book on the side.
We always watched the Friday night fights together
on the old console black-and-white TV.
The Gillette song and that announcer with the high
nasal voice and my father
leaning out of his chair, already an old man to me,
but sporty, with what seemed
like closets full of sporting shoes and sport coats
and even a camel's hair overcoat
I used to sneak a feel of every time I went into the hall
closet. He'd point out Jake La Motta,
call him "the possum" because he could play dead,

let a man batter him for what seemed
like hours, and then when the opponent dropped his guard
tear him apart. He had heart, it was said.
But all these guys seemed somehow tarnished to me, even Jersey
Joe. They were like my father's friends,
nice enough guys, who always treated me right, even if
I hated that they called me "little Jimmy."
I'd tell them my name is Michael
so then they'd call me Mikey, but they were okay.
Even the ones who were obvious bums
like Boots and Mary, and Frenchy, and all these characters
my father had grown up with and run
with and continued to help out till the day he died.
It was like living inside a
Damon Runyon story, and I dug the romance of it,
because despite the idea people
usually have who have never lived that life, it is romantic,
in fact, that's one of the appeals
of that world, any kind of underworld, the bookies
the petty crooks and over-the-hill
champs, there was a glamour and
a romance there, even with the old bags and bums like
Boots and Mary, hey, I used to see
them holding hands as they searched the ground for butts.
But it wasn't until Jackie Robinson
entered the big leagues that I found a hero of my own.
The man had something more than the romance
of the streets and sporting life and my father's friends
and closets of my home. The man had what
my father feared and desired most—"class"—the thing
my father's friends would toast him for.
And it was true that in our neighborhood my father had
some class and carried it as best he could.
But in the face of people more comfortable in this world
and self-assured, my father would get
awful humble, and almost do a kind of white man shuffle
that made me feel that maybe I wasn't
good enough either. He'd pretend that we were better off
where we were and among our own kind,
and we all grew up believing the other Americans, the ones
whose families had been here for a long time,
whose kids went to college and whose fathers and uncles

ran the businesses that really mattered—
we were taught they weren't as happy as we thought we were,
especially when we partied or married or
someone died. But inside, I knew it wasn't pride, it was
some unacknowledged form of ambition suicide.
Don't think beyond these streets, these ways of being or
you might get hurt. We knew our place.
And then Jackie Robinson entered major league baseball as the
first of his race, and I saw a kind of
dignity in the face of the obscenities that greeted him
every day on the field and it made my chest
swell with pride, which didn't make any sense since I was
obviously white and knew nothing about
this man except that he could stand up to the lowest forms
of hatred and not let it affect him,
at least not in any way I could see. And I saw a model for me,
when the kids would do the cruel things
kids can sometimes do, I would think of Jackie Robinson and I
would try to be heroic like him,
and sometimes it worked. Even when they called me a jerk
and a race traitor and all the rest,
because when we played stickball and each took on the persona
of our favorite players, I would
pick him, and the other white guys would berate me and try to
get me to react the way I usually did,
with my fists or my murder mouth or something that could be
turned to their amusement as long as
I was out of control. But when I took on his name for the game,
I took on his dignity too, and it
got me through their petty prejudices and opened up a whole
   new
world. Sometimes it even worked with
the girls. Until they too began to feel compelled to make
fun of one of their race who was inspired
by a man whose face was handsome and intense but happened
to be denser in its reflection of the sun
than one of us. Jackie Robinson was the guide to the
outside world for me, his example let me see
that what I was taught was not necessarily true, and what I
always suspected I knew might be. He gave
me a way to go beyond that world and to go deeper into me—
and when I came back, what I had learned

helped me to see that even the people I had left behind knew
these things too. When my cop brother
and my cop brother-in-law and my cop uncle and cousin and
boarder in my mother's house denounced
the riots in the '60s always in racist tones, I'd confront
them about the black friends they often
had in their homes and they would say, that's different,
that's LJ., he's my friend, he's not one
of them. Or when I'd point out how they often dressed and
spoke and drove the same cars and hung
out in the same bars and all the rest, they'd get hurt like
I had turned into some kind of foreigner,
one of those old-time Americans who didn't understand and
tried to grandstand with their liberal ideas
when they lived in wealthy suburbs and never had to deal
with the reality of our streets. They'd tell
me they didn't think they'd ever meet one of their own kind
as blind to what was real as me and then
they'd try and make me see that they didn't haven't anything
against the Jews and blacks and Italians
and homos and even the rich, because they all had friends or
even in-laws that fit those labels,
they'd try to tell me it's about being true to who you really are
no matter how far your people have come
or haven't come, and then they'd tell some story about how
it used to be and then they'd ask me
how come I never wrote those Damon Runyon stories about
    them
or more importantly about my father—
they figured I didn't bother because I got too far away
from what I'd been—when I moved
away from the old neighborhood after my father said I was
no good for wanting to marry a
black girl and having too many black friends—and then,
when I finally came back again,
so many years after I left him—this time we didn't
fight—because I asked him about
Boots and Mary, whatever happened to Louis the Lip or
Two Ton Tony—he talked all night
& it finally felt alright with him—he talked about how
his mother had been a "live-out maid"
when he was a kid—we never talked about politics or the

division that had driven us all into
fear and insecurity—I listened, he talked, and after I
left he called me up & asked if I had
enough to get my kids Xmas presents this year—I said I
did—I never took a dime from him
before, why should I start now—one of my sisters called
and told me because it was the only way
he could say I love you—so I called him back and said hey,
I could use two hundred & he said
it's yours—& I took the kids to see him with the
gifts his money made possible—
he was watching sports on the TV—and all of a sudden he
brought up Jackie Robinson—
how he always admired that man's dignity & a few days later
he called up the only brother he
had left and told him to take him to the hospital—
the doctor called my sister &
told her there's nothing we can find, we'll keep him
overnight and send him home—
& of course he died & this time when they tried to bring him
back he refused—hey, I don't know
why he wanted to die—that was a lot of years ago—all I
know is when I saw *Field of Dreams*
I started to cry—I didn't even know why—my father and
I never even tried to play any game—
but hey you know I'm not ashamed to carry his name—I hope
he feels the same.

MICHAEL LALLY

III. ～

CALLING ROLL

Sticks and stones will break my bones,

But names will never hurt me

The Riddle of Noah

You want to change your name. You're looking
for "something more suitable," words we can only guess
you've come by from television or teachers. All
your first-grade friends have names like Justin Mark
Caroline Emma or newly enrolled Xuan Loc
and yours, you sadly report, is Noah . . . nothing.

Noah *Hodges,* your middle name isn't nothing
your mother, named Hodges, reproves, but you go on looking.
Next day you are somebody else: Adam Stinger! The clock
turns back to my brother, Edward Elias, whose quest
to be named for his father (living names are death marks
on a Jewish child) was fulfilled by a City Hall

clerk. Peter Jr. went gladly to school all
unblessed. The names that we go by are nothing
compared to the names we are called. *Christ killer*! they mocked
and stoned me with quinces in my bland-looking
suburb. Why didn't I tattle, resist? I guessed
I was guilty, the only kid on my manicured block

who didn't know how to genuflect as we lock-
stepped to chapel at noontime. I was in thrall,
the one Jewish girl in my class at Holy Ghost
convent school. Xuan Loc, which translates as something
magical and tender—Spring Bud, a way of looking
at innocence—is awarded the gold bookmark

for reading more chapter-books than Justin Mark
or Noah, who now has tears in his eyes. No lack
of feeling here, a jealous Yahweh is looking
over his shoulder hissing, Be best of all.
What can be done to ease him? Nothing
makes up for losing, though love is a welcome guest.

Spared being burned at the stake, being starved or gassed,
like Xuan Loc, Noah is fated to make his mark,
suffer for grace through good works, aspire to something.
Half-Jewish, half-Christian, he will own his name, will unlock

the riddle of who he is: only child, in equal
measure blessed and damned to be inward-looking,

always slightly aslant the mark, like Xuan Loc.
Always playing for keeps, for all or nothing
in quest of his rightful self while the world looks on.

MAXINE KUMIN

Baptisms

Believing that people
were or became
what they were named,
they rose with the Sun,
called themselves Eagle,
Fox, Otter, Hawk, Wolf,
Bear and Deer.

Then new ones came,
those who named
themselves for forgotten memories,
great-grandfathers seeking
hard dominion over rock and stream,
ownership of forest and plain,
with names of Farmer, Smith and Weaver,
Joiner, Carpenter, Stoner, Wright.

Then they gave
the first people new names,
Government men and preachers smiled
as they christened Washingtons,
Wilsons, Garcias, Smiths—
and waited for them to change.

Yet even today,
when the newest names,
Citizen Band, Breeder Reactor,
Missile Range, Strip Mine and Pipe Line
have begun to move in,
residing where Bark Lodge, Wigwam

and Tipi, Wickiup and Hogan stood,
things have not ended as they should.

Somewhere, it is whispered,
at some ragged edge
of the unfinished land
the Sun is rising, breathing again
names which we have not yet heard,
names about to be spoken.

JOSEPH BRUCHAC

Freedom Candy

so what kind of name is Omar?
I ask this new boy at school
you name after a candy bar or what?
you know you too light to be milk chocolate

Omar looks at me and laughs
since that first smile
he's my best friend
maybe my best friend ever

folks call us the inseparables
like one of those old singing groups
my daddy is always talking
about

Omar is a muslim name
Omar tells me
I think it still sounds like a candy bar
like O'Henry, Baby Ruth, Mars or Almond Joy

maybe his momma should have named him Snickers
because of the way he laughs
Omar's name sounds like candy
and the way he acts is sweet to me

every teacher except Ms. Greenfield think so
Ms. Greenfield she don't like muslims
and the rest of us she calls natural born sinners
because of the way we talk and behave

Omar says we should tell Ms. Greenfield about herself
especially since it's Black History Month
so Omar stands up and says to Ms. Greenfield
how come you don't lead us somewhere?

why you not like Harriet Tubman?
why no field trips?
why no trips to the museum or zoo?
why we never go nowhere?

Ms. Greenfield she don't say nothing
she just look at Omar as if he is
the last muslim on earth
and about to die

I think of how Omar says muslims pray
five times a day and how cats have nine
lives and just maybe Omar might make it
to 3 o'clock or maybe he won't

suddenly Ms. Greenfield has one of those
fainting spells just like old Moses Tubman
and has to sit down behind her desk
she tells me to get some water

I feel free as I race down the hall
wondering how Omar can be so sweet
sometimes and get on everyone's
nerves the next

my daddy once told me M&Ms
melt in your mouth and your hands
especially if you colored
wait until I tell Omar

E. ETHELBERT MILLER

The Boots of Alfred Bettingdorf

Alfred Bettingdorf was a first-class twit. Twit, dork, squirrel, lead brain, shite-tooth: You name it, Alfred got called it. He slunk down the halls of our high school with a perpetual look of hunted malice. He hardly ever made it between classes without at least one un-provoked shove or verbal taunt. Yet he never retaliated. He'd just squint his beady eyes and shove his double-thick glasses further up his nose and bumble on in silence.

I was never one of his abusers. I don't say that to pat myself on the back; it's just that to me, guys like Alfred were too pathetic to attack. I tended to ignore him, as much out of embarrassment at his awkwardness as anything else.

Besides, I had other things to fret about. Like Suzie Sutton. Now there are pretty girls and pretty girls. But in 1965 in the tenth grade, there was only Suzie Sutton. My eyes were blinded to all else. I saw her in my study-hall daydreams. . . . I saw her while I bounced along in the back of the school bus. . . . I even saw her on the blackboard while the math teacher drew sine waves and bell curves. I was gone.

Not that I was the only one so afflicted. Suzie had the kind of build that made the physics teacher fumble for his slide rule: math-ematical perfection with a jiggle and a swish. She had long black hair that rippled in the wind, and eyes to match. Not dark. Black. Raven black. Suzie knew what she had, too—and just how to use it. Half the school was hot on her (the other half were girls, and probably a few of them shared the heat), but she always managed to keep her suitors panting in a pack.

In order to see her, I contrived elaborate routes between classes and after school. I knew her class schedule by heart, her locker number, where she met her friends. I even knew how many times she went to the john. When the bell rang to end a class I would dash madly to a selected point and then loiter there (still puffing from my run), casually adjusting the three-finger collar of my tai-lored shirt, staring out of the corner of my eye while she swirled past, surrounded by her circle of friends.

Oh, the joys that could be wrenched from a glimpse of those blood red lips, a passing fragrance from her hair! And then when she'd passed, a last lingering stare at her hips swaying on so fine and free above those achingly long legs. . . . Then another bell would ring and I'd limp into my next class.

Our school was an old brownstone affair, two-storied, institutional. The floors were wooden and creaked when trod upon. This made skipping classes somewhat difficult, as even the lightest tiptoe set the boards to sounding up and down the hallway. The only people who could move with impunity through the halls during class hours were debaters and a few selected jocks. Debaters, because they looked so glum and studious that nobody could imagine they were up to anything wrong. The jocks, because they were heroes to the school at large—teachers included—and heroes, they tell me, are hard to find. Whenever confronted by authority, the jocks swaggered a little bit harder and mumbled something about "Coach wants to see me" and they'd be waved on.

In the spring of the year, a new wrinkle in hallway freedom developed. There was to be an All School Talent Show, and those who volunteered to help prepare for it were allowed out of class. I didn't help, of course, but I took to carrying a couple of posters and an extra notebook around as cover for my own excursions.

I was still on the trail of Suzie Sutton, and grabbed at any excuse for better viewing or a potential opportunity for contact. The second-story windows on the south side of the building looked out over the school parking lot and it was from these windows that I bade farewell each day to the elusive Miss Sutton. I was so caught up in watching her that it took a while for me to realize how often I was seeing Alfred Bettingdorf. At first I figured it was coincidence, or just the fact that Alfred's gawky frame attracted attention wherever he went.

Then one day I finally realized what was up. Having just seen Suzie off for home in her pink Mustang (from a distance, of course), I turned away from my window vantage point and there was Alfred Bettingdorf lurking in a corner, licking his lips and still staring out at the parking lot. The hall was empty.

An instant flash told me Alfred—poor, puny, pathetic little Alfred—was hung up on the same chick I was. Against all reason, I felt a momentary bond of friendship.

I looked at him as I passed. He shied away, covering his torso with his notebook. That got to me. I stopped and his eyes narrowed. He kept his body covered. "She's something else, ain't she, Alfred?" My levity was forced.

His licked at his lips and said, "I got a right to watch," in his perpetual whine.

"Did I say you didn't? That's all you'll ever get to do, though."
Suddenly I felt low and I turned to leave.

"Same with you," he said, his voice a bit breathless and rising at
the end of the sentence.

I stopped and looked back. He swallowed and spoke—no whine
this time, just a bit of falter. "I mean . . . you watch her too. You
never get any closer."

It dawned on me that it would look very bad for my reputation
if this fact were discovered. I crooked a finger towards Alfred.
Instinctively, he cowered. "That's between you and me, buddy.
Understand?"

He nodded violently, glasses bobbing on his nose. I departed.

That was the end of it as far as I was concerned. But Alfred had
the same English class as I did. Two days later, old lady Olafson
gave us a writing assignment. I knocked out some drudgery about
life in a caddy shack and got the speechifying over as quickly as
possible.

When it was Alfred's turn, he stood up to a muted chorus of
hoots. Olafson glared for silence. Alfred stood knock-kneed at the
podium, pushing futilely at the heavy glasses sliding down his
lengthy nose.

He cleared his throat and from the back row Milnor imitated a
seal. Alfred's cheeks reddened. Then, with a grim, determined set
to his face he began to read.

> *Eddie was born in a Laundromat,*
> *or at least that's what he thought.*
> *He spent his days by the big machines*
> *where his parents worked and fought.*
> *A ten-foot counter, a two-tiered shelf*
> *and sixteen machines in a line.*
> *Eddie knew the scene like the back of his hand.*
> *It was staring at him all of the time.*

Alfred paused and caught his breath. Amazingly, the room was
quiet. He went faster, his thick lips framing an uneven row of teeth
and a thin stream of spittle spewing forth on the sibilants.

> *They said, "the boy's in the basement*
> *the boy's hiding out back . . .*

now what you gonna do
with a boy like that?"

Daddy was grey, kinda tired and fat.
And Ma, she had straggly hair . . .

What was this stuff? It sounded like a song, and not a bad one at that. I sat up straighter, tapping my foot to the cadence. The room was no longer quiet, and except for me and old lady Olafson grim-faced in a corner, Alfred seemed to have lost his audience.

. . . The street outside was a world apart,
left for bullies and groceries and school . . .
They said, "the boy's not in bed yet
the boy's getting fat . . .
now what you gonna do
with a boy like that?"

Alfred stuttered, losing the beat and finally stumbled to a halt. He wiped his mouth with the back of his hand and walked quickly down the aisle towards me, gripping the sheets of paper he'd been reading from and staring at his shoes. Olafson was already lambasting the loudest talkers and calling for the next volunteer, so I grabbed Alfred as he went by. Attention had turned to the front, where Big Brenda Phillips was still jiggling slightly from her passage to the front.

"Alfred, you write that stuff yourself?"

He blinked rapidly. "Sh—sh—sure," he said in a whisper. "I . . . write lots of stuff."

I looked at him with a cold eye, still not quite believing.

"Really," he said. "I got the idea from 'Grown Up Wrong.' Off the new Stones album."

"The what?"

"The new Stones album. Look." He ducked over to his seat and under cover of Big Brenda's chesty mew, scooted back and slipped a record jacket into my hands. I glanced toward Olafson's desk in a front corner of the room. She was occupied.

I turned the album around in my hands. "Where'd you get this?" I said. "I never saw this one."

"It's just out. Called *12 × 5*. It's great. Even better than their first." Alfred's hiss rose in volume as his enthusiasm swelled.

I glanced back at the front. The teacher was still occupied. "You a Stones fan?" It just didn't fit.

"Hey, yeah. Yeah, definitely." Alfred's eyes (as much as I could see of them through his glasses) gleamed. His voice rose. "Yeah. I play guitar and —"

"Sykes. Bettingdorf. What's going on over there?" A harsh voice from the front. Old lady Olafson stood up and peered out at us. Alfred shrank backwards. "No personal conversation you two. Save it for after class."

Scattered sniggers and a warbled "Bettingdorf—dorf—dorf—" trailed Alfred back to his seat.

My ears burned. My name had been publicly linked with his. I, Gabe Sykes, seemingly suave of dress and demeanor, publicly linked with scrawny, rumpled-shirted Alfred Bettingdorf. That he could write song lyrics seemed little consolation. His status was nil. I kept my eyes down on my desk, desperately hoping the incident would be forgotten.

My eyes focused. The Stones record still lay in front of me. A new one! I'd just about played the grooves off their first: *England's Newest Hitmakers*. A new Stones album! This was an event. I stared at the cover photo, imagining myself as Brian Jones. Blond and beautiful, hippest of the hip. I watched myself striding haughtily past Suzie Sutton, felt her tugging on my arm, begging for attention. A new Stones album!

The bell rang.

I had to hear it. Against my better judgment, against all social sense, I approached Alfred. He was smiling again, those strange full lips curled around his off-white teeth.

I held up the album. "Mind if I borrow this overnight? I got to hear this. I'll bring it back tomorrow, no sweat."

He scratched at his nose. "Yeah, you can borrow it. But just one night, you hear?"

I was already gone into the crowd of departing students. But I heard. I just didn't want our faces imprinted together in anybody's mind.

Alfred was right. The album was great. "Under the Boardwalk" was an instant favorite. I lay up in my bedroom and just let the needle drop back on it over and over.

If I were Brian Jones, I thought. I lay there imagining myself stretched out at seaside with Suzie's black eyes flashing into mine and the world going by somewhere at a distance. If I were Brian Jones . . .

The next morning I was watching the pink Mustang pull into the parking lot when I spotted an odd-looking shirt out of the corner of my eye. It was Alfred.

"What'd you think of the album?" His grin was wide and goofy.

"Uh, good stuff, Alfred. Good stuff. Just a sec'." We both paused and watched as a lithe figure with raven tresses whipping in the wind came strutting across the parking lot. Alfred sighed. I had more composure, but I felt the same. I turned away from the window.

Never any closer. Never anything more than a passing glance. Not a smile, not a touch, not even a sign of recognition. Hopeless. I felt at that moment as much a twit as Alfred.

After a moment of silence I handed back the album

"Like my shirt?" said Alfred proudly. I watched his little chest expand.

"Well . . ." I hesitated. Might as well tell him. "Tab collars just don't make it, Alfred." I said it as gently as I could. I was still feeling blue over Suzie.

"Oh, yeah?" His eyes flashed. "Jagger's wearing one. Look there." He pointed at the cover. Sure enough. "You telling me the Stones don't make it?" Damn. Sure enough.

It hit me in a flash. Provincials. We were all provincials. Our whole fashion pattern, the entire intricate structure of proper high school hipster–wear, the whole pattern built on the basic truth of the three-finger button-down collar, was all provincial. Arbitrary, conservative. I looked more closely at the picture of the Stones. Richards, Watts, none of them wore three-finger button-downs. Jones—Brian Jones—was wearing a flyaway collar! No buttons at all. A flyaway! My universe teetered. My hand shook. Then I focused and held firm.

I looked back at Alfred. He pushed his glasses up on his nose. His eyes looked different, more piercing. For the first time I saw a bit of what lurked beneath them. Hidden there, under all the fear and pain of being perpetually tormented, I saw an awareness of the forces—the capricious, herdlike forces—that bound and dictated our habits.

I stared. He blinked.

"Look at this." He pulled out a magazine photo of the Stones; a full-length shot. "Look at those shoes," he said. "You ever see anybody around here wear shoes like that?"

Richards wore boots. Scruffy black pointy-toed boots that disappeared up under his pants. Jagger had on what looked to be white Hush Puppies. Both were a far cry from the round-toed spit-shined wing tips that dominated our hallways.

"I'm gonna get me a pair of boots," he said. "Even if nobody else knows, at least I will. I'm gonna wear them for the Talent Show."

I was still stunned, still trying to rein in my racing thoughts. Provincials. Conservatives. Or . . . could it just be that nobody had the nerve to pick up on what was new? Could it be that this was how fashion changed? That one day an Alfred Bettingdorf saw a picture on a record and took a chance at being laughed at?

It was too much to swallow. I handed the picture back. "Sounds good, Alfred. Why don't you try that?" Still dazed, I started off down the hall.

Alfred called after me. "Gabe," he said, and I stopped. "I understand. It's harder for you. They don't laugh at you." He pushed his glasses up. "Me? I got nothing to lose."

I went on to study hall in a fog. There was a math quiz coming up that needed prompt attention, but I stared blankly at the same page for the rest of the hour. I wondered what Buddy Holly had looked like when he was in high school. A gawky kid with huge specs and a nasal voice. Or Jagger. Even Jagger. I remembered reading an interview where he said that when he was growing up he never knew if he was extraordinarily ugly or not. Those oversize lips, the sinuous curl of red against his teeth, a gash in his face almost as bad as Alf—I stopped. I had been about to say almost as bad as Alfred Bettingdorf.

At lunch that day everybody was talking about the Talent Show. The list of performers had finally been posted. I dropped my food tray on the table next to Jimmy Spees and sat down. Jacobson and the boys were roaring with laughter across from us.

"What's so funny, Jake?" I asked.

"Tell it again, Jake," said somebody at his side.

He stopped in mid-guffaw to explain. "They left off one of the performers' names," he said. "Suzie Sutton. Check this for an act. She comes out with just a bikini, a whip and a trained German shepherd. And a little background music, like maybe 'Ain't Too Proud to Beg.' And then she starts . . ."

I tried not to listen. Jacobson always was a little too graphic for me. I hummed to myself till I heard more bursts of laughter.

"Hey Jimmy," I said. "Who *is* performing?"

He shoved a list my way and I scanned it quickly. "No real surprises there."

"Except one," he said. "Look there. Madcap & the Laughs. Now who the hell is that? Only bands in this school are the Disasters and the Falling Rocks."

He was right. Nobody seemed to know who they were. Even the heaviest gossips were stumped. For a day or so, it was topic number one. Then I went back to thinking about more important things, like the way to Suzie Sutton's heart. Assuming there was one. She sure didn't seem to make very many people happy. I guess when you're beautiful you don't have to.

The following Monday, Alfred appeared in his new boots. "Had to go thirty miles to get these," he told me. "Nobody's got them like this around here."

He paid for his daring. After third hour a couple of the jocks noticed his foot-gear. By the end of the day they had half the senior class participating in a new game—step on Alfred's boots.

He wasn't at the window watching the pink Mustang depart that night and he wasn't at school at all the next day. When I saw him again he was limping and the boots were a mess. But he still wore them. And that hunted look in his eyes had been replaced by a sharp defiance, obvious immediately to anybody who cared to look. Few did.

"I beat them," he said. "Every one of them."

"How's that? Seems to me *they* got *you*."

"Uh-uh." He pointed at his feet. "I'm still wearing them, right? They had their fun, they did their damage. But I'm still wearing them. And now the laugh's on them." His lip curled in a sneer.

I pulled doubtfully at my ear lobe.

Alfred's fists clenched and unclenched. "Don't you see? One day they'll be wearing them too. And on that day they'll have to suffer with the fact that I—I, Alfred Bettingdorf—was wearing them first." He ran his fingers through his hair. "I'm letting my hair grow too. And practicing . . . every day."

"Practicing?"

"Guitar. I been telling you. I'm gonna enter that Talent Show. You just wait and see what happens."

"It's too late, Alfred." I really felt sorry for him now. Him and his delusions. "They've already got a full list."

"I know. I'm on it." He lowered his head and looked at me over his glasses. "We're Madcap & the Laughs."

"What!" I jerked back a step. "You mean it? You're the unknown band?"

"Well, not me alone. Got a couple of buddies from Central High who've been playing around together. It's a three-piece."

Alfred with buddies . . . in a band? This was more than I could process. This was definitely too much. Again I flashed on Buddy Holly.

"Alfred, they'll laugh you out of town. You know that."

He snorted. "So what's new. I been laughed at all my life. At least I'll know, even if no one else does. I'm gonna show those jocks. I'm gonna show Jacobson and Milnor and all those guys." His eyes were wide and glaring through his glasses. "And I'm gonna show that Suzie Sutton," he said. "I'm gonna show her she ain't the only thing going." His whole body was vibrating with excitement. "I gotta go."

He turned abruptly and ran down the hall, the clumping of his boots drowning out the creaking of the wooden floor.

I watched him go. Then I stood at the window for a long time while the cars pulled out one by one from the parking lot. The pink Mustang was still there. My stomach churned uncontrollably, sickness deep in my loins. I felt rash and desperate and ready for anything.

I straightened my three-finger collar and shined my Cordovan wing tips on the back of my pants leg. I took a step, then another. The floor creaked beneath me. I was walking steadily now, heart thumping, palms wet with sweat.

I caught up with her at the door of her car.

"Uh, Suzie. You got a sec'?" My voice sounded hoarse and weak. I cleared my throat.

She turned towards me in a swirl of ebony locks. A musky fragrance enveloped my head and I fought off dizziness.

"Yes?" she said, head cocked seductively at an angle. It was the first word she'd ever spoken to me.

"Uh . . . I was wondering . . ." I flashed my biggest smile. "I was wondering if you'd go to the Talent Show with me?"

There was a second of silence; an endless, heart-thumping second while we stood staring at each other. Her eyes burned into mine with black intensity. She smiled, and laughed—a mirthless chuckle. "Go with you?" she said. "You must be joking."

She opened the car door, got in, and was gone in an instant. I stood frozen to the spot, smile iced in place. Mercifully, I was numb. Except for the huge hunk of lead that clogged my throat.

I walked home that night. It took two and a half hours, but I didn't care. Anything to keep from existing. I told my mother I was sick and went straight to bed. The lead in my throat had passed to my stomach and I wondered if I could ever eat another meal. I considered flinging myself under a truck, or joining the navy. I knew I would never go to school again.

Towards dawn I thought of Alfred Bettingdorf. How often had he lain like this, victim of unbearable humiliation? Still sleepless, equal parts rage and shame, I switched on the radio. They were playing the new Stones single, "Time Is On My Side."

Alfred and those crazy boots. I rolled over and went to sleep.

Everybody went to the Talent Show. Numerous parties were scheduled for afterwards. Jimmy Spees knew of one at some girl's house and Jacobson was having a kegger down by the river. I felt like getting wild.

The acts were nothing special. A thin, anemic Senior girl played Chopin to yawns and twitching. The football team did a silly skit about cheerleaders. There were two bad comedians and some very ordinary rock-'n'-roll from the Disasters.

Suzie and her friends held center stage most of the night. Prancing and posing like uncrowned royalty, they whirled in a ceaseless circuit of male attention. I felt sick to my stomach just watching, but still the attraction was there. I knew what they said about the spider and fly—but now it didn't help.

Madcap & the Laughs was scheduled last. I was certain Alfred would be pathetic, but I felt I owed it to him to stay and watch.

The lights dimmed. The M.C. shouted "Madcap & the Laughs" and there they were, churning their way through "Time Is On My Side." A well-pimpled boy with long bangs beat out a rough-and-ready rhythm on his drums. The bassman was a moon-faced fellow of enormous girth whose cheeks expanded and contracted in a soundless parallel to the song's tempo.

But Alfred—Alfred Bettingdorf, first-class twit—was everybody's focus of attention. His hair was combed down in his eyes and he'd left his glasses at home. I doubt he could see beyond his mike stand. He wore a tab-collar shirt and a vest that looked like something off the cover of *England's Newest Hitmakers*. And his toes tapped rhythm in scuffed black boots that disappeared up the leg of his pants.

Alfred could play. He was no Keith Richards, and his voice bore little resemblance to Jagger's, but he had the phrasing down—and he knew exactly how it all should look.

I was astounded.

They banged to a halt and went into something new, something I'd never heard. Alfred shook his hair as he sang. And then I realized I'd heard those words before:

> *They said, "the boy's in the basement*
> *the boy's hiding out back . . .*
> *Now what you gonna do*
> *with a boy like that?"*

It was an Alf original. The one he'd read in Olafson's English class. The arrangement was more than the band could handle, but still—this thing kicked. Suzie and her crowd were pointing and making faces, oblivious to anything but their own safe standards of hipness. She was up near the front of the stage, wearing a patrician sneer, when Alfred suddenly stomped his foot and the band changed gears.

It was another Stones song, the final cut on *12 × 5:* "Suzie Q." That took nerve. I looked over to where Suzie stood, wondering what she thought. She was laughing; openly, shamelessly laughing. One of her friends mimicked Alfred—but not nearly as well as Alfred was mimicking Jagger.

Then Alfred, bat-eyed and nerveless, picked out that mass of raven black hair from the crowd and sang "Suzie Q" straight at it.

Suzie's laughter froze, and under his strutting, nearsighted, saliva-spewing spell, her smile vanished. *He* was singing to *her*. In front of a crowd. "Oh, Suzie Q," wailed Alfred in a guttural drawl, drawing his lips thickly around his teeth, "Tell me, who needs you?"

His own words again!

She shrank back into the wall and edged along it towards the rear, her haughtiness tempered momentarily with shame.

I looked at the rest of the crowd. Everybody seemed to think it was a joke—Alfred Bettingdorf, always good for a laugh. Nobody paid it much attention, except to ridicule. Couldn't they see? Couldn't they hear? This kid had something. Rough, yes. Derivative, certainly. But here was raw talent far above whatever else we'd been watching. But nobody noticed. They couldn't see past Alfred Bettingdorf, first-class twit.

The Laughs stopped. A few hands clapped. Far more stayed in pockets while their owners jeered. The lights came up and the show was over. I suddenly realized I didn't feel like partying. Not at all.

I walked up to the stage, with Suzie and her crowd alongside. I barely noticed. Alfred was putting his guitar back in its case. Suzie pushed past me and and stood staring for a moment at Alfred, her fists clasping and unclasping. "Creep," she snapped. Alfred smiled into the case.

She turned away again, and the ugly set to her mouth softened into a vast, insincere smile. She waved across at somebody on the far wall and her whole retinue of camp followers departed in her wake.

I waited until the stage area cleared and Alfred was locking his case. "Alf," I said. "Hey, Alf."

He blinked vaguely towards me. "That you Gabe?"

"Alf, that was incredible. You've got Jagger down cold. You're a performer."

He blushed and kicked idly with his foot. "Thanks," he said. "I'm glad somebody knows."

We stood there for a minute.

"I heard of a party Suzie Sutton's going to," he said at last. "I got no hope, but you could probably get in."

I looked behind me to where she was sweeping grandly out of the room. "No," I said. "I don't think so. I got other things to do." I stood there a minute, thinking. "Say Alf, where did you say you got those boots?"

DANIEL GABRIEL

Say What?

I got a message from
        a couple of hurt
        Negroes, who were
        very good at being
        Negroes (Good Negroes, like Aime Cesaire described).

Completely embalmed smiling
mummy handles
for animal toilets

So just as
The Wholly Book
& Holly Wood
have told us
& like the
Minister sd
Certainly, God
is real
& we have all
seen
Charlton Heston
&
Jeffrey Hunter

So just as these old Negroes
had imagined and hoped
& believed

Not only was there a God
But Heaven too.

So when these Good Negroes died
their Negro goodness
shot them straight up
to Heaven.

But by then Heaven had been privatized
& Affirmative Action
was over!

AMIRI BARAKA

Sangre 14

Sterling, Colorado

"On Saturdays we would go to town
after picking potatoes all week

and the Anglos would laugh at us
and call us dirty Mexicans,"
my mother tells me

as she sits and crochets
surrounded by the red, white, and blue ribbons
won at the State Fair

A picture of John F. Kennedy
smiles from the wall

Her busy, brown hands
pull pulling the thread
from the spool on her carpet

A portrait of Jesus
stares from the wall

The needle flick flick flickering
as she loops the laughter
and pulls the thread, pulls thread
and she loops the Saturdays
and pulls and pulls the thread
as she loops and loops the laughter
and Saturdays in Sterling
into yet another doily

LEROY V. QUINTANA

The Loss of a Culture

Not the trip to a land where words are pronounced as you were taught to pronounce them. Not the adage your grandmother serves you at dinner. The language you speak as a child, flushed down the toilet bowl. Your mother-tongue sounds as foreign to you as any language you do not understand. Forgotten as the lifestyle you once had. Latin engraved on darkened school desks. What do you tell yourself when you find yourself alone at night? The uneaten bread becomes stale. The avoided meeting of a one-night stand, dreadful. Squashed tomato on the floor sinks into the tiles of your perfection. You forget the past but the past will not forget you. You sit on broken chairs and get cramps when you are about to say something intelligent. If you collapse and smash your head on the floor, it will not be from lack of proper diet, it will be your ancestors who will shoot you from behind.

ANTONIO D'ALFONSO

Coffee

stream rises over my nose
against this night
cold empty room as wide as my throat; eases/flows
river a mocha memory from aunt ora's
kitchen. she made it in the
big tin percolator and poured the brew into thick
white fist-sized mugs and
put lots of sugar and milk in it for me and
the other kids who loved it better than chocolate
and the neighbor woman used to tell her and us
it wasn't good for young colored children
to drink. it made you get blacker
and blacker

WANDA COLEMAN

Horns on Your Head

The further you venture from the house,
Mother said, the fewer people you'll know.
Everyone on this block has either heard
of you or has seen you at one time. But
on the next block maybe only one person
will recognize you. Then there are hundreds
of blocks where no one knows you exist.
And it goes on that way until you get
to Nebraska, where it goes even worse.
There, the people never met a Jew before.
They think you have horns, & will want
to look for them. That's why you should never move
too far away from me. You don't want
strangers to always be touching your head.

HAL SIROWITZ

The Middle Classes

They say memory enhances places, but my childhood block of small brick row houses grows smaller every year, till there is barely room for me to stand upright in my own recollections. The broad avenue on our corner, gateway to the rest of the world, an avenue so broad that for a long time I was not permitted to cross it alone, has narrowed to a strait, and its row of tiny shops—dry cleaners, candy store, beauty parlor, grocery store—has dwindled to a row of cells. On my little block itself the hedges, once staunch walls guarding the approach to every house, are shrunken, their sharp dark leaves stunted. The hydrangea bush—what we called a snowball bush— in front of the house next to mine has shrunk; its snowballs have melted down. And the ledges from each front walk to each drive- way, against whose once-great stone walls we played King, a kind of inverse handball, and from whose tops we jumped with delec- table agonies of fear—ah, those ledges have sunk, those leaps are nothing. Small.

In actuality, of course, my Brooklyn neighborhood has not shrunk but it has changed. Among the people I grew up with, that is understood as a euphemism meaning black people have moved in. They moved in family by family, and one by one the old white families moved out, outwards, that is, in an outward direction (Long Island, Rockaway, Queens), the direction of water—it seems not to have occurred to them that soon there would be nowhere to go unless back into the surf where we all began—except for two of the old white families who bravely remained and sent reports in the outward directions that living with the black people was fine, they were nice people, good neighbors, and so these two white families came to be regarded by the departed as sacrificial heroes of sorts; everyone admired them but no one would have wished to emulate them.

The changes the black families brought to the uniform block were mostly in the way of adornment. Colorful shutters affixed to the front casement windows, flagstones on the walkways leading to the porch steps, flowers on the bordering patches of grass, and quantities of ornamental wrought iron; a few of the brick porch walls have even been replaced by wrought-iron ones. (Those adja- cent porches with their low dividing walls linked our lives. We girls visited back and forth climbing from porch to porch to porch, peeking into living room windows as we darted by.) But for all these proprietary changes, my block looks not so very different, in essence. It has remained middle class.

Black people appeared on the block when I lived there too, but they were maids, and very few at that. Those few came once a week, except for the three families where the mothers were school-teachers; their maids came every day and were like one of the family, or so the families boasted, overlooking the fact that the maids had families of their own. One other exception: the family next door to mine who had the snowball bush also had a live-in maid who did appear to live like one of the family. It was easy to forget that she cleaned and cooked while the family took their ease, because when her labors were done she ate with them and then sat on the porch and contributed her opinions to the neighborhood gossip. They had gotten her from the South when she was seven-teen, they said with pride, and when her grandmother came up to visit her the grandmother slept and ate and gossiped with the family too, but whether she too was expected to clean and cook I do not know.

It was less a city block than a village, where of a hot summer evening the men sat out on the front porches in shirtsleeves smok-ing cigars and reading newspapers under yellow lanterns (there were seven New York City newspapers) while the wives brought out bowls of cherries and trays of watermelon slices and gossiped porch to porch, and we girls listened huddled together on the steps, hoping the parents would forget us and not send us to bed, and where one lambent starry summer evening the singular fighting couple on the block had one of their famous battles in the master bedroom—shrieks and blows and crashing furniture; in what was to become known in local legend as the balcony scene, Mrs. Hoch-man leaned out of the open second-floor casement window in a flowing white nightgown like a mythological bird and shouted to the assembled throng, "Neighbors, neighbors, help me, I'm trapped up here with a madman" (she was an elocution teacher), and my mother rose to her feet to go and help but my father, a tax lawyer, restrained her and said,"Leave them alone, they're both crazy. To-morrow they'll be out on the street holding hands as usual." And soon, indeed, the fighting stopped, and I wondered, What is love, what is marriage? What is reality in the rest of the world?

The daughters of families of our station in life took piano lessons and I took the piano lessons seriously. Besides books, music was the only experience capable of levitating me away from Brooklyn with-out the risk of crossing bridges or tunneling my way out. When I was about eleven I said I wanted a new and good piano teacher, for the lady on Eastern Parkway to whose antimacassared apartment I went for my lessons was pixilated: she trilled a greeting when she opened the door and wore pastel-colored satin ribbons in her curly gray hair and served tea and excellent shortbead cookies, but of teaching she did very little. So my mother got me Mr. Simmons.

He was a black man of around thirty-five or forty recommended by a business acquaintance of my father's with a son allegedly possessed of musical genius, the development of which was being entrusted to Mr. Simmons. If he was good enough for that boy, the logic ran, then he was good enough for me. I was alleged to be unusually gifted too, but not quite that gifted. I thought it very advanced of my parents to hire a black piano teacher for their nearly nubile daughter; somewhere in the vast landscape of what I had yet to learn, I must have glimpsed the springs of fear. I was proud of my parents, though I never said so. I had known they were not bigoted but rather instinctively decent; I had known that when and if called upon, they would instinctively practice what was then urged as "tolerance," but I hadn't known to what degree. As children do, I underestimated them, partly because I was just discovering that they were the middle class.

Mr. Simmons was a dark-skinned man of moderate height and moderate build, clean-shaven but with an extremely rough beard that might have been a trial to him, given his overall neatness. A schoolteacher, married, the father of two young children, he dressed in the style of the day, suit and tie, with impeccable conventionality. His manners were also impeccably conventional. Nice but dull was how I classified him on first acquaintance, and I assumed from his demeanor that moderation in all things was his hallmark. I was mistaken: he was a blatant romantic. His teaching style was a somber intensity streaked by delicious flashes of joviality. He had a broad smile, big teeth, a thunderous laugh, and a willing capacity to be amused, especially by me. To be found amusing was an inspiration. I saved my most sophisticated attitudes and phraseology for Mr. Simmons. Elsewhere, I felt, they were as pearls cast before swine. He was not dull after all, if he could appreciate me. And yet unlike my past teachers he could proclaim "Awful!" with as much intrepidity as "Beautiful!" "No, no, no, *this* is how it should sound," in a pained voice, shunting me off the piano bench and launching out at the passage. I was easily offended and found his bluntness immodest at first. Gradually, through Mr. Simmons, I learned that false modesty is useless and that true devotion to skill is impersonal.

Early in our acquaintance he told me that during the summers when school was out his great pleasure was to play the piano eight hours in a row, stripped to the waist and sweating. It was January when he said this, and he grinned with a kind of patient longing. I recognized it as an image of passion and dedication, and forever after, in my eyes, he was surrounded by a steady, luminous aura of fervor. I wished I were one of his children, for the glory of living in his house and seeing that image in the flesh and basking in the luxuriant music. He would be playing Brahms, naturally; he had told me even earlier on that Brahms was his favorite composer. "Ah, Brahms," he would sigh, leaning back in his chair near the piano bench and tilting his head in a dreamy way. I did not share his love for Brahms but Brahms definitely fit in with the entire picture—the hot day, the long hours, the bare chest, and the sweat.

Mr. Simmons had enormous beautiful pianist's hands—they made me ashamed of my own, small and stubby. Tragicomically, he would lift one of my hands from the keyboard and stare at it ruefully. "Ah, if only these were bigger!" A joke, but he meant it. He played well but a bit too romantically for my tastes. Of course he grasped my tastes thoroughly and would sometimes exaggerate his playing to tease me, and exaggerate also the way he swayed back and forth at the piano, crooning along with the melody, bending picturesquely over a delicate phrase, clattering at a turbulent passage, his whole upper body tense and filled with the music. "You think that's too schmaltzy, don't you?" laughing his thunderous laugh. The way he pronounced "schmaltzy," our word, not his, I found very droll. To admonish me when I was lazy he would say, "*Play* the notes, *play* the notes," and for a long time I had no idea what he meant. Listening to him play, I came to understand. He meant play them rather than simply touch them. Press them down and make contact. Give them their full value. Give them yourself.

It seemed quite natural that Mr. Simmons and I should come to be such appreciative friends—we were part of a vague, nameless elite—but I was surprised and even slightly irked that my parents appreciated him so. With the other two piano teachers who had come to the house my mother had been unfailingly polite, offering coffee and cake but no real access. About one of them, the wild-eyebrowed musician with the flowing scarves and black coat and beret and the mock-European accent, who claimed to derive from Columbia University as though it were a birthplace, she commented that he might call himself an artist but in addition he was a slob who could eat a whole cake and leave crumbs all over the fringed tapestry covering her piano. But with Mr. Simmons she behaved the way she did with her friends; I should say, with her friends' husbands, or her husband's friends, since at that time women like my mother did not have men friends of their own, at least in Brooklyn. When Mr. Simmons arrived at about three forty-five every Wednesday, she offered him coffee—he was coming straight from teaching, and a man's labor must always be respected—and invited him to sit down on the couch. There she joined him and inquired how his wife and children were, which he told her in some detail. That was truly dull. I didn't care to hear anecdotes illustrating the virtues and charms of his children, who were younger than I. Then, with an interest that didn't seem at all feigned, he asked my mother reciprocally how her family was. They exchanged such trivia on my time, till suddenly he would look at his watch, pull himself up, and with a swift, broad smile, say, "Well, then, shall we get started?" At last.

But my father! Sometimes my father would come home early on Wednesdays, just as the lesson was ending. He would greet Mr. Simmons like an old friend; they would clap each other on the shoulder and shake hands in that hearty way men do and which I found ridiculous. And my father would take off his hat and coat and put down his *New York Times* and insist that Mr. Simmons have a drink or at least a cup of coffee, and they would talk enthusiastically about—of all things—business and politics. Boring, boring! How could he? Fathers were supposed to be interested in those boring things, but not Mr. Simmons. After a while Mr. Simmons would put on his hat and coat, which were remarkably like the hat and coat my father had recently taken off, pick up his *New York Times*, and head for his home and family.

And my father would say, "What a nice fellow that Mr. Simmons is! What a really fine person!" For six years he said it, as if he had newly discovered it, or was newly astonished that it could be so. "It's so strange," he might add, shaking his head in a puzzled way. "Even though he's a colored man I can talk to him just like a friend. I mean, I don't feel any difference. It's a very strange thing." When I tried, with my advanced notions, to relieve my father of the sense of strangeness, he said, "I know, I know all that"; yet he persisted in finding it a very strange thing. Sometimes he boasted about Mr. Simmons to his friends with wonder in his voice: "I talk to him just as if he were a friend of mine. A very intelligent man. A really fine person." To the very end, he marveled; I would groan and laugh every time I heard it coming.

Mr. Simmons told things to my father in my presence, important and serious things that I knew he would not tell to me alone. This man-to-man selectivity of his pained me. He told my father that he was deeply injured by the racial prejudice existing in this country; that it hurt his life and the lives of his wife and children; and that he resented it greatly. All these phrases he spoke in his calm, conventional way, wearing his suit and tie and sipping coffee. And my father nodded his head and agreed that it was terribly unfair. Mr. Simmons hinted that his career as a classical pianist had been thwarted by his color, and again my father shook his head with regret. Mr. Simmons told my father that he had a brother who could not abide the racial prejudice in this country and so he lived in France. "Is that so?" said my mother in dismay, hovering nearby, slicing cake. To her, that anyone might have to leave this country, to which her parents had fled for asylum, was unwelcome, almost incredible, news. But yes, it was so, and when he spoke about his brother Mr. Simmons' resonant low voice was sad and angry, and I, sitting on the sidelines, felt a flash of what I had felt when the neighbor woman being beaten shrieked out of the window on that hot summer night—ah, here is reality at last. For I believed that reality must be cruel and harsh and densely complex. It would never have occurred to me that reality could also be my mother serving Mr. Simmons home-baked layer cake or my father asking him if he had to go so soon, couldn't he stay and have a bite to eat, and my mother saying, "Let the man go home to his own family, for heaven's sake, he's just done a full day's work." I also felt afraid at the anger in Mr. Simmons' voice; I thought he might be angry at me. I thought that if I were he I would at least have been angry at my parents and possibly even refused their coffee and cake, but Mr. Simmons didn't.

When I was nearing graduation from junior high school my mother suggested that I go to the High School of Music and Art in Manhattan. I said no, I wanted to stay with my friends and didn't want to travel for over an hour each way on the subway. I imagined I would be isolated up there. I imagined that the High School of Music and Art, by virtue of being in Manhattan, would be far too sophisticated, even for me. In a word, I was afraid. My mother wasn't the type to press the issue but she must have enlisted Mr. Simmons to press it for her. I told him the same thing, about traveling for over an hour each way on the subway. Then, in a very grave manner, he asked if I had ever seriously considered a musical career. I said instantly, "Oh, no, that sounds like a man's sort of career." I added that I wouldn't want to go traveling all over the country giving concerts. He told me the names of some women pianists, and when that didn't sway me, he said he was surprised that an intelligent girl could give such a foolish answer without even thinking it over. I was insulted and behaved coolly towards him for a few weeks. He behaved with the same equanimity as ever and waited for my mood to pass. Every year or so after that he would ask the same question in the same grave manner, and I would give the same answer. Once I overheard him telling my mother, "And she says it's a man's career!" "Ridiculous," said my mother disgustedly. "Ridiculous," Mr. Simmons agreed.

Towards the end of my senior year in high school (the local high school, inferior in every way to the High School of Music and Art in Manhattan), my parents announced that they would like to buy me a new piano as a graduation present. A baby grand, and I could pick it out myself. We went to a few piano showrooms in Brooklyn so I could acquaint myself with the varieties of piano. I spent hours pondering the differences between Baldwin and Steinway, the two pianos most used by professional musicians, for in the matter of a piano—unlike a high school—I had to have the best. Steinways were sharp-edged, Baldwins more mellow; Steinways classic and traditional, Baldwins romantically timeless; Steinways austere, Baldwins responsive to the touch. On the other hand, Steinways were crisp compared to Baldwins' pliancy; Steinways were sturdy and dependable, while Baldwins sounded a disquieting tone of mutability. I liked making classifications. At last I decided that a Baldwin was the piano for me—rich, lush, and mysterious, not at all like my playing, but now that I think of it, rather like Mr. Simmons'.

I had progressed some since the days when I refused to consider going to the High School of Music and Art in Manhattan. If it was to be a Baldwin I insisted that it come from the source, the Baldwin showroom in midtown Manhattan. My mother suggested that maybe Mr. Simmons might be asked to come along, to offer us expert advice on so massive an investment. I thought that was a fine idea, only my parents were superfluous; the two of us, Mr. Simmons and I, could manage alone. My parents showed a slight, hedging reluctance. Perhaps it was not quite fair, my mother suggested, to ask Mr. Simmons to give up a Saturday afternoon for this favor. It did not take an expert logician to point out her inconsistency. I was vexed by their reluctance and would not even condescend to think about it. I knew it could have nothing to do with trusting him: over the years they had come to regard him as an exemplar of moral probity. Evidently the combination of his being so reliable and decent, so charming, and so black set him off in a class by himself.

I asked the favor of Mr. Simmons and he agreed, although in his tone too was a slight, hedging reluctance; I couldn't deny it. But again, I could ignore it. I had a fantasy of Mr. Simmons and myself ambling through the Baldwin showroom, communing in a rarefied manner about the nuances of difference between one Baldwin and another, and I wanted to make this fantasy come true.

The Saturday afternoon arrived. I was excited. I had walked along the streets of Manhattan before, alone and with my friends. But the thought of walking down Fifty-seventh Street with an older man, clearly not a relative, chatting like close friends for all the sophisticated world to see, made my spirits as buoyant and iridescent as a bubble. Mr. Simmons came to pick me up in his car. I had the thrill of sliding into the front seat companionably, chatting like close friends with an older man. I wondered whether he would come around and open the door for me when we arrived. That was done in those days, for ladies. I was almost seventeen. But he only stood waiting while I climbed out and slammed it shut, as he must have done with his own children, as my father did with me.

We walked down broad Fifty-seventh Street, where the glamour was so pervasive I could smell it: cool fur and leather and smoky perfume. People looked at us with interest. How wondrous that was! I was ready to fly with elation. It didn't matter that Mr. Simmons had known me since I was eleven and seen me lose my temper like an infant and heard my mother order me about; surely he must see me as the delightful adult creature I had suddenly become, and surely he must be delighted to be escorting me down Fifty-seventh Street. I would have liked to take his arm to complete the picture for all the sophisticated world to see, but some things were still beyond me. I felt ready to fly but in fact I could barely keep up with Mr. Simmons' long and hurried stride. He was talking as companionably as ever, but he seeemed ill at ease. Lots of people looked at us. Even though it was early April he had his overcoat buttoned and his hat brim turned down.

We reached the Baldwin showroom. Gorgeous, burnished pianos glistened in the display windows. We passed through the portals; it was like entering a palace. Inside it was thickly carpeted. We were shown upstairs. To Paradise! Not small! Immensely high ceilings and so much space, a vista of lustrous pianos floating on a rich sea of green carpet. Here in this grand room full of grand pianos Mr. Simmons knew what he was about. He began to relax and smile, and he talked knowledgeably with the salesman, who was politely helpful, evidently a sophisticated person.

"Well, go ahead," Mr. Simmons urged me. "Try them out."

"You mean play them?" I looked around at the huge space. The only people in it were two idle salesmen and far off at the other end a small family of customer, father, mother, and little boy.

"Of course." He laughed. "How else will you know which one you like?"

I finally sat down at one and played a few timid scales and arpeggios. I crept from one piano to another, doing the same, trying to discern subtle differences between them.

"Play," Mr. Simmons commanded.

At the sternness in his voice I cast away timidity. I played Chopin's "Revolutionary Etude," which I had played the year before at a recital Mr. Simmons held for his students in Carl Fischer Hall—nowadays called Cami Hall—on Fifty-seventh Street, not far from the Baldwin showroom. (I had been the star student. The other boy, the musical genius, had gone off to college or otherwise vanished. I had even done a Mozart sonata for four hands with Mr. Simmons himself.) Sustained by his command, I moved dauntlessly from Baldwin to Baldwin, playing passages from the "Revolutionary Etude." Mr. Simmons flashed his broad smile and I smiled back.

"Now you play," I said.

I thought he might have to be coaxed, but I was forgetting that Mr. Simmons was never one to withhold, or to hide his light. Besides, he was a professional, though I didn't understand yet what that meant. He looked around as if to select the worthiest piano, then sat down, spread his great hands, and played something by Brahms. As always, he *played* the notes. He pressed them down and made contact. He gave them their full value. He gave them himself. The salesmen gathered round. The small family drew near to listen. And I imagined that I could hear, transmogrified into musical notes, everything I knew of him—his thwarted career, his schoolteaching, his impeccable manners, his fervor, and his wit; his pride in his wife and children; his faraway brother; his anger, his melancholy, and his acceptance; and I also imagined him stripped to the waist and sweating. When it was over he kept his hands and body poised in position, briefly, as performers do, as if to prolong the echo, to keep the spell in force till the last drawn-out attenuation of the instant. The hushed little audience didn't clap, they stood looking awed. My Mr. Simmons! I think I felt at that moment almost as if he were my protégé, almost as if I owned him.

We didn't say much on the way home. I had had my experience, grand as in fantasy, which experiences rarely are, and I was sublimely content. As we walked down my block nobody looked at us with any special interest. Everyone knew me and by this time everyone knew Mr. Simmons too. An unremarkable couple. At home, after we reported on the choice of a piano, Mr. Simmons left without even having a cup of coffee. He was tired, he said, and wanted to get home to his family.

Later my mother asked me again how our expedition had been.

"Fine. I told you already. We picked out a really great piano. Oh, and he played. He was fantastic, everyone stopped to listen."

My mother said nothing. She was slicing tomatoes for a salad.

"I bet they never heard any customer just sit down and play like that."

Again no response. She merely puttered over her salad, but with a look that was familiar to me: a concentrated, patient waiting for the proper words and the proper tone to offer themselves to her. I enjoyed feeling I was always a step ahead.

"I know what you're thinking," I said nastily.

"You do?" She raised her eyes to mine. "I'd be surprised."

"Yes. I bet you're thinking we looked as if he was going to abduct me or something."

The glance she gave in response was more injured than disapproving. She set water to boil and tore open a new bag of potatoes.

"Well, listen, I'll tell you something. The world has changed since your day." I was growing more and more agitated, while she just peeled potatoes. Her muteness had a maddening way of making my words seem frivolous. She knew what she knew. "The world has changed! Not everyone is as provincial as they are here in Brooklyn!" I spit out the last word. I was nearly shouting now. "Since when can't two people walk down the street in broad daylight? We're both free—" I stopped suddenly. I was going to say free, white, and over twenty-one, an expression I had found loathsome when I heard my father use it.

"Calm down," my mother said gently. "All I'm thinking is I hope it didn't embarrass him. It's him I was thinking about, not you."

I stalked from the room, my face aflame.

I went to college in Manhattan and lived in a women's residence near school. For several months I took the subway into Brooklyn every Wednesday so I could have a piano lesson with Mr. Simmons, it being tacitly understood that I was too gifted simply to give up "my music," as it was called; I slept at home on my old block, then went back up to school on Thursday morning. This became arduous. I became involved with other, newer things. I went home for a lesson every other Wednesday, and soon no Wednesdays at all. But I assured Mr. Simmons I would keep renting the small practice room at school and work on my own. I did for a while, but the practice room was very small and very cold, and the piano, a Steinway, didn't sound as lush as my new Baldwin back home; there was an emptiness to my efforts without the spur of a teacher; and then there were so many other things claiming my time. I had met and made friends with kindred spirits from the High School of Music and Art, and realized that had I listened to my mother I might have known them three years sooner. The next year I got married, impulsively if not inexplicably; to tell why, though, would take another story.

Naturally my parents invited Mr. and Mrs. Simmons to the wedding. They were the only black people there, among some hundred and fifty guests. I had long been curious to meet Mrs. Simmons but regretably I could not get to know her that afternoon since I had to be a bride. Flitting about, I could see that she was the kind of woman my mother and her friends would call "lovely." And did, later. She was pretty, she was dressed stylishly, she was what they would call "well-spoken." She spoke the appropriately gracious words for a young bride and one of her husband's long-time students. In contrast to Mr. Simmons' straightforward earnestness, she seemed less immediately engaged, more of a clever observer, and though she smiled readily I could not imagine her having a thunderous laugh. But she fit very well with Mr. Simmons, and they both fit with all the other middle-aged and middle-class couples present, except of course for their color.

Mrs. Simmons did not know a soul at the wedding and Mr. Simmons knew only the parents of the boy genius and a few of our close neighbors. My mother graciously took them around, introducing them to friends and family, lots of friends and lots of family, so they would not feel isolated. I thought she overdid it—she seemed to have them in tow, or on display, for a good while. I longed to take her aside and whisper, "Enough already, Ma. Leave them alone." But there was no chance for that. And I knew how she would have responded. She would have responded silently, with a look that meant, "You can talk, but I know what is right to do," which I could not deny. And in truth she was quite proud of knowing a man as talented as Mr. Simmons. And had she not introduced them they certainly would have felt isolated, while this way they were amicably received. (Any bigots present successfully concealed their bigotry.) My mother was only trying to behave well, with grace, and relatively, she succeeded. There was no way of behaving with absolute grace. You had to choose among the various modes of constraint.

For all I know, though, the Simmonses went home and remarked to each other about what lovely, fine people my parents and their friends were, and how strange it was that they could spend a pleasant afternoon talking just as they would to friends, even though they were all white. How very strange, Mr. Simmons might have said, shaking his head in a puzzled way, taking off his tie and settling down behind his newspaper. It is a soothing way to imagine them, but probably false.

I had always hoped to resume my piano lessons someday, but never did. And so after the wedding Mr. Simmons disappeared from my life. Why should it still astonish me, like a scrape from a hidden thorn? There were no clear terms on which he could be in my life, without the piano lessons. Could I have invited the Simmonses to our fifth-floor walk-up apartment in a dilapidated part of Manhattan for a couples evening? Or ask him to meet me somewhere alone for a cup of coffee? At what time of day? Could my parents, maybe, have invited the Simmonses over on a Sunday afternoon with their now teen-aged children and with my husband and me? Or for one of their Saturday night parties of mah-jongg for the women and gin rummy for the men and bagels and lox for all? Could Mr. Simmons, too, have made some such gesture? Possibly. For I refuse to see this as a case of *noblesse oblige:* we were all the middle classes.

But given the place and the time and the dense circumambient air, such invitations would have required people of large social imagination, and none of us, including Mr. and Mrs. Simmons, had that. We had only enough vision for piano lessons and cups of coffee and brief warm conversations about families, business, politics, and race relations, and maybe I should be content with that, and accept that because we were small, we lost each other, and never really had each other, either. Nonetheless, so many years later, I don't accept it. I find I miss him and I brood and wonder about him:

where is he and does he still, on summer days, play the piano for
eight hours at a stretch, stripped to the waist and sweating?

LYNNE SHARON SCHWARTZ

Right Off the Bat

My mother's a lesbian. That's the first thing I want you to know
about me. I know it's not really about me, but it sort of is, and,
anyway, I like people to know right off the bat so they don't get
weird on me later when they find out.

Like Brenda for instance. Brenda used to be my best friend at
my old school and then one day she just stopped talking to me.
For no reason. I mean we didn't have a fight or anything, like the
time she told Richard Culpepper I liked him which was a lie. We
didn't speak for almost a whole week that time. But this time there
was no reason. I mean she crossed the hallway when she saw me
coming and everything. I finally cornered her in the bathroom between homeroom and first period and asked her what was wrong.
She said, "Go away, my mom says I can't talk to you anymore.
Your mother's a dyke."

Dyke is a bad word for lesbian, like yid is a bad word for Jew.
I'm Jewish too, which is another thing that makes me different.
Being Jewish means I go to temple instead of church, only we
hardly ever go anyway, and we have *Chanukah* and Passover instead
of Christmas and Easter. Being a lesbian means my mom loves
women instead of men. Not everyone knows these words. Sometimes my mom says dyke when she's talking to her friends on the
phone or something, but she says that's okay. Lesbians can say dyke
but straight people can't. I don't really understand that. I don't
understand a lot of what my mom says or does. She's not like
anyone else's mother I've ever met.

Like even what we eat. My mom won't let me eat school lunches,
though sometimes I save up my allowance and buy one and throw
out the lunch she's packed for me. At my old school I liked macaroni and cheese the best with chocolate pudding for dessert.

My mom's not the world's greatest cook, and we always fight
because she wants me to eat weird stuff like tofu which is this
white square that looks like soap and tastes like nothing. Just to
get her to make me a Swiss cheese sandwich is a big deal, because
she always has to give me a lecture about dairy products and how
they clog you all up.

If I'm lucky Linda will be around and tell my mom just to lay off. I like Linda. Linda's the reason we moved here in the first place, so my mom and Linda could be together. Linda's like, well she's part of the family. She's my mother's, well, they use the word lover, but it's not like she's Casanova or anything. Lots of kids have single parents and lots of kids' moms have boyfriends. My mom has a girlfriend.

We have two bedrooms in our new house. My mom and Linda have one and I have the other. When we moved here my mom said I could paint my room any color I wanted. I said pink. She said any color except pink, but Linda said that wasn't fair and anyway, I'd grow out of it sooner or later. We have a kitchen and a living room and a big yard, and a cat named Pat-the-cat. Pat-the-cat sleeps with me and Linda sleeps with my mom.

Linda found us the house and then we moved here. I like it better than my old house. My old house was really an apartment and I didn't have a room. My mom had her room and I had half the living room and my clothes were in the hall closet. I slept on a futon that we folded into a couch during the day. A futon is a weird kind of mattress my mom says is good for your back. Anyway, I like the new house better—it's bigger and I have my own room, but I kind of liked it when it was just me and my mom. Except Linda was there most every weekend anyway, and once in a while we'd go to her house, but I didn't like that so much. I couldn't see any of my friends, and even though I packed things to do like books to read or records to listen to, it always worked out that what I really felt like doing was at home. I mean, how should I know on Friday afternoon when I'm packing up my stuff, that on Sunday morning I'd be just dying to hear my new Whitney Houston album? My mom would just tell me to stop *kvetching*— that's a Jewish word for complaining—but I never dragged her off to spend a weekend with one of my friends. Then she'd see what it was like.

Anyway, now we all live together and I know your next question—you don't even have to ask it—where's my father—right? Well this will probably shock you, but I don't have a father. I have a donor. A donor is a man who gives sperm to a sperm bank so a woman can have a baby. Oh I know all about the birds and the bees. My mom told me.

You see twelve years ago, no, make that twelve years and nine months ago, my mom decided that she wanted to have a baby. And she'd been a lesbian for a long time, so she certainly wasn't going to do it the old-fashioned way. That's what she calls it, you know how they do it in the movies and stuff. So she used alternative insemination.

She's into all kinds of alternative stuff—that's what people call her lifestyle—but that makes her kind of mad. How come straight people have a life and gay people have a lifestyle, she asked Linda once and Linda said, "I don't know, maybe because gay people have hair and straight people have hairstyles?" My mother thought that was hysterically funny. Personally I didn't get it at all, but she and Linda giggled for a good fifteen minutes over that one, until I rolled my eyes and said, "Children!" which made them laugh even more. I swear they can be so immature sometimes, much worse than me and my friends.

Anyway, what I was going to say was some people call it artificial insemination but my mom gets really mad at that. She gets mad pretty easy. She says it's not artificial, it's alternative. And there's nothing artificial about me. The way it works, see, is my mom got the sperm from the sperm bank and put it into a turkey baster and when her egg popped out, she popped the sperm in, and the rest, as they say, is history.

Only my mom would say herstory. She's always changing words around so they're not sexist but I forget sometimes. Anyway, I don't think it's all that important, but my mom gets mad when I say that. Like I told you, practically everything makes her mad. Like the fact that I want to wear make-up, for example. I'm not really ugly or anything, but I'm not exactly Whitney Houston either. It's bad enough being different in all the ways I've already told you about. It would really help to at least be able to look halfway normal. So just a little eye make-up and some blush, I asked her. I don't want to look loose or anything.

But my mom as usual had a fit, and went on and on about women's oppression, one of her favorite topics. She ranted and raved about how women are supposed to look a certain way and if we spent half the energy we spend on our bodies on our brains we could probably overthrow patriarchy, whatever that is, and really change the world.

Well, you know, by that time I was sorry I asked. It would have been a lot easier to just buy the stuff, put it on in the girls room at school and wash it off before my mom got home from work. But Linda was great. She's the only one who knows how to calm my mother down in these situations. "But Darlin'," she said—that's what she calls my mom—"Darlin', you're just laying your own trip on her, the same way your mother laid her own trip on you. Leave her be. She's got to make her own decisions about things. And besides, you wouldn't look so bad in a little lipstick yourself."

"Yeah," I said, "and anyway you're always saying how oppression is not having any choices so if you don't let me wear make-up, you're oppressing me."

I knew my mother wouldn't be able to argue with that one, and I felt pretty proud of myself for thinking of it, but she just shook her head and said that was different and I didn't understand. Anyway, it doesn't really matter because she finally gave in and Linda even showed me how to put eyeliner on straight.

My mom doesn't know about things like that. She never wears dresses or anything, but Linda does—just on special occasions. Like last year they got all dressed up to celebrate their anniversary, at a big fancy restaurant. I wanted to go too, but my mom said it was their special night, for just the two of them. She promised to bring me a surprise home from the restaurant if I wanted. I asked for something chocolate. Anyway, Linda got all dressed up in this royal blue dress with a big black belt around the waist. She even put her hair up on top of her head and wore these really cool silver earrings that have three interlocking loops and a ball in the middle. They kind of reminded me of an atom with a nucleus and protons and electrons orbiting around. Anyway, she looked really awesome.

My mom on the other hand, well she's not exactly the world's greatest dresser. All she ever wears are jeans and flannel shirts. And not designer jeans either—nerdy jeans from Bradlees. And in the summer she wears T-shirts with sayings on them like *I Am A Woman. I Can Bleed For Days And Not Die.* That's a white T-shirt she has with red splotches on it that stand for blood I guess. She made it herself. It's gross. Anyway, you get the picture. I mean her wardrobe is really pathetic. So that night she wore a pair of black jeans, a white jacket, a red shirt and a white tie. You probably think that's really weird, a woman wearing a tie, but lots of my mom's friends do. I'm kind of used to it I guess. Anyway, I can't imagine my mother in a dress. First of all she has these really hairy legs she refuses to shave, and second of all, what would she wear on her feet? She only has work boots, sneakers, and green flip flops for the summer.

So Linda and my mother got all dressed up that night. I took their picture and then off they went to have a good time. Only they didn't. Here's what happened: I guess they were in the restaurant eating their dinner and everything, and some punks figured out they were lesbians. They were probably doing something dumb, like holding hands. Anyway, while they were eating, I guess the punks scoped out which car was theirs, which wouldn't be too hard to do, since my mother has all these bumper stickers that say things like *I Love Womyn's Music,* and *You Can't Beat A Woman,* and one with purple letters which just says *We Are Everywhere.* It's kind of embarrassing when she takes me some place, but I don't know if I'm more embarrassed by the bumper stickers or by the car. It's not even a car really, it's a truck, a beat up old pickup because we aren't exactly rich or anything. So I bet my mother's old pickup with all her bumper stickers stuck out like a sore thumb in the parking lot of that fancy restaurant with all the Mercedes Benzes and Cadillacs and whatever other kinds of cars rich people drive.

Well, by the time these punks, or whoever it was got done, my mom's truck had four slashed tires. My mom was so mad she wanted to kill somebody. Linda just got really sad and started to cry. That's what always happens—my mom gets mad and Linda gets sad. I get both, but this time I got mad, just like my mom. I mean, it was their special night and they weren't hurting anybody or anything; they were just going out to have a good time. But then something happened inside of me, and I got really angry at my mother. I mean, if she would just shave her legs or put on a dress or quit holding Linda's hand on the street or something, these things wouldn't always be happening to her.

Me and my big mouth. As soon as I said it, I knew I shouldn't of. My mom tells me it's important to say how you feel, and then when I do, she always gets mad at me. "Haven't I taught you anything?" she yelled. Then she started pacing up and down the living room delivering one of her famous speeches about oppression and blaming the victim. And then all of a sudden she just stopped. Maybe she saw I wasn't really listening because she came over to the couch and sat down next to me and held my hand.

"Roo," she said, and I knew she couldn't be too mad if she was calling me Roo—that's my nickname from *Winnie the Pooh.* See, when I was a baby, my mom carried me around in a snuggly and she felt like Kanga with her baby Roo. My real name's Rhonda, after my grandma Rebecca, and my nickname's Ronnie. Anyway, my mom said, "Listen Roo, I know it's hard for you to understand why I live my life the way I do. You think if I just put on a skirt and shaved my legs everything would be okay. Well, your Great Aunt Zelda and your Uncle Hymie thought the exact same thing with their fancy Christmas tree on their front lawn, and still their neighbors in Poland turned them in to the Nazis for a buck fifty a piece. Remember Brenda, Ronnie? You don't need friends like that. Listen Roo," She said again, "if I only teach you one thing in your whole life, it's be yourself. Be straight, be gay, be a drag queen in heels, or a bulldyke like your old ma, but be whoever you are and be proud of it, okay? Life's too short to pretend you're someone you're not, and then spend all your time worrying about what's going to happen if you get caught. I spent too many years in the closet, and no tire-slashing assholes are going to push me back."

She made a fist and smacked it into her hand, hard. But she didn't hurt herself or anything. My mom studies karate, which is another weird thing she does. I watched her in her class once, where we used to live. It was pretty cool to see her punching and kicking and everything. My mom's small, and kinda skinny, but she's a lot stronger than she looks. Her teacher was a lesbian too. I could just tell by her short hair and the way she shook my hand.

Which leads me to the next question I know you're thinking about—do I think I'm gonna be a lesbian when I grow up? I don't know. I know my mom wants me to be, even if she doesn't exactly say so. But one night I heard her talking to Linda when she thought I was sleeping. It was pretty easy to listen in on them in the old house because we only had the two rooms. Anyway, it was right after this boy Phillip called me up for the math homework because he was out sick. My mother handed me the phone with this who's Phillip look in her eye and later that night I heard her talking to Linda.

She said, "I hope Ronnie doesn't have to go through her teens and early twenties being straight like I did before she comes out. The thought of adolescent boys running around the house gives me the creeps. I haven't even talked to her about birth control yet. Or AIDS. Oh Goddess, (that's what my mom says instead of oh God) oh Goddess I feel like I just got her out of diapers and already boys are calling her up on the phone."

Then I heard Linda say, "Relax, Darlin'. Ronnie's got a good head on her shoulders. And besides, we know how to get rid of any fifteen-year-old boys we don't like. We just start with a little of this . . . and a little of this . . . and before you know it, they'll run home screaming to their mamas." Then I heard my mother laugh—Linda's the only one who can make her laugh—and then they didn't talk anymore.

Meanwhile, I didn't bother telling my mother that Phillip is a real nerd and I wouldn't go out with him if he paid me a million dollars. Well, maybe I would, just once, but he'd have to put the money up first—in cash. Anyway I wouldn't kiss him for all the tea in China, like my Aunt Myra would say. I've never kissed a boy. I've only gone out with a boy once, this guy Billy from my old school. We went out and he bought me ice cream and then he asked if he could kiss me. "Kiss me?" I said. "Are you kidding? We've only been going out for thirty-five minutes." We didn't go out again after that.

I don't know, kissing boys seems really gross and kissing girls seems really weird. Maybe I'll be a nun, except my mom says Jews can't be nuns. I don't know. I guess I'm kind of young to worry about it too much. That's what Linda says anyway. She says just be yourself and see what happens. I said to her, who else would I be, Whitney Houston, and she laughed—Linda laughs at my jokes most of the time, unlike my mom.

But really I kind of know what she means, because I used to pretend I came from a normal family. I even made up a father and pretended he was away on business trips a lot just so the other kids wouldn't tease me for being so different and all. I never told my mom that—I could just imagine what she would say.

So anyway, that's all about me. I wanted you to know right off the bat so I wouldn't have to worry about you pulling a Brenda. Do you think your mom will let us be friends?

LESLÉA NEWMAN

French Girls Are Fast

French girls are fast
I find this out
before I know what it means
Two days in the Irish-Catholic school
my mother thought would keep me safe from sin
and the name is following me around.
Frenchie, hey, Frenchie,
ooh la la
the Irish boys leer
staring at the roundness
I am not ashamed of—
the Irish girls still properly flat
beneath their uniform jackets

I learn quickly to sneer
light my cigarette with a wooden match
flicked against the brick school wall
taste the smoke, roll it over my tongue
and exhale upward in a gesture
of exquisite boredom
I tighten my face, turn
to look them up and down
and spit out the prayer
of this place—
eat it, assholes

Years later it is a grandmother
who accuses me
and I hear it again
French girls are fast—
who am I to say otherwise
my belly pushing outward
with her grandson's child

She admonishes me
not to rest my hands on my belly
You'll ruin the baby
touching yourself like that . . .

My hands fly away for a moment
like frightened birds
looking for another place to perch
then settle back down
She shrugs and turns away

Later she digs out a blanket
she bought at Niagara Falls
from those Indians, you know,
she tells me, shaking her head,
clicking her tongue
but the blanket is nice, she says,
you can use it

I will not tell her now
my father's family is Indian,

that the blood was mixed in me
generations ago
My hands accept the white wool,
finger the stripes
of red, yellow, black, green
I draw it over me, the child,
my unruly hands, feel my body slowing,
getting ready for the long push ahead

CHERYL SAVAGEAU

My Rough Skinned Grandmother

My rough skinned grandmother
woke me up in the morning by
stroking my face with a warm
callused hand, scrubbed my skin clean
off when I took a bath. She would say, "Here
more dirt, there on your ankle, more
dirt." Her thumb rubbed soiled
flesh like thick brown wood
carvings off my body, until my skin
was a tender pink slate. When I ate dinner
she grabbed chicken legs from me
and scolded me for not sucking the meat
down to the bare bone. Eating
my leftovers, she'd tell me stories
of when she was my age and had to
eat fried roaches like crisp candy,
on her birthdays, a boiled egg
on a chipped plate.

My rough skinned grandmother told
me not to cry when she tore my baby teeth
out of my mouth. I could hear them rip from
their root; she said crying should be
saved for death, happiness, or any other good
reason but not for the loss of teeth.

My rough skinned grandmother
washed the rice with a quick
whooshing hand, rinsing the grains

again and again until the water
was clear. When she cooked, she beat
the tough meat tender with a fist
and sang nursery rhymes at the same time.
In the summer, she dropped
live, snapping crabs into a vat of hissing
water. Their pink shells turned a freckled
red as their arms became limp, drifting downward.

My rough skinned grandmother had a
chunk of skin missing from her arm
as if a pair of teeth had bitten straight
through her bicep. She carved her own muscle
with a butcher knife to make a healing
broth for her father. She never felt the pierce
of blade as he lay dying by daylight.

My rough skinned grandmother walked with me
past grown men sitting on crates in front
of convenience stores, holding
a cool St. Paulie Girl in their chapped
white hands as they yelled,
"ching chong ching chong"
like hot bells ejaculating
in my ear. She pretended
not to understand: she didn't speak
English but she understood
thunderous voices
from the gentle kind,
and she knew when to cross a street.
But she was no meek grandmother
Once on a night walk across a dark overpass,
she had me tucked beneath her
elbow. A man began to
follow the wind behind us. She shifted
her plump body around and roared Chinese curses,
her voice booming like a long string
of lit, flailing firecrackers. After
he ran away, she stroked my forehead
with her warm, callused hand,
my rough skinned grandmother.

TINA CHANG

Kemo Sabe

In my dream I take
the white man
slap him
til he loves me.
I tie him to the house
take his land
& buffalo.
I put other words
into his mouth
words he doesn't understand
like spoonfuls
of smashed lima beans
until his cheeks
bulge.
Chew now, dear
I say.
I flick his throat
until he swallows.
He works all day
never leaves the house.
The floors shine
the sheets are starched.
He wipes grime
from the windows
until clouds dance
across the glass.
He feeds me
when I'm hungry.
I can leave whenever
I want.
Let him struggle
for his dignity
this time
let *him* remember
my name.

DIANE GLANCY

Dictionary of Terminology

It's got to help you out
a bit
to know that when
you crack your dictionary
open
to look up the
word criminal or
thug or beggar man
thief
you see my picture
instead of yours
or my brother's picture
or nephew niece
or son
instead of yours
or in that thesaurus
where the term
teenage pregnancy
has my sister's hair
or my daughter's face
or my niece's clothes
and her frown
or the brown
of her skin
& the black of
her eyes
staring down
the threat
of you
looking
for words
to fit
the pictures
you take
in your
mind
to ignore the publishers
the owners of the books
and the words

and the pictures
manufactured
to keep you
behind
the one who's
kicking your
behind
and replacing
your thoughts
w/ grave
thoughts
at ATMs
or restaurants
or washing windows
w/ a squeegee
creating my own
job

TONY MEDINA

A New Story

Several years ago,
I was a patient at the VA hospital
in Ft. Lyons, Colorado.
I got a message to call this woman,
so I called her up.
She said to me,
"I'm looking for an Indian.
Are you an Indian?"
"Yes," I said.
"Oh good," she said,
"I'll explain why I'm looking
for an Indian."
And she explained.
"Every year, we put on a parade
in town, a Frontier Day Parade.
It's exciting and important,
and we have a lot of participation."
"Yes," I said.
"Well," she said, "Our theme
is Frontier,

and we try to do it well.
In the past, we used to make up
paper-mâché Indians,
but that was years ago."
"Yes," I said.
"And then more recently,
we had some people
who dressed up as Indians
to make it more authentic,
you understand, real people."
"Yes," I said.
"Well," she said,
"that didn't seem right,
but we had a problem.
There was a lack of Indians."
"Yes," I said.
"This year, we wanted to do it right.
We have looked hard and high
for Indians but there didn't seem
to be any in this part of Colorado."
"Yes," I said.
"We want to make it real, you understand,
put a real Indian on a float,
not just a paper-mâché dummy
or an Anglo dressed as an Indian
but a real Indian with feathers and paint.
Maybe even a medicine man."
"Yes," I said.
"And then we learned the VA hospital
had an Indian here.
We were so happy,"
she said, happily.
"Yes," I said.
"There are several of us here."
"Oh good," she said.

Well, last spring
I got another message
at the college where I worked.
I called the woman.
She was so happy
that I returned her call.

And then she explained
that Sir Francis Drake,
the English pirate
(she didn't say that, I did)
was going to land on the coast
of California in June, again.
And then she said
she was looking for Indians . . .
"No," I said. No.

SIMON J. ORTIZ

IV. ~

PLEDGING ALLEGIANCE

This land is your land,

this land is my land

The Poets

1965–1968

In the gymnasium the balls spun
from their fingers like spiders' silk,
fine and unconquerable. Legs woven
in threads of hope, they jumped,
came down on silent sneakers,
dashing any hopes we had of winning.
They were the blacks, the black blacks
who had the advantage of being born black.

Dunbar, the high school that sent
a jingle in a broken tongue to colleges
on full scholarships. Dunbar, the high
school that we watched march here
to smash us once again, we black boys
with all these white boys too thick
to dance like a knife in the air,
to open, cut, slice a tangled history.

Breath held back "nigger" in the air
over the bleachers. Breath held back
"wino junkies" under the old clock
over the hollering wooden floor where
we sang pep songs in German, peeping
inside our shirts and ties at our own
magic. The Dunbar Poets made baskets
while strolling, dreaming of rivers.

"Coach, we can't do nothing with
these darkies from Dunbar. Coach,
their bodies ain't bodies. They are
songs from somewhere unfair to us."
We, the black folk at Polytechnic,
wished from the white sea of equality
that Dunbar would stamp blackness
all over this stiff building to save us.

The lead had opened so wide it was
too hard for The Poets to keep from
laughing. They slapped their hands
and did the slow jazz of black boys
walking away from an easy game.
In the streets, we watched them stride
away in long leather coats to get high,
too brilliant to live, too brilliant to die.

AFAA M. WEAVER

Seven Horses

When I was a pencil of a girl
I had seven horses, one
for each day of the week.

Thunder, Lightning, Sun
and Moon, East Wind
North Wind and Red Roses.

Only I could see them,
roan and black, grey,
palomino, dapple, white

and the strange one
the flying red horse
from the Mobil sign.

I rode them to school,
home, to the store.
I rode them down the slopes

of rocky night. In adolescence
I never mooned over horses.
Later, they were something cops

rode at us in demonstrations.
I'd sooner ride a cow.
No, it was not horseflesh

but power I craved
and speed. I longed to gallop
out of our tight mortgaged house

furnished with shouts and razors,
out of the smoke of frustrations
burning like old tires.

I wanted to stick out my neck
and gallop at full tilt off
any map I had ever seen.

MARGE PIERCY

The Last Wild Horses in Kentucky

In separateness only does love learn definition
ROBERT PENN WARREN

We stand at the bus stop. Eyeing my son and me,
the other children are quiet and they look hard.
It's not their first day of class. My finger ends tighten
over me at six years: cowbarn, outhouse, backdoor,
cornbread, woodpile, chickenhouse. I rode a plowhorse
named Snip, no big yellow bus. Our greyhound, Queenie,

uncurled from under a forsythia bush outside the kitchen,
leaping to race me but my father held her by the collar.
Before I rode off, he told me about the last wild horses
in Kentucky. Scoured out of hills, they were roped,
tied down, nostrils clamped shut. Their neck veins pulsed
like salmon jumping upstream. The mares all aborted.

I know beyond that word. Hanging limp as morning
wet grass, my son's hands are smooth not toughened
from milking a cow as mine were by the time I went
to first grade. I want to double-fence a pasture to protect
him like my father did to keep our stallions apart in order
to keep them spirited for breeding. Eric waits but strains

to see beyond the corner and I pull him back, fearing roads
I cannot see him travel. The day must come when I will force

his snowsuited body out without immunity into January
mornings so cold milk jugs would freeze if I left them out
on the doorstep. Can I be ready with a message to pin on him
as his boots scale snow tracking maps I have not traced?

Boarding the bus, Eric twists around to me from the landing
and I reach out to touch his shoulder, then stand waving him
out of sight. My stomach cupped in my hands, I bow my head
and let my son go. Knowing how wild horses are broken,
I ask that he remember the soles of his bare feet running
through the bluegrass blooming over the hills in Hardin County.

VIVIAN SHIPLEY

Learning Silence

By the time I am in first grade, I know enough
to be frightened, to keep my hands folded
on my desk and try to be quiet "as a mouse."
I am nervous most of the time,
feel sick to my stomach.
I am afraid to raise my hand, afraid
to ask for the bathroom pass, afraid
of the bigger children, but most of all,
afraid of Miss Barton who does not like me.

We read the *Dick and Jane* books. The world of these books,
painted in bright primary colors, seems so free and perfect.
When I open the pages, I feel I can walk through them,
like Alice stepping through the looking glass,
into that clean world,
those children with their wide open faces,
their blonde curls, their cute, skipping legs,
their black-and-white dog with its perky tail,
their big, white house with its huge lawn of manicured grass.
In those books, I can forget Miss Barton and her icy
eyes and the grimy, shopworn classrooms of P.S. 18,
with their scarred wooden desks,
their dark green blackout shades,
reminders of the war that has just ended.
In that house, where even the doghouse is perfect,
there would be no reason to be afraid.

I try to be good. I try to be quiet.
I hope Miss Barton will not curl her lip
when she looks at me.
I would gladly turn into Jane
if some magic could transform me,
make me blonde and cute, instead of sad
and serious and scared, with my sausage curls
my huge, terrified eyes,
my long nose, my dark, olive-toned skin,
the harsh cheap cotton of my clothes.

MARIA MAZZIOTTI GILLAN

Home Training

for Marguerite

I remember how they clung
to the white door of the Frigidaire:
lessons that swung in and out
with every trip for baloney
or green Jell-O.

"Intelligence is like a river:
the deeper it is,
the less noise it makes."
"Do unto others as you
would have them do unto you."

To an eight-year-old, they seemed
to spread from the kitchen
like flat snails that traveled
by night, affixed themselves
at eye level, surprising us
as we climbed stairs
and turned corners.

Even the laundry chute
bore a message: "Perseverance
is the secret to success."
It was as if my mother were afraid
that walls without explanations

would give us the wrong idea
about playing outside.

While she slept afternoons
in her night nurse's uniform,
Rudyard Kipling held forth
on the door of my bedroom
about boys becoming men,
and a pair of slender praying hands
held out reminders about serenity,
things one can and cannot change.

I had not yet read about
white men with guns in India
or declared boycott on church.
But I felt I was old enough
to drop my dirty underwear
down a hole without instruction.

I did not know then
about the power of signs,
how two words posted
on every Jim Crow rest room
from Ohio to Arkansas
on my mother's childhood vacations
had meant squatting in fields,
or holding pride between one's legs
like an eighteen-hour vise.

My grandfather held it
straight through from Toledo
to the Voting Rights Act.
One day he pulled up
in our driveway in Rochester
unable to say hello,
then drove his pastel '58 Chevy
straight to the hospital,
where they unlocked his bladder
with a catheter.

I did not know then about
the dog-eared petition

that white neighbors signed
against our moving in,
or how the hammered circles
of my father's bare feet on the floor
had something to do with
his walking hat in hand
to every bank in the city,
finally needing a white patron
to co-sign a loan
for a pharmacy that hung
his own name in red letters.

I did not know how
the chase for polite proverbs,
the embrace of cliché,
the laying on of hands to placards
printed in white men's language
was my mother's set of instructions
for nuclear weapons,
her own code of war
for ramming the atoms
of forbidden existence,

her way of clearing a circle
for the perfectly ordinary,
where brown children could dream
free of police dogs,
where her son could kiss a white girl
and not pay at the neck,
where "please" and "thank you"
were tickets held at gunpoint
and her fence line of red roses
gave the world deadly warning.

Now my sister's small daughter
runs free as dirt in the yard
before being given a bath. I watch her,
a brown girl in a white basin
with promise foaming at her shoulders,

while above her hang sayings
taped to tile by my sister,

an enduring ritual
of words cleansing walls.

BRUCE A. JACOBS

Half-Breed's Song

for Janet Campbell Hale

Late March. The High Plains.
The idyllic intrudes briefly.
The playful Dakota sun burnishes
the hoar frost on cedars
and winter's nightmares are melting.
Kids are tightrope walking
the snow-packed streets to school.
A sudden warm wind gently shakes
the neighbor lady's clothesline
flock of blue, white, and pink panties.
I pull out the snarls and braid
my burden of waist-length hair.
When I first left home
more than a quarter of a century ago,
I had a flat-top with wings.
I took a job in a Reno casino
making change for fools at the slots.
My sister has a photo of me from those days.
What a strange, muscular clown I was.
Striped, button-down shirt. Hush Puppies
and pressed corduroy slacks
and that goofy flat-top with wings.

No men wore braids back then
and I was ashamed of my Indian blood.
Grandfather . . . no shit, sometimes
I still am.

ADRIAN C. LOUIS

Mestizo

Sometimes a fierce dichotomy
severs me in half:

within the privileged weather
of a marble city built

beside a calm, blue sea,
I find luxury in the visa

of white skin; huge, ornate
doors open slowly

on sumptuous feasts, eloquent
speech, and I am privy

to the ivory fables of an
empowered class . . .

But in the jagged mountains
burn a thousand

campfires throughout the night;
I know the censored grief

of the poor, the oppressed
citizenry of color,

those "expendables" whose lives
are miracles of survival,

whose deaths are statistics locked
in blood-stained files

buried in the minds of the secret
police. Always the wretched

gather and march toward that place
of shining domes,

immaculate boulevards.
Always I appear,

by turns, defender and invader:
my clothes elegant

and tattered, my flags sovereign
and imperiled,

one hand half-opened,
and one hand half-closed

ALFRED ENCARNACION

Tangerine

Thanks to the unrelenting rigidity of public school teachers during the Eisenhower years, when Clementine Orvalle was half-dragged by the principal into our third-grade classroom in the dead of winter, she was seated right next to me. Miss Keeler, who never walked through the wilderness of our tiny desks without a yardstick clutched in her hand, and who had a bald spot on the back of her head that she attempted to hide with a wispy bun of dyed, red hair, insisted on alphabetical order.

"What a pretty name," Miss Keeler oozed out at this latest surprise, patting Clementine Orvalle on the head. "Thank you for bringing us a new friend, Mr. Merdley," our teacher quacked on in her rough falsetto. "Remember, children, the word principal is spelled with a 'pal' at the end."

As she spoke, she prodded the intruder down the aisle between the *O*'s and the *M & N*s, as we in my aisle had dubbed ourselves. My last name was Mullineau, love-legacy from a Mohawk grandmother who eloped with a Frenchman.

Until this morning, as I flew with my husband out of the dirty snows and bitter winds of New York City to Aruba's hot moonscape and blue waters, Clementine Orvalle had mostly remained a dark silence beneath all the lava flows and blossoming reconstructions of memory. But the tall, mulatto stewardess, with her sloped cheekbones and Nefertiti neck, looming at the end of the airplane aisle that reminded me of old school aisles, pulled me back as surely as any archeologist into lost and splendid ruins. Miming how not to drown if we crashed, the stewardess made me think of Clementine, made me think she could be Clementine grown into a beautiful woman, made me hope she could be.

"Clementine," Miss Keeler instructed the speechless and wide-eyed little black girl on that winter's day thirty years ago, "you sit here next to Laurel."

That meant that T.J. Ottington III, a central torment in my

eight-year-old, half-breed life, had to move. As soon as Miss Keeler turned her back with its double-gauge shotgun spine shooting up its middle, I swung my face towards T.J. and stuck my tongue out so far I could touch the dimple in my chin. I could see that Clementine Orvalle saw the tongue and was tracing exquisitely minute patterns on the floor with her floppy yellow galoshes dripping mud and snow.

"Don't you know that's a pickaninny you'll be sitting next to, dum-dum?" T.J. Ottington III hissed at me as he banged his books, crayons, and stubby red pencils on the desk behind him, starting a chain reaction of students, from the O's on, moving back one seat, slamming their desk tops down hard and dropping things, I knew, on purpose.

"She's a Negro," I whispered prissily to T.J. "Abe Lincoln freed her."

"Tangerine," T.J. taunted, jutting out his opalescent jawbone in the direction of Clementine, fluttering his pale eyelashes and crossing his blue eyes until only bulging white and the tiny, red stitching of capillaries showed.

I looked at Clementine Orvalle with renewed interest. Why would she be called a tangerine, is what I wanted to know. No longer making pictures with her boots, Clementine was glaring straight at T.J., her rough unruly hair spiked out in a dozen black pigtails, each one with a different colored clip at the end. When T.J.'s eyes returned from the middle of his head, he grinned. He had noticed what I had missed at first, the trembling that vibrated ever so lightly across Clementine's lower lip.

"Silence, silence!" Miss Keeler's voice was cracking loudly along with the yardstick she was smashing down on the vast plateau of her desk. "Clementine, sit! Laurel, share your crayons with Clementine until we can get her some of her own. It's coloring time."

Everyone fell as silent as when we had to huddle together in the hallway during air-raid drills, burying our faces in our raised knees and waiting for the atom bomb to kill us before we turned ten. But worse than the atom bomb was Miss Keeler's yardstick, which she had used on every boy in the class except T.J., and even on two of the girls. Each time she whipped one of us into tears or wet pants, she cut a notch into the stick with a pearl-handled jackknife. But she knew enough not to touch T.J. He was the doctor's son, the only one who would have dared to tell.

Gradually the room started to fill up with whispers again, and then with quiet voices.

"If you go through the year without being hit," I explained to Clementine Orvalle, "Miss Keeler takes you out for a banana split."

I, myself, didn't know what a banana split was. My family was too poor for such gastronomical frivolities, but I pretended that I knew, and was trying my best to see that I ate this ambrosia of my wildest imaginings at the end of third grade.

Clementine's mouth opened up in a lopsided smile and a flashing of teeth with some gaps where second teeth were still jagging through.

"I don't care about any banana split," she drawled. "I come from New Orleans. We eat beignets down there."

New Orleans? Beignets? I placed a yellow crayon on Clementine's desk and watched as she pressed two brown fists against the tears that shone across her cheeks, tears she had kept from T.J.

"What's beignets, anyway?" I asked her, my way of letting her know that I wouldn't mention the tears to anyone, not even to her.

"They're donuts, only better," Clementine said, pulling her tears away on her fists and picking up the crayon.

She gave me a sidelong glance and started coloring on some pale green construction paper. The yellow streamed out of the crayola like rays from the sun, hot rays I had begun to think I would never see again, the winter seemed so long. By the time Clementine had finished she had expanded the green of the paper with a golden, interlocking puzzle of Louisiana herons, fleshy ladies tossing their skirts and derrières up in the air in the midst of a cancan, African kings blowing on saxophones as they galloped bareback on winged zebras, floating coffee cups, and little Negro girls waving scimitars over their heads. Silently, I stretched my arm across the stick figures I had begun on my own rectangle of paper. I was hopelessly in love.

"What is this, Clementine?" Miss Keeler was standing between us like an eclipse. "What are these women doing? Disgusting! Zebras with wings, cups that float, naked legs, how dare you?"

For the first time in the history of the third grade, Miss Keeler lay down her yardstick. She bent her switchblade-body over Clementine's desk and swiped up the paper, slowly and deliberately ripping it across the bold line of the ladies' rear ends.

"Don't ever let me see you draw anything naked again, or you won't have a rear end left!" Miss Keeler yelled, taking up the yardstick once more and cracking it against the desk where the pale green paper had been.

Clementine sat frozen as the winter outside, the yellow crayon concealed inside her motionless fingers as Miss Keeler strode back to her own desk.

" 'Killer' Keeler had a sledding accident when she was little," I whispered in the same adult tone I had heard my mother use when she explained why Miss Keeler was an old maid. "She can't get married or have babies. That's why she doesn't like naked things."

"Yeah, Tangerine," T.J. Ottington III echoed me from behind. "You're lucky the old witch didn't whop you with the stick."

But Clementine didn't answer either one of us, just continued to sit there with her stricken face.

Even in the wan light of February falling so feebly through the square panes of the schoolroom windows, there was a glow that flickered along the ledge of Clementine's cheekbones and across her wide, serious brow. I imagined I saw some orange in that flickering. Maybe that's why T.J. called her a tangerine. Maybe if you could taste a Negro, that's what she would taste like, an exotic fruit imported for the winter months. I wouldn't put it past T.J. to run his tongue over a Negro, even though Clementine Orvalle was the first Negro I could ever remember seeing in our small northern town.

Then again, on days when I stayed home ill with measles or mumps, I liked to listen to my mother's old 78s with their white and wine-colored middles, listen as they spun hypnotically around the silver spindle of the phonograph. One of my favorites was "Tangerine," Frankie belting out "she is all they claim, with her eyes of night and her lips as bright as flame." And wasn't that Clementine Orvalle sitting right across from me, her long-lashed eyes nearly black and her mouth bitten red and trembling like fire?

Just then, Clementine moved. Very slowly, so slowly I could have screamed, the hand with the crayon in it made its way to the deep pocket of her summery, flower-bedecked, out-of-place dress. When the hand levitated back out of the pocket it was empty and light as bird bones. Inside the pocket the unseen, yellow crayon bulged against a sprig of cotton violets.

Now I was biting *my* lip, as Clementine Orvalle treated me to another one of her flashing, lopsided smiles. But I was no tattletale, and, besides, I was so enthralled I would have given her all my crayons, eager to see what else she might draw that was naked, magical, and wicked.

"What is it, T.J.?" I heard Miss Keeler's aggravated quack fast-approaching down the aisle.

"Clementine stole Laurel's yellow crayon," T.J. piped up in his best choir boy's voice. "It's in her pocket."

"Is that true, Clementine?" Miss Keeler's face had turned as purplish-red as her hair. "Is it?"

I was shaking my head "no," frantically trying to get some words out. Clementine just looked at her, the lopsided smile still on her face. When Miss Keeler saw the smile, for the second time in the history of the third grade she lay down the yardstick, grabbed Clementine Orvalle by her black pigtails and yanked her out of her chair, slammed her across the top of her desk and pulled up her flowery dress so that her white cotton underpants showed. Up and down raged Miss Keeler's hand across Clementine in the position of her cancan ladies, the hand so swift and angry it seemed more like bee's wings than a human hand. Half the class was crying, none louder than I, until Miss Keeler jerked the screaming Clementine Orvalle to her feet again. I quickly looked away so she would not see that I had watched her shame.

"Pocahontas," I heard T.J. laugh at my tears.

The next morning when I came to school and opened my desk top there was a large white sheet of paper inside, crowded with yellow drawings done by the unmistakable hand of Clementine, ghostly trees dripping Spanish moss, steamboats with calliopes floating above clouds, piano men with striped hats playing pianos upside down, dancing girls with my face, and two caricatures, one of T.J. Ottington III and one of Miss Keeler, both in the nude, as hard as that was for me to imagine. At the bottom of the paper Clementine Orvalle had painstakingly printed FRIENDS FOR LIFE?

I shut my desk top in a hurry so Miss Keeler wouldn't see, and nodded my head at Clementine sitting in the O's. Her coppery face opened up to me with that lopsided smile of hers, her teeth flashing, her black eyes snapping defiance. I knew right then and there that I was never going to get to eat a banana split at the end of third grade, that thanks to Clementine Orvalle, and to the Tangerine of Frankie's song, I was about to partake of more sustaining ambrosias.

SUSAN DEER CLOUD CLEMENTS

Between Holi and Halloween

Mira waved at Sudhir and Preeti from the kitchen window as Sudhir backed their red Chevrolet out of the driveway.

She continued to wave as the car drew out of sight, feeling extraordinarily happy. For once, breakfast hadn't been an ordeal. Preeti had been quite cheerful, almost animated, unlike her usual sullen self—stacking up the plates in the sink, even giving Mira a peck on her cheek before she left. Perhaps it was because Sudhir's mother, Madhu, had gone away for a few days to visit her relatives in New Jersey, she reasoned as she washed up. Or perhaps it was because Sudhir had finally agreed to increase Preeti's curfew time to 8 P.M. Or perhaps Preeti was just growing up. She prayed the fragile peace would last.

Mira went up to her bedroom and started assembling her puja things, lighting the diyas and the incense, garlanding the statues of Parvati and Siva, Lakshmi and Vishnu, and the large portrait of Lord Krishna with flowers. She performed all her actions slowly, delighting in the soft comfort this daily ritual gave her. It was the time of day she loved best; the quiet, empty house became completely hers for those few hours, absorbing the atmosphere of devotion—pure, untainted, Indian. The smell of burning sandalwood incense began filling the house, and as she began praying, her troubles seemed to fall away, becoming more and more insignificant as she entered a reunion with her God, her keeper and the source of all her strength. Yes, she had a lot to be thankful for. They lacked nothing, they were one of the more well-off Indian families in the area. Their house was an object of envy among their friends. Yet they lived very simply, in ways most of their Indian friends didn't understand, not updating their electronic equipment or their car. Making do with an old nineteen-inch television set, an ancient phonograph that scratched all their records, and a 1985 Chevrolet that had rusted in all the wrong places, they could afford to take trips back to India whenever they could get away and be generous with the presents and money that they sent to relatives back home.

Materially, no, there was nothing she lacked. Spiritually, however, she was in a desert. Not naturally acquisitive, she was beginning to have less and less in common with her Indian friends, who seemed to have made the acquisition of material goods their sole object, even leaving their children with baby-sitters in order to become two-income families so they could afford to buy more things. And most of the American stay-at-home mothers she knew either watched soap operas all day or played bridge with each other. Mira had never watched a soap opera in her life, and she had never played cards. Her list of groceries was simple, and she never changed brands, so coupon-clipping had no attraction for her, nor did conversations about prices and quality and where to buy what. Tomatoes and carrots and yogurt were the same wherever you bought them.

The days that used to be so full of happiness and warmth for her—Divali, Holi, Dussehra, and Janmashtami—were now bleak little affairs between Sudhir and her. Once, a few years ago, Mira had tried to re-create the spirit of Divali in their house. She had cooked for days, producing the traditional sweets and other foods eaten on Divali, and decorated the house with lit candles and flowers. On the driveway, she had drawn three large swastikas—the Hindu symbol for well-being and prosperity—in red and yellow powders. It had felt almost like home. Then Preeti had marched in angrily, saying, "Ma, someone around here really hates us." "Why?" Mira had asked. "Haven't you looked outside? There are three large swastikas in the driveway. Must be the local skinheads." "But I did those myself," Mira said. "It's for health and prosperity. We always make swastikas on Divali—*swastika* is a Sanskrit word."

Preeti had turned into a raving lunatic. "Ma, you're crazy, you know that? That's what the Nazis used in Hitler's time—how can you not know these things? When you see it here, it stands for hate and racial prejudice. It's what they warn us about in school. I can't believe it. My own mother . . ." Preeti dashed outside in a rage and stamped all over the swastikas with her feet. Mira watched from the window, her eyes filling with tears. Powdery puffs of red and yellow color rose from the ground, swirled in clouds around her outraged child. The colors blurred, then blended, becoming a dull earth orange. It seemed to Mira that her child had turned evil, grinding out all that was fine and good and true within herself. Mira was filled with bleakness, all the gay colors around her suddenly turning lifeless and strange. Perhaps it was then that she had given up hope.

These days, on Divali, Sudhir and she would light a diya furtively together, as if enacting some pagan rite, and pop sweetmeats into each other's mouths, their minds filled with the scenes of Divalis long past: the weeks of preparation culminating in happy faces around long tables, bright clothes, houses lit up with diyas—on garden paths, around flower beds, on the front step, in every window—and children waving sparklers at each other, and luscious mouthwatering things to eat, and overwhelming happiness in the conviviality and the sharing of blessings. On Holi, Mira would childishly sprinkle colored dye onto Sudhir's fawn-colored socks, reminding him of the festival of spring. It was her small tribute to the buckets of colored water people would joyfully and teasingly hurl at each other on Holi day all over India. And he would tug playfully at her chunni after dinner and say, "Must be Holi—I had colored socks this morning." These days, both of them sadly remembered days when the world, as in a storybook fantasy, could be colored the way you wanted it to be—vividly splashed in fiery tones of red and yellow, green and blue. And how the most misanthropic of men would on that one day become children, allowing themselves to be doused with colors and flinging their own buckets of colored water at whomever they wished. No, spiritually Mira was starved. Her life was lived in such isolation that she wondered, sometimes, where she would be without a daughter like Preeti.

She meditated quietly, grounding herself, her spirit—until she heard Chuck, their neighbor's college-age son, yell at his dog in the backyard. She rose slowly and looked out of the window. The boy was lounging in a hammock, throwing sticks for the dog, headphones stuck to his ears, a can of beer by his side. Dropped out for a year, just like that. Wants to find himself. Hah! And now he sits under trees drinking beer all day. Mira shook her head, then went in to bathe and dress.

As she put on her salwar-khameez, she thought about Preeti again. There had been another sharp exchange at dinner the previous evening. Mira and Sudhir were vegetarians, and Preeti, refusing to eat their food, had recently begun picking up things for herself at the supermarket on her way home from school. She had brought back a steak. Mira looked at the thing, still dripping blood, and felt sick.

"Preeti," she said, "don't forget to use the other pan, the pan I bought for your meat, to broil it."

"Yes, Ma," the girl had obediently replied.

Yet when Mira came down, Preeti had obviously forgotten all about the other pan and had put her steak into the tray her mother used. The steak sizzled and sputtered in the broiler. The smell of burning flesh was nauseating.

"Preeti, how many times have I got to remind you? You can't use the same things as us for your food. We can't eat from something that has had meat cooked in it. You know all this. Why do I have to keep repeating things?"

"Ma, I didn't forget," Preeti replied. "This is my house. You make me feel like an outcast, something dirty and filthy, just because I eat meat. I'm not going to cook things in separate pans just because you're vegetarian."

"Preeti," Mira said wearily. "Please just listen to me. It's not me—it's our religion, our culture. In India, people don't even allow meat to be cooked in the house if they're vegetarians."

"Ma, this isn't India, it's America—get it? America!" she shouted. "Liz's parents are vegetarian too, and they don't act like this. Her mom even has all of us over for turkey on Thanksgiving. It's just you, you and your crazy ideas." Preeti was banging the cabinet drawers shut as she looked for some cutlery. "Why can't you be more like my friends' moms? *Why?*"

God knows she had tried, Mira thought. But every attempt brought forth only rebuff and scorn. Sudhir and she had struggled so hard in the beginning to understand this new world they had become part of. They had barely moved to Ohio from Bombay when, a year later, Preeti was born. Three years later, everything was still foreign and strange: the shopping malls; the supermarkets; the realtors' offices, where you simply had to sign a form saying you wanted a particular house you'd seen, for it to be yours in the time it took to dream it up; the body-freezing, mind-numbing winters. Then there were all the machines: to wash, to dry, to cut, to grind, to dust, to clean the plates, even to cut the grass. Life was so easy now, wasn't it, her sisters would remark enviously in their letters from home. Easy, yes, Mira reflected. But so lonely.

In Bombay, every domestic activity involved a human being: the hamal, who dusted and polished the silver and the furniture; the cook, who grumbled all morning long about the rising prices and the decreasing quality of food; the ayah; the cleaner, who came to do the bathrooms; the tailor, who came on his once-a-week visits and sat at the sewing machine in a corner of the guest bedroom, plied with constant cups of steaming tea and an ashtray for his foul-smelling beedis, mending and darning, replacing buttons and broken zippers; the dhobi, who arrived to take the week's laundry away and always complained about the quality of sunlight nowadays—so sharp it made all the white sheets yellow, like itself; the biscuit-seller, who came on his weekly visit with a flute in his mouth and a huge black trunk on his head, which he would open to reveal layers of black trays filled with different kinds of biscuits—all these many transactions conducted sometimes within the space of a day, often to such tunes as "You Are My Sunshine," played in unison on harmonicas by a group of beggar children in the courtyard below, to whom one occasionally and exasperatedly threw a bagful of coins, hoping that would silence them. How could one get to know this country, Mira puzzled, since all the daily activities of life were performed by machines, not by people?

In the absence of human teachers, the supermarkets became Mira's guides through the mysteries of American culture. In the Bhagavad-Gita, it is written that you are what you eat. And where else could you see what Americans ate but in the supermarket? Mira could tell you more about the sort of mother who bought frozen packaged fried chicken for her kids for dinner and the kind who bought raw chicken to batter and fry at home than the chief market research person at any food corporation. She could tell at a glance the kind of person who used Arm & Hammer detergent and the kind who used Era, and why; the kind who chose Equal over Sweet'n Low, and so on and so forth. Disinfectants, detergents, toilet paper, all were endless sources of fascination for Mira. Every package was like a book to her, opening up a fresh experience, a new feel for the sensibilities of the American consumer.

She went as often as she could, always deliberately forgetting something from her list so that she would have to return the next day. The order of things was puzzling: if she found the logic in it, she was convinced, she would have begun the process of unraveling the mysteries of the American temperament. Why, she wondered, was the bottled water next to the laundry things? Who would know to look for herbs and spices next to the children's school stuff—crayons and notebooks and such? The shoe polish, which she needed often since Sudhir insisted on having his shoes polished every day, was next to the Raid range of insect killers. The sugar was next to the flour but the rice was aisles away, tucked between the mayonnaise and the pickles. What was their logic, she wondered?

She would watch women reading the packages for their contents, men rushing through aisles, filling the carts seemingly at random, without ever looking to see what was in the packages they bought. She saw women pore through coupon booklets with the shrewdness of investors while their children clamored for cookies and candies. She heard the clerks at the cash registers discuss with one another their evening dates, while they mechanically punched in apples and pears, spinach and beans. She lingered in the aisles, eavesdropping on conversations, picking up all kinds of facts about the way people related to each other, the kinds of things they quarreled about, the kinds of things that made them happy. Sometimes it didn't make any sense. Like when couples argued furiously over brands of detergents, sodas, and popcorn, then settled their differences according to random statements like "But that's what my mom uses!" or "My ex-girlfriend stuffed my shoes with that stuff," or "Those people are anti-abortion fascists." Once, while she was staring at a young couple as they fought, the man turned around and glared at her: "Get a life, lady," he said. Yes, she admitted as she backed away from them in alarm. Life. It was life, precisely, in her new adopted country, that continued to mystify her.

The first time she had felt this keenly was when she had been reading fairy tales to four-year-old Preeti—silly stories about handsome young princes swept off their feet by beautiful young girls, and inquisitive little girls who get eaten up by wolves. There seemed to be no purpose to them. Why should she fill her daughter's head with all this nonsense? So she started telling Preeti stories about Lord Krishna as a young boy—how he used to tease the shepherdesses and steal curds from people's houses and how one day, when Krishna was playing in the dirt, his friends came up to his mother, Yashodhara, and told her that her son was eating dirt. When Yashodhara called the boy, he said, "Mother, I haven't been eating dirt." But his friends insisted that he had. So Lord Krishna said to his mother, "If you don't believe me, look." And when he opened his mouth, she saw the whole universe there, all its galaxies and moons and stars, and the earth itself and all its rivers and mountains and cities.

At school, when the teacher told Preeti and her classmates about the earth, she described it as so large and round the human eye could never see all of it in one glance. Preeti piped up, "But Yashodhara did." The teacher wanted to know who Yashodhara was. So Preeti told them the story. But everyone laughed at her. And the teacher said, "Your mother shouldn't be telling you stories about boys who steal and tell tales on their friends. You know what we call them—tattletales. And she shouldn't be telling you lies—no boy could ever contain the whole universe in his mouth."

"But he was a god," Preeti cried.

"You can't be a naughty little boy who steals and be a god," the teacher said.

So Mira received a note from the teacher saying that her child's educational progress would be seriously hindered if Mira didn't stop telling her stories about naughty little boys who are really gods. They were immoral in essence, and part of what the school tried to do was to inculcate a sense of ethics in the children. Such contributions from parents didn't help. She enclosed a list of storybooks, with the name and telephone number of a bookstore in town, and strongly recommended that Mira take a trip there as soon as possible.

Then there was the time when Mira sent a tray of Indian sweets she had prepared for Divali to Preeti's school. In her note to the teacher, Mira explained that Divali was a very auspicious festival for Indians because it was when Rama and Sita returned to their home in Ayodhya after fourteen years of exile in the jungle. These sweets were traditionally prepared as part of the special foods made for the occasion. She thought Preeti's friends might enjoy them. The teacher wrote back a polite note saying she had found her story interesting, but they didn't celebrate other countries' festivals in their school. The tray of sweets was untouched. Even the red ribbon she had tied around the Saran-Wrapped tray was exactly as it had been—as if the tray had never left the house.

Then one day, when Preeti's friends came over in the afternoon, she gave them ladoos and spiced tea. Preeti had said to have brownies and milk ready, but Mira didn't know how to make brownies, and on the ready-mix package at the supermarket they had looked heavy and thick and unnaturally brown. The children didn't like the ladoos and they couldn't drink the spiced tea and Preeti came to her crying hysterically after they had left, saying that she'd never have any friends.

The complaints from Preeti continued to grow. She would come into the house freezing because she'd left her coat behind in her locker. When Mira demanded to know why she persisted in returning to the house in this half-dressed condition, Preeti said she couldn't wear clothes that smelled of Indian food anymore. She complained that all her woolen things had absorbed the smells of Mira's cooking and that her classmates shunned her as soon as she entered the class, saying, "Here comes the stinker." "Mom, you don't understand. I'm dark, so I'm dirty. And being dirty means being smelly. And being smelly means being bad. That's how kids think." Mira was so puzzled by this logic, she called the school to ask how the children could think that being dark meant being dirty. The teacher—a different one this time—was immediately apologetic, explaining that kids were sometimes cruel because they didn't understand subtle differences between people. Yes, she was aware of some of the problems Preeti had been facing but, unfortunately, she could only attempt to deal with overt challenges. The more subtle put-downs Preeti would have to address on her own, the teacher said.

Her first meeting with Preeti's teacher on parents' day made her feel so bad, she never went again. Preeti said, Mom, please don't wear a sari. It's so tacky. Haven't you got anything else? They rummaged through her closet, but there were only saris and salwar-khameezes. I could wear one of those, Mira suggested. They're almost like what the Chinese women wear, loose trousers with long tunics. Mom, I don't want you to look Chinese, I want you to look more American, Preeti fretted. But this was a dead-end issue; Mira went in her salwar-khameez, which, with the long floating scarf, looked almost like a sari. She sat in the back of the room just listening, listening. And what she heard really frightened her. The parents seemed to be attacking the teacher. Why did you give my child such a low grade last semester? Why can't you make her do better in English? My child's bright; something's wrong with this school if my kid's not doing well. My kid's not getting the push she needs here. Boys seem to do better in your class than girls. My child's discriminated against because she's pretty. My boy's not do-ing well here because he's so shy and no one's helping him. On and on and on. These parents were blaming the teacher for their child's poor grades. They were rude to the teacher and they were full of anger. Mira had never seen anything like it. Where she came from, teachers were like gods. You dressed up in your best clothes when they asked to see you, and you were more polite to them than to anyone else in your life. They held the keys to the children's futures and one wanted only their goodwill. As a parent, one would never have tried to aggravate the teacher.

"Mrs. Kapur, have you got anything to say?" the teacher asked her.

"No, no," Mira said softly. "Thank you for the trouble you take with Preeti," she said, wanting to make amends for the rudeness of the other parents. But the teacher only sighed in relief and turned to someone else, as though she hadn't heard what Mira had said, as though it made no difference what Mira said. Some parents glared at her. This was a forum for complaints, not for appreciation.

She tried to approach some of Preeti's friends' parents at a coffee break. But they sailed past her, either ignoring her completely or saying, "Hello, Mrs. Kapur," and moving on. "What a pretty cos-tume," one woman said, and walked on before Mira could even say thank you. She didn't bother to return after the coffee break and left quickly in her car, wishing Sudhir had gone instead. He might have handled things better.

Preeti's first Halloween costume was another hurdle. "It's got to be scary, Mom, really scary," Preeti said.

Mira thought and thought. What sort of a culture was this that made you dress your children up to look horrible and frightening? Then she asked, "Evil also?" Preeti's six-year-old mind hadn't quite grasped the implications of that and, feeling the word "evil" must be something really bad, she said, "Yes, evil also."

The only scary and evil figure Mira knew was Ravana, the demon who abducted Sita from her husband in the jungle and carried her off to his palace. So she made a grotesque little Ravana costume for Preeti though it hurt her to dress her child in it, so intense were the true Hindu's feelings against this mythological figure. It was an odd choice by any standard. The other Indian parents stared at her, as though this were a gross violation of religious sense, and the American kids didn't have the patience for the story. Ravana was not someone they had ever come across at Halloween.

Gradually, Preeti had begun to reject her. Mira wasn't like her friends' mothers, and everything she did and said was wrong. She noticed the hate in Preeti's eyes when her friends walked into the house and saw a sari-clad woman. They'd giggle behind Preeti's back. "Preeti's mom's so weird. What a funny costume!" And Mira would hear them and not know what to do.

Once when Preeti and she had gone shopping, Preeti lured her into a clothes shop, begging and pleading with her to try on the dress in the window. Mira kept looking at it, thinking how could she. She didn't even like it. "Please, Preeti, I can't, I can't," she kept saying, feeling she would rather die than get into that dress. Finally, to please Preeti, she had tried it on and just cringed to see herself exposed like that, legs, arms, whatnot, a person without any shame. She ripped it off, horrified at herself, nearly in tears. At that moment, she vowed that she would not try to be an American mother. She would try to be the best Indian mother she could possibly be, but she couldn't, she wouldn't, be anything else.

She liked to think of the sitaphal, or custard apple, she had once seen in the supermarket. They called it cherimoya. She stood in front of the carefully wrapped fruits in wooden crates, with thick wads of colored tissue paper separating them, and was thrown completely off track. Sitaphal grew only in India, so she had always been told. What was it doing here? It was the goddess Sita's favorite fruit, and thus acquired the name *sitaphal*. Its crabbed green-black exterior mocked her here in its smart wooden crate and its pink tissue paper. She yearned for a taste and, after much wrestling with her sense of economy, bought one for $10 and devoured it as soon as she got home, rejoicing in the memories it brought forth. When she went back to the supermarket the following week, the crate was still there. It was full, with the exception of one hollow space, where the one she had bought the previous week had lain. They were rotting, those sitaphals, unfamiliar, unknown. No one had bothered to introduce the American consumer to the delicious, custardy sweetness that lay under their crabbed exterior.

Like the sitaphal, she was an unknown. Her reluctance to embrace American culture was reciprocated, for American culture, most certainly, would not embrace her. She turned instead to her own Indianness, letting it become the standard on which to base all her thoughts and actions, proudly painting the bindi on her forehead every morning, despite warnings from her friends that "dot-buster" gangs had become extremely threatening in public places. She and Sudhir became strictly vegetarian, even cutting out the occasional fish and chicken dish from their diets, and Mira started going to an Indian homeopathic doctor. She began to mistrust everything in a culture that so thoroughly excluded her, her way of thinking, her way of life. And gradually that mistrust turned to fear—fear at what this society could do to her family. As Preeti grew older, the feeling intensified. Now it kept her awake at night, barely able to think about Preeti and what tomorrow might bring, so estranged had they become from each other.

Mira thought of all these things and felt sad, sad that she was not American in a way that would be helpful to her child. Yet she had tried to be everything her own mother had been and more, taking all the trouble necessary to ensure that Preeti learned about her own culture. The sitar player lived three towns away, the kathak dance teacher lived nearly thirty miles away, the Hindi teacher visited the area only once every two weeks, staying in a different town every time he came. It didn't matter to Mira. She would drive anywhere, go any distance, to provide whatever she felt her daughter needed. And it hurt when Preeti said, "You're only doing this because *you* want it. You never do what *I* want."

Mira put her sneakers on and instantly felt herself enter her secret persona. She was brisk and smart in her freshly ironed salwar-khameez. It was Tuesday—time for her shift at the emergency telephone counseling service. Her sneakered feet squeaked with purpose against the polished wooden floor, her mind was alert, her whole being quickened in anticipation. This was when she secretly met America, for neither Sudhir nor Preeti nor any of her friends knew of her clandestine appointments at the hot line every Tuesday at ten o'clock in the morning.

BEENA KAMLANI

Strange Country

When we drove off in a shower of confetti
and popping flashbulbs
I never pictured this destination.
My great-aunts, stitching fifteen hours a day
for seven cents an hour in Iowa factories
used to write home to Volovchisk:
You should see how America is filled with gold!
Someone should have warned me

how lonely it is to be newly married.

Like the women urged by men
to leave the gleaming pots in the scrubbed kitchen,
give away a grandmother's carved bookshelf,
kiss parents good-bye and walk out from paved streets
to cross the Blue Mountains step by step
and plant virgin prairie with children's graves

to be a wife is to be an exile

I said I love him. Yes, I love him.
But the words no longer have weight and purpose
like *library book,* or *bank statement.*
Strange that this man I've chosen for a lifetime
I've known only one year, or two,
not like a sister or high school friend,
and strange to think that when I die
I'll be buried among strangers.

I planted my life like a garden
my name and work grew weedy and blooming around me.
But now people call me by his mother's name
and tell me I must be *so happy*

and grateful, because *finding someone to love*
makes me *a better person.*

But what if I don't want to be a better person?
What if marriage is only the second-best thing that ever
   happened to me
and *forever* is easy but a week is endless?
What if I want to drive off with no map
the road black with rain
and lightning splitting the sky?
When I hear my voice seek his approval

I want to smash all the mirrors

like an immigrant
from a country that no longer exists
who refuses to learn the new language.

JULIE PARSON-NESBITT

Roomers, rumors

My mother took in roomers. Salesmen mostly.
I wrote my poems on their invoices,
their expense reports, pink and green.

Once a week we changed their beds.
Washed the smelly towels. Cleaned.
Rummaged their things, prying.

I have a right to know, Mother said.
I didn't think so, but I was curious.
Their lives were just expense reports.

Smells of unwashed socks and aftershave.
Photo of a child visited five years ago.
Girlie magazines, detective fiction,

maps of where they had to go.
Mother always knew where they had been.
His wife left him for a butcher. He caught

his girlfriend in bed with his brother.
He did time for bad checks in Wisconsin.
He was drinking and ran off the road.

The only one I ever befriended was three
years older than me and pregnant,
up to Detroit for her husband's job at Ford's.

I held her when she miscarried.
Her blood soaked my blouse.
Her screams made furrows in my brain.

No more women, Mother said. Men
are easier. I slid past them in the hall.
I made myself invisible and kept silent.

By this time I was a roomer myself
in my parents' house, spinning lies
around myself, a cocoon inside which

I altered beyond their guessing. I hid
my poems from her, slipped my journal
into the wall and went on the road

selling my dreams to anyone, to you.

MARGE PIERCY

Language Difficulties

One of the great tragedies of my childhood was my inability to
communicate with my grandfather's parrot. I spoke English; it
spoke two languages: Neopolitan and Quechua. This parrot, if at
all possible, was even older than my grandfather, who was the
oldest person on earth. He had purchased him or her from an
Indian in the Amazon region of Brazil where my grandfather was
then engaged in building up and losing his second fortune. The
bird's pale chartreuse feathers, the exact color of a Nehi lemon/
lime soda, feathers which perhaps were once as lustrous as the
plumes in Montezuma's crown, now appeared as lifeless and uneven
as the fur of an elderly housecat.

My grandfather's parrot had its own room, freshly carpeted with newsprint every day, in my aunt's home in the Bronx. I, in my brief circumscribed existence, had never seen a room quite like this; the rooms I'd been acquainted with held furniture. This one contained only Bronx sunlight slanting through the windows on opposite sides, and, dead center on a perch, the bird itself. To me, this room was like a small temple in which the parrot was a kind of oracle. Every time I visited my aunt's house, I also made sure to check in on the parrot. I'd say the expected, "Polly wanna cracker?" (Hope, as we know, springs eternal.) The parrot, in response, would cock its head, shift sideways like a Balinese dancer, and scream piercingly. I never got much closer to him or her than three feet; my grandfather told me that his parrot had a mighty overbite that could cut Brazil nuts in half and would surely detach one of my fingers. This depressed me, since I always had the barely controlled urge to smooth the parrot's feathers.

My grandfather's parrot would speak words only to its owner. My grandfather himself was practically as exclusive. He was a man who, after his dreams of gilded palaces flew away, resigned himself to a life of earthbound toil. Beginning his journey as a student of architecture, he ended up as a master mason, a craft that paid handsomely but did not confer upon him the status of gentleman. Even though my grandfather thought that America was a nation of savages, he initially wanted to make a good impression.

My grandfather was also a man who loved beautiful things, objects in both the animate and inanimate categories. His taste in furniture was imperial; I particularly remember a pair of Venetian candelabra, eighteenth-century, the kind of "objets" corporate raiders fill their homes with or donate to the Metropolitan Museum of Art—black basalt cherubs grappling thickets of ormolu. His taste in women, to the constant dismay of my grandmother, was democratic.

The man himself contrasted startlingly with his universe of preferences. He was of medium height and without an ounce of fat. Due to the fact that he was outdoors most of the day, his skin had acquired a deep coppery hue. It stretched across his face with its high cheekbones and proud beak of a nose like fine saddle leather run through at the stress-points with networks of minute creases. For many years I thought my grandfather was a Mexican or an American Indian. When I was in grade school my father gave me a book on ancient Egypt. When I opened the pages dealing with the mummies and came upon the pharaoh Rameses, asleep in his coffin, I saw a close copy of my grandfather.

I am told that when he was a younger man he favored suits with vests. In old age, he wore the same type of thing day in, day out: a plaid cotton shirt, usually dark blue, and a pair of baggy pants held up by suspenders, the kind with clip fasteners. Outdoors he added a hat that, though clean, needed to be reblocked.

My grandfather had never acquired the habit of stillness; until the age of ninety-eight, his final year, he rowed a boat, hiked eight miles a day. Even when he sat down his eyes, as bright, dark, and piercing as a hawk's, lit and darted everywhere. I got the feeling that whatever those eyes contacted was, in some obscure but final way, annihilated.

Over the years, the old man gradually ceased to relate to most of his family. He considered his two elder sons fools and slovenly; his only daughter, who in middle age was no longer beautiful, had a volcanic temper exactly like his own. He now spoke only to my father, who was handsome, spoke English like Lowell Thomas, and wore three-piece suits tailored by his wife's bare knuckles, as splendid as anything a banker might own. I, on the other hand, was a fat little kid who was always asking questions. "Grandpa," I'd say, "tell me what the jungle is like did you ever go out hunting with the Indians did they teach you how to use a blowgun blowguns are these truly neat hollow reeds they put an arrow in 'em and they dip the arrow in some kinda poison and they go *phoot!* and bingo a monkey falls out of a tree did they really pay you in gold bars when you were working in Rio de Janeiro what size were they as big as a brick or maybe you could put 'em in your pocket when you were inspecting the stonework on the Woolworth building didn't you ever look down and get really dizzy I'd get dizzy I wouldn't be able to stand it!"

My grandfather would get up, smash his gray felt hat onto his coppery skull, collect the parrot, and say, "I'm a going for a walk."

KATHRYN NOCERINO

The Welcome Table

Three nights a week, when I was seventeen, my father took me downtown and made me shout "monkey," and "nigger," and "coon." He made me shout these things, he said, because he loved me. "Put your heart into it," he told me whenever my voice would falter. "Go on. Get with it. Give it everything you've got."

It was 1960, a touch-and-go time in Nashville. An activist named James Lawson was organizing students from the black colleges, and, because my father sold greeting cards to black-owned variety stores, he had gotten word of the lunch-counter sit-ins that were about to get underway. He had decided to hook up with the integration movement because he couldn't resist the drama of it. "This is history," he said to me one night. "The world is going to change, Ed, and someday you'll be able to say you were part of it."

He had volunteered my services as well because he knew I was at an age when it would be difficult for me to stand up for right, and he wanted me to get a head start on being a man of conscience and principle.

Our job was to prepare the students for the abuse they were sure to get. So, on those nights, in classrooms at Fisk University, we stood over the young men and women and did our best to make their lives sad. My father was a handsome man with wavy hair and long black eyelashes. He had a friendly smile and a winning way about him, but when he started his taunting, his face would go hard with loathing.

"Get the niggers," he would shout. "Let's get these monkeys out of here."

At his urging, I would join in. "Nigger," I would say, and my jaw and lips would tighten with the word.

We would pick at the students' hair. We would shove at them and pull them down to the floor.

When the workshop leader called our demonstration to a halt, we would help the students up, brush off their clothes, and laugh a bit, just to remind them that we were playacting. But always there would be heat in their eyes, because, of course, it was all different for them.

One of the students was a young man named Lester Bates. He had a reddish tint to his hair, and his hands were broad and long-fingered. One night, during a break, he clamped his hand around my wrist. I was holding a bottle of Coca-Cola, and he said to me: "Don't drop it. Hold on, boy. Keep a grip."

I could feel my hand going numb, my fingers tingling, and just when I was about to drop the bottle, Lester grabbed it. "This is going to get ugly," he said. "You know that, don't you? This whole town is going to explode." He took a drink from the bottle and handed it back to me. "Days like this make a body wonder what kind of stuff a man is made of."

He stood there, watching, and I did the only thing I could. I raised the bottle to my lips, and I drank.

I wanted to feel good about what we were doing—my father and I—but I hated him for bringing me into those classrooms. I hated him because he made my life uncomfortable. Some nights, on the way home, he would imagine a car was trailing us, and he would pull to the side of the street just to make sure we were safe. "There are limits," he said to me once, and he said it in a way that made it clear that he was one who knew those limits, and I was one who did not.

My father was Richard Thibodeaux, but that wasn't his real name. The previous spring, he had fled a scandal in New Hampshire. He had managed a cemetery there, and in the harsh winters, when the ground was so frozen that graves were impossible to dig, the corpses were preserved in charnel houses until the spring thaw. Then, sometime in April, assembly-line burials began: the air shook with the raucous sound of the heavy machinery digging the plots, the cranes hoisting concrete liner vaults from flatbed trucks. Sometimes, in the rush, the wrong bodies were put into the wrong graves, a fact that came out when one of the gravediggers spilled the news.

After that, we didn't stand a chance. It was a small town, and the rumors were vicious. We were cannibals, devil worshipers; we all had sex with corpses.

"How can we live here now?" my mother said one night to my father. "You've ruined us."

So we came south to Nashville. My mother, who had been there once to visit the Grand Ole Opry, chose it for its friendliness.

"Anywhere," said my father, "away from this snow and ice."

Any city, he must have been thinking, large enough to forget its dead.

Our first morning there, we left my mother in the motor-court cabin we had rented, and went looking for a cemetery. "That mess in New Hampshire," my father said. "Let's put it behind us."

Nashville was brilliant with sunshine. My father put the top down on our Ford Fairlane 500, a '57 Skyliner with a retractable hardtop, and we drove past antebellum estates with guitar-shaped swimming pools and manicured lawns landscaped with azalea bushes and dogwood trees. My father whistled a Frank Sinatra tune—"Young at Heart"—and for the first time since we had left New Hampshire, I believed in what we were doing.

"Don't think I'm a wicked person," my father said.

"I don't," I told him.

"People make mistakes, Ed." He lifted a hand and rubbed his eyes. "This must seem like a dream to you."

"It's something interesting," I said. "Something I might read about."

"That's you." He slapped me on the leg. "Steady Eddie. Just like your mother."

My mother was at a time in her life when her looks were leaving her, but, instead of complaining, she had developed a habit of surrounding herself with beautiful things. In New Hampshire, she had learned how to do eggshell art. She would take an egg and poke a hole in each end with a pin she had saved from an old corsage. Then she would insert the pin and break the yolk, hold the egg to her mouth, and blow out the insides. She would soak each eggshell in bleach, dry it, and then spray it with clear acrylic paint.

The paint strengthened the shell, and my mother could then use cuticle scissors to cut away a section: an oval, or heart-shaped, or teardrop opening into the hollow egg. Inside the shells, she painted background scenery, and then with plaster of Paris built platforms on which she could position miniature figures, some of them only a quarter of an inch tall, to create scenes she would then name "Chateau Against Snow-Covered Mountains," "Collie Waiting by Stone Wall," "Skier Sliding Down Icy Slope." It was a precise and painstaking art, each motion calculated and sure. The shells were surprisingly strong, and she rarely broke one. If one did happen to shatter, she would throw it away and start again. "Why curse your mistakes?" she said to me once. "Why not look at them as new opportunities?"

My father had come to Nashville hoping for a new start in life, and it didn't take him long, that first morning, to find what he was looking for: a cemetery and the headstone of a child who had died at the age of two in 1920, the year of my father's birth.

"That's going to be my name now," he said. "Richard Thibodeaux. It's a good southern name, don't you think?"

"What about your old name?" I asked him. "What about my name?"

He said he would go to the county clerk's office and get a copy of Richard Thibodeaux's birth certificate. Then he would pay a visit to the Social Security Administration and apply for a card under his new name. If anyone got curious about why, at his age, he was just then getting around to applying for a card, he would tell them his parents had been Baptist missionaries, that he had been born in Tennessee, but had gone with his parents to South America where he had spent nearly all his adult life carrying out their work.

"What about me?" I said. "What's my story?"

My father put his finger to his lips and thought a moment. "That's a snap," he finally said. "I met your mother, the fair and pious daughter of a coffee plantation owner, an American from New Orleans, married her, and nine months later, you were born. You were a delicate child, given to fevers and ailments of the lungs. Finally, we had no choice but to send you back to America, away from the tropics, to live with your aunt in Memphis." He put his arms around me and pressed me to him. "And now here we are, united again. You see how easy it is? I'll tell anyone who gets nosy we're starting a new life."

And that's what he did. Once he had the birth certificate and the social security card, the rest was a breeze. We rented a modest home, and my father became Richard Thibodeaux, region five sales representative for the Glorious Days Greeting Card Company. He finagled some school forms from a print shop he knew and concocted a set of records for me. He gave me a near-perfect attendance record at Memphis East High School, excellent marks in citizenship, better grades than I had ever been able to manage.

"There," he said. "Now, you're set. A completely new profile. *Alacazam.*"

He wanted to make sure no one ever linked our name with what he had begun to call "that misery in New Hampshire."

"I lost my self-respect there," he said to me. "That's the worst thing that can happen to a man."

My mother's eyes sparkled when she learned our new last name. "Penny Thibodeaux," she said, and I knew, like me, she had fallen in love with the elegant sound of those three syllables.

In school, when teachers called me by my full name—Edward Thibodeaux—I answered "yes, sir," or "yes, ma'am." I developed a soft-spoken gentility and impeccable manners. The change of climate, my father said, had done us a world of good.

It was a sweet time for us there in Nashville. Saturday evenings, we drove downtown to the Ryman Auditorium and took in the Opry. My father's favorite singer was Hawkshaw Hawkins. He was tall and lean, and he wore his cowboy hat cocked back on his head.

My mother preferred Jan Howard because she was graceful and had a sweet smile. After the show we would cruise down Broadway, the top down on our Skyliner. We would drive by the music and record shops, and sometimes my mother would slide over next to my father, and I would lay my head back and close my eyes and let the night air rush over my face and give thanks for Nashville and the second chance we had hit upon there.

"The Athens of the South," my father said once. "Milk and honey. Folks here know style when they see it."

Each day at noon, whenever he was on his route, he would find a public rest room where he could change his shirt.

"You can tell a man by his clothes," he explained to me. "A tidy man lives a tidy life."

He wore suspenders, and linen suits, and wingtip shoes he polished and buffed each night before going to bed. He had monogrammed handkerchiefs and ties. He carried a new leather briefcase full of sample cards, and when he swept into stationery shops and drug stores, he doffed his Panama hat, and said to the ladies behind the counters, "It's a glorious day for Glorious Days."

The Glorious Days Greeting Card Company specialized in sensitivity cards: genteel messages to commemorate birthdays, anniversaries, weddings. Selling them, my father said, made him feel he was contributing to the general celebration of living. He had been occupied too long with the burying of the dead, with mourning and grief.

"A gloomy Gus is a grumpy Gus," he said one day. "But that's all behind me now. Nothing but blue skies. Isn't that right, Ed? Hey, from here on, we're walking the sunny side of the street."

I know my father didn't mean to make trouble for me but, of course, that was the way it all worked out. Some boys at school had seen the two of us going through the gates at Fisk University, and before long, the word was out that I was a "nigger lover."

One day, a boy named Dale Mink said a group was going downtown to stir up a ruckus. He was the center on our basketball team and an honor student. He had already won a scholarship to Vanderbilt. Even now, I don't think he was a thug; he was just caught up in the ugliness of those days. The way of life he had always known was changing, and he was afraid. "Those nigras think they can get away with this," he said to me. "You're either with us, or you're not."

The lunch-counter sit-ins had been going on for over a week.

Downtown, at Kress's, McClellans, Woolworth's, and Walgreens, black students were occupying stools even though the ten-cent stores had chosen to close their counters rather than serve them.

My father came and went through these stores, selling Glorious Days greeting cards. Each evening, at dinner, he told us how the students sat there, studying for their classes. They were remarkable, he said—"as sober as judges"—the young men in dark suits with thin lapels and white shirts as bright as Judgment Day, the girls, poised, as they unwound their head scarves and folded their duffle coats over the backs of their stools.

Sometimes, my father said, a waitress would call him back to the kitchen and set him up with a hamburger and a Coca-Cola, on account of she knew him as a man on the road who needed a hot lunch.

"You actually do that?" my mother said one night. "You sit there and eat while those poor kids do without?"

In those days, my father had a smugness about the new life he was inventing for us. He was so sure of the right direction we were taking, he had convinced himself that we deserved special liberties.

"I never thought," he told my mother. "Call me an idiot. Lord alive."

My mother was, by nature, a cheerful woman, and once we had left New Hampshire, she did her best to believe her life had been handed back to her. She worked part-time in an arts-and-crafts shop, and afternoons, when I came home from school, she asked me to help her with her eggshells. She sensed, better than my father, how brutal these times would become—how they would ruin people—and she was determined to maintain a certain beauty and delicacy in my life. She showed me how to transform a quail egg into a basket by cutting out a handle and adorning it with pearls and velvet ribbons. Together, we made eggs into cradles and lined them with lace.

This all seemed to me a terribly womanly thing to do, but slowly her optimism won me over. When I watched her paint background scenes on the eggshells—amazed at how a few strokes could create trees, clouds, blades of grass—I fell in love with the way vast landscapes yielded to her slightest effort. When I was with her, I believed she could shrink anything that was difficult or immeasurable.

"Proportion," she told me. "That's the key. Making things fit."

Finally, she let me paint scenes of my own and, when I did, my fingers tingled with the delicacy of their motions. In New Hampshire I had fallen into some trouble—vandalism, truancy, petty thievery—and I convinced myself that each gentle stroke I made was saving me from a life of violence and mayhem.

I rode downtown that day with Dale Mink. In Kress's, a gang of boys from the high school were prowling behind the students at the lunch counter. The boys' shirt collars were turned up, and their heel taps were clacking over the tile floor. Somewhere in the store a radio was playing WSM. Later, I would learn that the station's call letter came from its original owner, The National Life and Accident Insurance Company, whose motto was "We Shield Millions." But I didn't know that then. I only knew I was in a place I didn't want to be. I was there because things were getting hot for me at school—"nigger lover"—and, like most people, I wanted my life to be easy and sweet.

The radio went off and one of the boys stepped forward, closer to the students, and he said in a low, steady voice, "Get your coon asses off those stools."

The students refused to turn their heads or let their shoulders slump with shame. I noticed, then, that one of the students was Lester Bates. He closed the book he had been reading and put his hands on the edge of the counter. The girl next to him turned her head just a fraction of an inch, and I could see her lips move. "This is it," she said.

The high school boys were squawking now: *nigger* this and *nigger* that. Some of them were jostling the students. Dale Mink elbowed me in the side. I knew he was waiting for me to join in the jeering. If there is one thing I would want people to understand, all these years later, it would be this: I didn't want to be Dale Mink, only something like him.

So I shouted, "Nigger."

I had done it hundreds of times with my father at training sessions.

"Nigger," I shouted, and I convinced myself it was only a word, that I was only one voice swallowed up by the voice of the mob.

But then the gang surged forward and I saw Dale Mink latch onto Lester Bates. Dale jerked him backward, onto the floor, and soon I heard the dull thuds of punches and kicks finding cheekbones and ribs.

I'm ashamed to think now of the fear I helped cause Lester Bates, and those other young men and women. I have never been able to watch news films from those days and, until now, I have kept my part in them a secret.

When I got home that afternoon, my mother was waiting for me so we could finish an eggshell we had been working on that week. It was a dining room scene. We had lined the inside of the shell with wallpaper, and we had built a table and four chairs from balsa wood. We had upholstered the chair seats with velvet ribbons and made a tablecloth from lace. My mother had brought home three miniature figures from the arts-and-crafts store: a man, a woman, and a young boy.

"Here's your father and me," she said. She put the miniature man and woman into adjacent chairs. Then she handed the miniature boy to me. "And here's you. Go on, Ed. Have a seat."

I didn't know where to put the boy who was supposed to be me. After the scene at Kress's, I didn't know where I belonged. I closed my hand around the figurine and felt it press into my palm.

"There was a fight at Kress's today," I said. "At the lunch counter. A bunch of boys from school went down there, and I went along. I said some things, and now I wish I hadn't."

My mother put her hand over my fist. "Don't let yourself get caught up in this," she said. "Listen to me. People have to live their lives the best they can. We've had too much trouble as it is."

"I can't forget it," I said. "How do you forget something terrible you've done?"

"You do whatever you have to do to get beyond it." My mother opened my fist and took the figurine and sat it in the chair whose back was turned to us. "There," she said. "It's cozy, isn't it? Inviting. Let's call this one 'The Welcome Table.'"

"There's nothing on the table," I said. "We're not doing anything."

My mother thought a moment. "We're waiting."

"For what?"

"Who knows?" She snapped her fingers. "Hey, Buster Brown, get out of your shoe. The sky's the limit. For whatever's going to happen next."

Because my mother worked at the arts-and-crafts store, she had made some friends. One of them was a woman named Dix Gleason, and sometimes in the afternoons she would drop by for a visit. My mother was thrilled and worried on these occasions, happy for the company, but afraid her hospitality would fall short of Dix's approval. "You'd think she'd give a party notice," she said the first time Dix's car pulled up to our curb. "Heaven's sake. What do I have in the kitchen? Mercy, let's see. What I can whip up to suit Miss Dix?"

Dix Gleason was a loud woman who left lipstick stains on my mother's drinking glasses. She called me *Eddie* in a whiny voice like Topo Gigio, the mouse puppet on "The Ed Sullivan Show," and she called my mother *Henny Penny*, a nickname I knew my mother despised.

"Like I was some hysterical old dame," she said to me once. "Honestly. The idea."

Some afternoons, Dix brought her husband, The Commodore.

Commodore Gleason was an accident reconstruction specialist for the highway patrol. He was intimate with the facts of crash and disaster. At accident scenes, he measured skid marks, gauged road conditions, interviewed survivors. He calculated the speed of travel, the angle of impact, reconstituted the moment of poor judgment or unfortunate circumstance.

"I can raise the dead," he boasted to us once after he had testified at a coroner's inquest. "I can bring them back to that moment where everything is A-okay. They're driving a Chevrolet down Route 45, just before eight P.M. The road is dry, visibility is fifteen miles, their speed is fifty-eight miles per hour."

If he could only leave them there, he said, happy and safe in their ignorance. But he knew too much. He knew that thirty miles up the road a Pontiac was streaking their way, that they would meet head-on at the top of a hill just before sunset.

"It's a burden to know as much as I do," he told us. "Take it from me: Men are fools more often than not."

I was afraid of The Commodore. He had a way of making me feel nothing in my life would ever be safe.

Once he came to my school and showed a blood-and-gore film about highway safety and traffic fatalities. He was snappy and regulation in his uniform: necktie firmly knotted, collar tips pointed, badge gleaming, trousers pressed, belt buckle polished. He told us about head-on crashes, decapitations, body bags.

"I know what you're thinking," he said. "You're thinking this can't happen to me. That's what we all think. That's why we have to prepare ourselves for every hazard. Even you cool cats. Hell, you think you'll live forever."

One afternoon my mother had sent me to the store for ice cream, and The Commodore had insisted we take his car. "You drive, sport," he said to me.

Before I could start the car, he jerked the keys from the ignition.

"Imagine the moment, Edward." He shook the keys in his hand as if they were dice. "That instant of horror when you know you're losing control. Your speed is too high, the road is too slick, the curve is too sharp. You're at that place you never dreamed you'd be. Brink of disaster, pal. One wrong move, and you cross over. Too late to get yourself back to safe ground. What do you do?"

"Don't panic," I said.

"And?"

"React."

He tossed me the keys. "O.K., Speedy Alka-Seltzer. Let's see if you've got any fizz."

The afternoon my mother and I finished "The Welcome Table," out doorbell rang.

"Ding-dong," Dix Gleason shouted. "It's Dix and The Commodore."

The Commodore was off-duty. He was wearing a salt-and-pepper sports coat and a bolero tie with a silver horseshoe clasp. His black hair was shiny with tonic.

"Sport," he said to me. "I'd say you've been in some trouble."

"Trouble?" my mother said. "There's been no trouble here."

The Commodore pointed to my shirt pocket where a corner had been torn away in the melee at Kress's. "I don't imagine your mama sent you to school with your pocket like that. And that lip of yours. Looks a little fat to me. Like it got in the way of someone's fist."

"You might as well come clean," Dix said. She was wearing a lavender cowgirl dress with golden fringe along the bottom of the skirt. "You can't put anything past The Commodore."

A stray punch had clobbered me at Kress's, but I didn't want to admit any of this to The Commodore. Luckily, my mother came to my rescue. "Just a scuffle," she said. "You know boys."

"Tempers are on the boil," The Commodore said. "What with the nigras all up in the air. I hear there's been some nasty business downtown today."

My mother was always on edge whenever The Commodore was around but on this afternoon she looked close to coming apart. She bustled about, pulling out chairs for Dix and The Commodore at our dining table, going on and on about the eggshell we had just finished and what a funny thing it was that it was a miniature scene of people sitting around a dining table, and here we were sitting around a regular-sized table.

"Like a box inside a box," she said. "Or those hand-painted Russian dolls. Oh, you know the ones I mean. Take off the top half and there's a smaller doll inside. Five or six of them like that all the way down to the tiniest one—no bigger that the first joint of your pinky finger, Dix—and the funny thing is, even though the last one is so much smaller than the first one, their features are exactly the same."

The Commodore picked up "The Welcome Table" eggshell from its ornate stand, and held it with his thick fingers. "I bet there'd be something different," he said. "Something small, practically impossible to pick out. I bet I'd find it."

"Be careful with that," Dix said, and she said it with a hardness to her voice like a woman who had lived too long with a reckless man. "You bust that and Henny Penny might lose her head."

"It must take a world of patience." The Commodore set the eggshell back on its stand. "I'd say you'd have to have a ton of love to pay such close attention to things."

My mother ran her hand over our tablecloth. "Why, thank you, Commodore." A blush came into her face as if she were a young girl, unaccustomed to compliments. "That means a great deal coming from someone with your keen eye."

It had been some time since my mother had been able to enjoy friends. In New Hampshire, when the truth of my father's mismanagement became public, she closed our blinds and refused to answer the telephone or the doorbell. Now, despite Dix's forwardness and The Commodore's suspicious nature, she was thankful for Nashville and the chance it had given her to be gracious and hospitable. When she came from our kitchen that afternoon, the serving tray held before her, the dessert cups filled with sherbet, the coffee cups chiming against their saucers, she might as well have been offering her soul to The Commodore and Dix, so desperate she was to have people admire her.

The Commodore had gone out on the porch to smoke a cigarette.

"Run get The Commodore," my mother told me. "Tell him his sherbet's going to melt."

He was sitting on our porch glider, a cigarette hanging from his lip. He was reading a Glorious Days greeting card my father had left there. "Listen to this, Edward. 'May your special day be filled with sunshine and love.' Now that is a beautiful sentiment." He folded the card and tapped its spine against his leg. "Your daddy's not like me, is he?"

"No, sir. I suppose he's not."

"What you have to decide," he told me, "is whether that's a good thing."

I wanted my father to be noble and full of goodness. "He's been helping the Negroes organize the lunch-counter demonstrations," I said.

The Commodore took a long drag on his cigarette. "How about you? What do you make of that?"

I touched my finger to my sore lip. "It's caused me some grief."

"Understand, I don't have anything against the nigras." He flipped his cigarette butt out into our yard. "But people here are set in their ways. I'm only telling you this for your own good. Whatever happens with this integration mess, your daddy has to live here."

When The Commodore said that, something lurched and gave inside me. The life we had invented for ourselves cracked and began to come apart. For the first time, I could see the raw truth of my family: We were cowards. If things didn't work out for us here, as they hadn't in New Hampshire, we could go somewhere else. We could choose a new name. We could do it as many times as we needed to—move away from ourselves, like opening one of those Russian dolls and finding another one inside. I saw us shrinking with each move we made until we got down to the smallest people we could be, the ones that wouldn't open, the ones made from solid wood.

The Commodore laid the greeting card on the porch glider. "Edward, your daddy ought to take care. You be sure to tell him what I said."

We were eating sherbet when my father came home. We heard his car pull into the driveway, and my mother smiled and said to me, "How's that for luck? Your father's home early. Won't he be surprised to see we've got company?"

"Your husband?" Dix said. "My stars. We finally get to meet the mister."

My father came through the door and walked right up to the dining table and sat down across from The Commodore as if he had been expected. He kept his head bowed, and I could tell something was wrong. His hands were on the table, and his fingers were trembling, and the eggshell was wobbling on its stand. We all bowed our heads, as if we were asking a blessing, and for a long time no one spoke.

Then my mother said, "Richard?" And she said it with the cautious tone I remembered from New Hampshire.

My father still wouldn't raise his head, and I'm not sure he even knew there were other people sitting at his table, people he didn't know and wouldn't care for once he did. "I saw a boy killed today," he said, and his voice was barely a whisper. "That's all I want to say about it."

"Killed?" my mother said, and I think she knew, even then, that trouble had found us.

That's when The Commodore spoke. "An accident?"

Dix slapped his arm. "Mr. Thibodeaux said he doesn't want to say any more about it."

When she said that, her voice steeled with warning; I could tell she had never gotten used to The Commodore's intimacy with accidents and deaths, hated him for it, no doubt, in ways she might not even have known.

But The Commodore wouldn't keep quiet. "I hope you weren't involved with it. That's all I'll say."

My father raised his face, and I could tell he was trying to hold himself together. His jaw was set and his lips were tight, but his eyes were wet and I could see he was crying.

"Probably some of that nigra mess," The Commodore said. "Is that it, pal?"

It was clear to me, then, that The Commodore hated something about my father, feared it, perhaps, and I decided it was the fact that my father was a careless man.

"If it is," The Commodore went on, "you asked for your trouble. Like those hot-rodders who think the speed limit means everyone else but them. They don't see the danger. Buddy, you get out there on the wild side, something's bound to go wrong. Hell, you know it. I wouldn't think you'd have any call to cry over that."

"What's your name?" my father said to The Commodore. He turned to Dix. "Is this your husband?"

He wasn't crying now; his voice had that edge to it I recognized from the sit-in training sessions.

"His name's Commodore Gleason," Dix said. "We're friends of your wife. Dix and The Commodore."

"The Commodore's with the highway patrol," my mother said.

"He does accident reports," I told my father, hoping to explain The Commodore's interest in the boy's death and somehow make my father feel better about all this.

"What do you do at an accident scene?" he asked The Commodore.

"I put it all together," The Commodore said. "Gather the facts, pal. Tell you how it happened."

"Talk to the survivors, do you?"

"That's right."

"Tell them you're sorry for their trouble?"

The Commodore gave a little laugh. "Say, what kind of a bastard do you think I am?"

"Do you mean it when you say it?" my father asked. "When you tell them you're sorry?"

"Listen, pal."

"Do you?"

"I'm there to get at the facts." The Commodore slapped his palm down on the table, and the eggshell wobbled again, and my mother put her hand to her mouth. "I'm there to get at the truth, pal. It's my job to know things." The Commodore stood up and pointed his finger at my father. "Just like I know what you're up to with the nigras. It's people like you who'll ruin the South. Even your own boy knows that. He's been clubbing niggers downtown today."

It's funny how your life slows down during the moments you wish you could speed away from and leave behind you forever. I could see the smallest details: the way the gold fringe on Dix Gleason's dress turned silver in the sunlight slanting through our window, my mother wetting her finger and rubbing a spot of sherbet that had stained her white tablecloth, the way one string of The Commodore's bolero tie was shorter than the other, my father's shoulders sagging as if all the life had left him.

"Is that true, Ed?" he said to me.

I remembered the way I had shouted "nigger" at Kress's, how I had pushed my way out of the mob once the fighting had started. I had run outside and started walking, wanting to get as far away from Kress's as I could. I had walked and walked, and then I had caught a city bus and come home, and now The Commodore had lied about me, and because I felt so guilty about my part in the trouble downtown, because I wanted all this between The Commodore and my father to stop before it went too far, and The Commodore found out all there was to know about us—that our name wasn't Thibodeaux, that my father had made mistakes in New Hampshire, that we had tried our best to bury these facts—I said, yes, it was true.

My father slumped down in his chair. "I'm sorry," he said. "Folks, I'm sorry for all of this."

And The Commodore said, "Damn straight you're sorry. I could have told you that from the get-go."

The boy who died that day was not a Negro as we all had first believed. It was, as I would find out later, Dale Mink. He had come from Kress's, jubilant, the way he was after a basketball victory. He must have been feeling pretty full of himself. He was seventeen years old, a basketball star on his way to Vanderbilt, and he had the juice of a fist fight jazzing around in his head. When he ran out into the street and saw my father's car, he must have been dazzled by how quickly misfortune had found him.

It was, my father finally told us, something he had played over in his head time and time again after he told his story to the police: the street had been wet with rain and the police vans had pulled up to Kress's. The officers were gathering up the black college students, arresting them for disorderly conduct, and the white boys who had attacked them were spilling out into the street. They were raising their arms and shaking their fists. My father glanced into his rearview mirror and noticed the way the skin was starting to wrinkle around his eyes. When he finally looked back to the street, there was Dale Mink, and it was too late for my father to stop.

My mother and I didn't know any of this when Dix and The Commodore left our house.

"He knows about you now," my mother said to my father. "He'll tell it over and over. And then where will we be?"

"Were you there?" my father asked me. "At Kress's?"

"I went with a boy from school. I didn't hit anyone. I said some things. That's all."

"You said things? Provoked those poor students? What did you say?"

I let my face go wooden, the way Lester Bates had when he gripped the lunch counter, and the taunting had begun. "Things you taught me," I said.

My father lifted his hand and, with his finger, brushed a piece of lint from his eyelashes. I wanted to think that he was an unlucky man—"Trouble knows my name," he had said in New Hampshire—but I could see he was actually a man of vanity. I knew that was a dangerous thing to be in the world. It meant forgetting others and concentrating only on yourself, and, when that was the case, all kinds of lunatic things could happen.

"I'm hungry," my father said. "I swear, Penny. I'm starved."

We were sitting at our dining table and outside the light was fading. The eggshell was still upright in its stand and what I remembered was how, when my father first sat down, we all bowed our heads and stared at it. I like to believe now that each of us, even The Commodore, was thinking what a lovely scene. "Inviting," my mother had said earlier. The people around the miniature table seemed cozy and content. We must have looked at them with a desperate yearning. They were so small. They were so far away from us and everything that was about to happen in our home.

LEE MARTIN

High School: San Martin

Howard Miyata was my boyfriend for awhile.
We walked school halls
holding hands.
The cowboys, the chicano-bashers,
they let us be,
because the Japanese owned land,
farmed,
drove new cars,
and that made them white,
or almost same-as-white,
and so the cowboys didn't count it
as somebody taking one of their women.

Howard's skin was as pale as mine,
swimming in a summer creek
his body smooth and lean
his hair short and black and straight,
mine long and curly and red.

Miguel Martinez, the boy they killed
in a parking-lot riot,
had pale skin, black hair,
an Anglo girlfriend, too.
But his parents were wetbacks,
he picked in the fields,
spoke with an accent.
A tall blond boy
in cowboy boots
hit him with a chain,
and his face became whiter,
and his hair became red.
They watched him bleed
and his blood never touched them.

RENNY CHRISTOPHER

On the Subway

The young man and I face each other.
His feet are huge, in black sneakers
laced with white in a complex pattern like a
set of intentional scars. We are stuck on
opposite sides of the car, a couple of
molecules stuck in a rod of light
rapidly moving through darkness. He has
or my white eye imagines he has the
casual cold look of a mugger,
alert under hooded lids. He is wearing
red, like the inside of the body
exposed. I am wearing old fur, the
whole skin of an animal taken and
used. I look at his raw face,
he looks at my dark coat, and I don't
know if I am in his power—
he could take my coat so easily, my
briefcase, my life—
or if he is in my power, the way I am
living off his life, eating the steak
he may not be eating, as if I am taking
the food from his mouth. And he is black
and I am white, and without meaning or
trying to I must profit from his darkness,
the way he absorbs the murderous beams of the
nation's heart, as black cotton
absorbs the heat of the sun and holds it. There is
no way to know how easy this
white skin makes my life, this
life he could break so easily, the way I
think his back is being broken, the
rod of his soul that at birth was dark and
fluid, rich as the heart of a seedling
ready to thrust up into any available light.

SHARON OLDS

V. ⌇

SCHOOL DAZE

School days, school days

Dear old golden rule days

In the Elementary School Choir

I had never seen a cornfield in my life,
I had never been to Oklahoma,
But I was singing as loud as anyone,
"Oh what a beautiful morning. . . . The corn
Is as high as an elephant's eye,"
Though I knew something about elephants I thought,
Coming from the same continent as they did,
And they being more like camels than anything else.

And when we sang from *Meet Me in St. Louis,*
"Clang, clang, clang went the trolley,"
I remembered the ride from Ramleh Station
In the heart of Alexandria
All the way to Roushdy where my grandmother lived,
The autos on the roadway vying
With mule carts and bicycles,
The Mediterranean half a mile off on the left,
The air smelling sharply of diesel and salt,

It was a problem which had dogged me
For a few years, this confusion of places,
And when in 5th grade geography I had pronounced
"Des Moines" as though it were a village in France,
Mr. Kephart led me to the map on the front wall,
And so I'd know where I was,
Pressed my forehead squarely against Iowa.
Des Moines, he'd said. Rhymes with coins.

Now we were singing "zippidy-doo-dah, zippidy-ay,"
And every song we'd sung had in it
Either sun or bluebirds, fair weather
Or fancy fringe, O beautiful America!
And one tier below me,

there was Linda Deemer with her amber waves
And lovely fruited plains,
And she was part of America too
Along with sun and spacious sky

Though untouchable, and as distant
As purple mountains of majesty.

"This is my country," we sang,
And a few years ago there would have been
A scent of figs in the air, mangoes,
And someone playing the oud along a clear stream.

But now it was "My country 'tis of thee"
And I sang it out with all my heart
And now with Linda Deemer in mind.
"Land where my fathers died," I bellowed,
And it was not too hard to imagine
A host of my great uncles and -grandfathers
Stunned from their graves in the Turkish interior
And finding themselves suddenly
On a rock among maize and poultry
And Squanto shaking their hands.

How could anyone not think America
Was exotic when it had Massachusetts
And the long tables of thanksgiving?
And how could it not be home
If it were the place where love first struck?

We had finished singing.
The sun was shining through large windows
On the beatified faces of all
Who had sung well and with feeling.

We were ready to file out and march back
To our room where Mr. Kephart was waiting.
Already Linda Deemer had disappeared
Into the high society of the hallway.
One day I was going to tell her something.
Des Moines, I was saying to myself,
Baton Rouge. Terre Haute. Boise.

GREGORY DJANIKIAN

Sixth Grade

The afternoon the neighborhood boys tied me and Mary Lou
    Mahar
to Donny Ralph's father's garage doors, spread-eagled,
it was the summer they chased us almost every day.

Careening across the lawns they'd mowed for money,
on bikes they threw down, they'd catch us, lie on top of us,
then get up and walk away.

That afternoon Donny's mother wasn't home.
His nine sisters and brothers gone—even Gramps, who lived
    with them,
gone somewhere—the backyard empty, the big house quiet.

A gang of boys. They pulled the heavy garage doors down,
and tied us to them with clothesline,
and Donny got the deer's leg severed from the buck his dad had
    killed

the year before, dried up and still fur-covered, and sort of
poked it at us, dancing around the blacktop in his sneakers,
    laughing.
Then somebody took it from Donny and did it.

And then somebody else, and somebody after him.
Then Donny pulled up Mary Lou's dress and held it up,
and she began to cry, and I became a boy again, and shouted
    Stop,

and they wouldn't.
Then a girl-boy, calling out to Charlie, my best friend's brother,
who wouldn't look

Charlie! to my brother's friend who knew me
Stop them. And he wouldn't
And then more softly, and looking directly at him, I said,
    Charlie.

And he said Stop. And they said What? And he said Stop it.
And they did, quickly untying the ropes, weirdly quiet,
Mary Lou still weeping. And Charlie? Already gone.

MARIE HOWE

The Jacket

My clothes have failed me. I remember the green coat that I wore
in fifth and sixth grades when you either danced like a champ or
pressed yourself against a greasy wall, bitter as a penny toward the
happy couples.

When I needed a new jacket and my mother asked what kind
I wanted, I described something like bikers wear: black leather and
silver studs with enough belts to hold down a small town. We were
in the kitchen, steam on the windows from her cooking. She listened so long while stirring dinner that I thought she understood
for sure the kind I wanted. The next day when I got home from
school, I discovered draped on my bedpost a jacket the color of
day-old guacamole. I threw my books on the bed and approached
the jacket slowly, as if it were a stranger whose hand I had to
shake. I touched the vinyl sleeve, the collar, and peeked at the
mustard-colored lining.

From the kitchen mother yelled that my jacket was in the closet.
I closed the door to her voice and pulled at the rack of clothes in
the closet, hoping the jacket on the bedpost wasn't for me but my
mean brother. No luck. I gave up. From my bed, I stared at the
jacket. I wanted to cry because it was so ugly and so big that I
knew I'd have to wear it a long time. I was a small kid, thin as a
young tree, and it would be years before I'd have a new one. I
stared at the jacket, like an enemy, thinking bad things before I
took off my old jacket whose sleeves climbed halfway to my elbow.

I put the big jacket on. I zipped it up and down several times,
and rolled the cuffs up so they didn't cover my hands. I put my
hands in the pockets and flapped the jacket like a bird's wings. I
stood in front of the mirror, full face, then profile, and then looked
over my shoulder as if someone had called me. I sat on the bed,
stood against the bed, and combed my hair to see what I would
look like doing something natural. I looked ugly. I threw it on my
brother's bed and looked at it for a long time before I slipped it
on and went out to the backyard, smiling a "thank you" to my
mom as I passed her in the kitchen. With my hands in my pockets

I kicked a ball against the fence, and then climbed it to sit looking into the alley. I hurled orange peels at the mouth of an open garbage can and when the peels were gone I watched the white puffs of my breath thin to nothing.

I jumped down, hands in my pockets, and in the backyard on my knees I teased my dog, Brownie, by swooping my arms while making bird calls. He jumped at me and missed. He jumped again and again, until a tooth sunk deep, ripping an L-shaped tear on my left sleeve. I pushed Brownie away to study the tear as I would a cut on my arm. There was no blood, only a few loose pieces of fuzz. Damn dog, I thought, and pushed him away hard when he tried to bite again. I got up from my knees and went to my bedroom to sit with my jacket on my lap, with the lights out.

That was the first afternoon with my new jacket. The next day I wore it to sixth grade and got a D on a math quiz. During the morning recess Frankie T., the playground terrorist, pushed me to the ground and told me to stay there until recess was over. My best friend, Steve Negrete, ate an apple while looking at me, and the girls turned away to whisper on the monkey bars. The teachers were no help: they looked my way and talked about how foolish I looked in my new jacket. I saw their heads bob with laughter, their hands half-covering their mouths.

Even though it was cold, I took off the jacket during lunch and played kickball in a thin shirt, my arms feeling like braille from goose bumps. But when I returned to class I slipped the jacket on and shivered until I was warm. I sat on my hands, heating them up, while my teeth chattered like a cup of crooked dice. Finally warm, I slid out of the jacket but a few minutes later put it back on when the fire bell rang. We paraded out into the yard where we, the sixth graders, walked past all the other grades to stand against the back fence. Everybody saw me. Although they didn't say out loud, "Man, that's ugly," I heard the buzz-buzz of gossip and even laughter that I knew was meant for me.

And so I went, in my guacamole jacket. So embarrassed, so hurt, I couldn't even do my homework. I received Cs on quizzes, and forgot the state capitals and the rivers of South America, our friendly neighbor. Even the girls who had been friendly blew away like loose flowers to follow the boys in neat jackets.

I wore that thing for three years until the sleeves grew short and my forearms stuck out like the necks of turtles. All during that time no love came to me—no little dark girl in a Sunday dress she wore on Monday. At lunchtime I stayed with the ugly boys who leaned against the chainlink fence and looked around with propellers of grass spinning in our mouths. We saw girls walk by alone, saw couples, hand in hand, their heads like bookends pressing air together. We saw them and spun our propellers so fast our faces were blurs.

I blame that jacket for those bad years. I blame my mother for her bad taste and her cheap ways. It was a sad time for the heart. With a friend I spent my sixth-grade year in a tree in the alley waiting for something good to happen to me in that jacket, which had become the ugly brother who tagged along wherever I went. And it was about that time that I began to grow. My chest puffed up with muscle and, strangely, a few more ribs. Even my hands, those fleshy hammers, showed bravely through the cuffs, the fingers already hardening for the coming fights. But that L-shaped rip on the left sleeve got bigger; bits of stuffing coughed out from its wound after a hard day of play. I finally Scotch-taped it closed, but in rain or cold weather the tape peeled off like a scab and more stuffing fell out until that sleeve shriveled into a palsied arm. That winter the elbows began to crack and whole chunks of green began to fall off. I showed the cracks to my mother, who always seemed to be at the stove with steamed-up glasses, and she said that there were children in Mexico who would love that jacket. I told her that this was America and yelled that Debbie, my sister, didn't have a jacket like mine. I ran outside, ready to cry, and climbed the tree by the alley to think bad thoughts and watch my breath puff white and disappear.

But whole pieces still casually flew off my jacket when I played hard, read quietly, or took vicious spelling tests at school. When it became so spotted that my brother began to call me "camouflage," I flung it over the fence into the alley. Later, however, I swiped the jacket off the ground and went inside to drape it across my lap and mope.

I was called to dinner: steam silvered my mother's glasses as she said grace; my brother and sister with their heads bowed made ugly faces at their glasses of powdered milk. I gagged too, but eagerly ate big rips of buttered tortilla that held scooped up beans. Finished, I went outside with my jacket across my arm. It was a cold sky. The faces of clouds were piled up, hurting. I climbed the fence, jumping down with a grunt. I started up the alley and soon slipped into my jacket, that green ugly brother who breathed over my shoulder that day and ever since.

GARY SOTO

Ladies' Choice

A lot depends on your type of jacket—what neighborhood in the city you come from, what side of the dance floor you stand around, who you talk to, who talks to you. There are girls here who say no right to your face and others who sort of look you up and down and then kind of laugh. You can tell them apart easy enough just by looking at their hair. The dooper girls wear their hair down, most of the time parted down the middle. They look like they've just washed it. When they dance it swings around behind them in clouds and waves. The greaser girls always wear their hair up—teased, ratted, and sprayed. It never moves when they move. You have to be careful dancing with them because sometimes that spray gets into your eyes and makes them tear something awful. They're the ones who look at you sideways and smile to themselves.

Though you can never really tell. The number of city girls here at the dance is always getting smaller, or at least it seems like that. Girls' hair keeps getting longer, and sometimes it seems like everybody is washing it and combing it down the middle. So you just guess and make your shot.

But like I just said, what counts is the jacket. The doopers wear all the strange kinds. They wear lumber jackets that look like big red-and-white or black-and-white checkerboards, and they wear CPOs that look just like lumber jackets but without the squares. Then there are jackets that look like coats the kid's mother bought him so he'd have something nice to wear to funerals. Only the real numbnuts wear those, and if they're smart they take them off and carry them over their arms, or better yet they stash them in a corner and hope somebody walks off with them. You don't usually see guys with coats back at these dances week after week. None of the girls will have anything to do with them.

Sometimes I'll be walking around, like I am right now, and I'll see a group of guys find one of these kids' coats wadded up in the bleachers like a furry ball, and I'll watch the guys pull it out and go through its pockets, and then maybe one of the guys will have to spit, so he'll do that in the lining, and then another of the guys will hock on it or blow his nose, and then somebody will kick the coat out onto the dance floor where another guy will step on it and then kick it further out, and after the dance on the way out I'll see the loons asking the priests if they have seen their coats anywhere, and it's funny and pathetic and really kind of sad. I know these guys have probably never been to this kind of sock hop before, and after the experience they probably won't be back either.

See, everybody wears their jacket, and if you ever take it off you tell your friends to guard it with their lives. The priests and the men from the Fathers' Club and the Holy Name Sodality check your shoes upstairs in the gymnasium balcony. It costs a quarter, and they do it because they don't want their basketball court all scuffed up. They don't touch jackets, even like now in the middle of winter, because they don't want the responsibility. Plus, nobody would check their jacket anyway. A guy wears his jacket to show everybody who he is.

The greasers wear suedes and leathers. Expensive threads. They come from all over the North Side of the city, sometimes even from the suburbs, though usually the greasers from the suburbs are crazy, wanting to get into fights all the time. They're almost as stupid as the kids who wear their mothers' coats, and you can tell them easy from the city greasers because try as they might they never exactly look right. They're always a step behind, wearing what we wore yesterday. They're the greasers whose pants look brand new when we're washing them out or their hair is still long while we're getting closer cuts. They don't exactly know what to say to you if you talk to them. The dead giveaway is if they smoke filtered cigarettes or use a lighter. Most greasers I know from the city never use lighters because lighters always leak that fluid out through your pants pocket and onto your leg, and then you get a round red sore spot like a ringworm. I had a lighter once—a good one, a Zippo—and it did exactly that. It was back when I was a kid. I threw the damn thing away or left it in my locker at school or gave it to a girl or something.

I first started coming to these dances last year when I was a sophomore. They're the only thing really going on in the city on Sunday nights. I had to show them my ID from school to prove I was a Catholic. You don't have to be a Catholic to get in, but Catholics pay fifty cents less. Then all that fall and winter I came here every Sunday night, taking the Clark Street bus south from my corner and transferring west at Addison by the ballpark, then getting off at Western Avenue and walking north. I know it would be more direct if I transferred at Irving Park, but I like going past the dark empty ballpark and then walking by Riverview on Western and Belmont. Riverview is the amusement park, the largest and greatest in the whole world. Not that I've been to any others, but that's what people say. From the street you can see the Ferris wheels and the Pair-O-Chutes tower and that good long dip of the Silver Flash roller coaster. You can hear people screaming from the Wild Mouse and Shoot the Chutes, and wave to the folks up on the Space Ride. LAUGH YOUR TROUBLES AWAY announces the big billboard. I like walking past the sounds and smells of the place, and I especially like all the bright lights.

Coming here to the dance is something I do every Sunday. It's a habit, I guess, but it's a good habit, and I like riding the buses sitting in the back row looking out at all of the different people and the city, and I like walking the extra mile or so past the big shining used car lots, with the prices painted on all the windshields, and then by Riverview there's always something going on outside the main gates, somebody showing off or laughing their troubles away or trying to sell you something, and then past that there is the big public school, Lane Tech, and the rest of the walk to the dance is dark and quiet and peaceful.

Some of the guys told me once that Lane Tech was built on top of a garbage dump, and they said every year the school building slips down just a little and that by the year 2000 the whole place will have sunk and be filled in with water from the lake. I think about that every time I walk past the place. It sorts of makes you wonder about what kind of ground it is you're walking on.

There's a guy now who's fast-dancing with a girl out in the middle of the floor, and the guy's big toenail is sticking out a hole in his sock. The greasers are around him in a circle, getting on him. What a stupid dooper, wearing a ripped pair of socks to a sock hop. The girl is looking down now to see what's causing all the commotion, and now she's blushing and walking right away. The dooper keeps on dancing. He shrugs and says to all of us, "Hey, knock it off, these are the socks I wear on Sundays." So a greaser asks him what he means. The guys says, "These are my holy socks," and I tell you that's pretty funny.

I guess I'm what you'd call a regular here, since I know mostly all of the guys. We hang around in the far corner, looking at people as they walk by. After we've checked them out, we start cruising. The outer fringes of the gym are filled with groups of guys just walking around checking things out. We look for genuine heartbreakers or girls we've never seen before or especially good dancers or jerks who're making fools of themselves.

The last are easy enough to spot. Some of these doopers must have learned to dance in Spazland by the way they flop their arms and kick their legs, and now just in front of me some bozo is whirling his lumber jacket over his head like he's a helicopter or something.

We're on the lookout for the mythical group of pretty girls, which is kind of like searching the forest for a bunch of unicorns. Everybody in the world knows there's no such thing. Groups of girls are like everything else—there are one or at the most two good-looking ones and the remainder are dogs. None of them will dance with you unless all her friends agree to dance so every now and then you have to make the sacrifice and dance with a dog. What you do then is get it over with as mercifully as possible.

But first there is the talking. Every group of guys has to have a talker—you know, somebody to walk over and break the ice. You need a face man—a guy who's good looking—to attract them to the guy delivering the spiel. I'm usually the third man, so I usually ask the third-best-looking girl, who is usually quiet, like me, and not a particularly high scorer in the looks department. As we dance we trade names and high schools and maybe streets where we hang out. It's hard to really get anywhere if you don't talk much. So after the song's over we just nod and kind of mutter thanks and see you, and I move on along.

The songs are records, 45s, that somebody, probably a young priest, plays over the PA. After a while you learn there is a kind of pattern to them. The sock hop begins with a lot of fast numbers, and the girls dance mainly with themselves while the guys just walk around, watching, and then there is a slow song and we make our first move then to get a dance, and then there are more fast songs and then a ladies' choice. In my time coming here I only got asked to dance once on a ladies' choice, and it wasn't a very pretty girl who asked me. She held me an arm's distance away and talked my ear off, saying I looked like her cousin from somewhere in Indiana who'd got himself killed in some kind of car crash, and I didn't say anything. I just danced with her. And when it was over the guys really kidded me.

Sometimes when I'm on the bus going home I think about these ladies' choices. I have a whole thing worked up. I'd be just walking around by myself, like I am now, and then I'd see a real pretty girl with nice long hair parted down the middle, and some guy would be bothering her, a real jerk, and then over the loudspeaker there would be the announcement that this song was a ladies' choice. The girl would turn to me then—there'd be a big smile on her clean, pretty face, and her big eyes would look up at me—and I'd stand tall and nod. Then we'd dance. The jerk would watch us. Then

I'd ask the girl if the jerk was bothering her, and she'd say yeah, and I'd tell the jerk to get lost. And if he didn't move quickly and there was a fight I'd beat the crap out of him, and the girl and several of her pretty friends and all the guys would watch me, and even if the priests and the men from Holy Name and all the jerk's friends broke it up and kicked me out and took away my card for good it still would be worth it because of course I'd wait for the girl outside and take her home. At her door I'd hold her hand and kiss her lightly on the lips, and I'd take her out the next Friday night—we'd go all out and go to Riverview—and I'd tell her as we rode the twin Ferris wheels and Bubble Bounce and Flying Turns and Crazy Dazy and Bobs and Strat-O-Stat and Tunnel of Love all about how I'd heard that Lane Tech was built on top of garbage, and we'd figure out together what that means, and we'd talk and really get to know each other, and we'd touch and kiss, and she would be my girl.

Of course that could never happen. It couldn't even happen in the movies. In the first place, the only girls who like me are greasers, the girls with the dark, dark eyes and the miles of makeup, all the hair spray and thick, too-sweet perfume. They know me like they know their brothers. They can see I'm not a jerk or a tough guy, that I'm quiet, even shy. It's just no good, going with these girls from my neighborhood. Sure, I date them and take them to movies at the Uptown or Riviera and afterwards buy them french fries and Coke, but I don't like talking to them and I'm afraid that if I get involved with one of them I'll end up having to get married to her, and that'll be the end of my life. Then I won't get any farther than the corner bus stop, and I'll be just like the rest of the goons who work in the filling stations and supermarkets and corner drugstores, and I don't want that. I don't know exactly what it is that I do want, but I know it isn't that. So I walk past the greaser girls on the dance floor, looking for that pretty long-haired girl.

But the dooper girls are afraid of my jacket. I wear a leather, a Cabretta. It took me two months of working in the paint store unloading cartons of gallons of paint and sweeping up at night to pay for it. In my neighborhood everybody wears a leather jacket. Mine's a fine one. I take perfect care of it. After I bought it before I even wore it outside I rubbed the leather with oil to make it soft. A leather jacket can last you the rest of your life if you treat it right. The dooper girls won't have anything to do with me, or if they do I soon realize they're playing games, just showing off in front of their friends. Afterwards when their parents pick them up in their big new cars that sit double-parked outside the gym every Sunday night the dooper girls will be talking about the greaser boy they danced with, how the cat had him by the tongue, how he didn't know what to say, and they'll laugh and feel important and daring because they'd done something they thought was dangerous, slumming with a greaser boy, and they'll talk about it all week long in their high schools out in the suburbs, and if I see them the next Sunday night at the dance they won't even remember it had been me.

The guys from the city hate them. They act like they think they're better than us. Sometimes when we dance with a group of them we can tell they're making fun of us behind our backs—they have these signals to one another, and they double-talk with words you can't understand. I walk away from them then, frustrated and angry, not knowing what I'd done or hadn't done, not understanding really what just took place or why it has to be this way, these differences, why they exist. And if I look back at them sometimes I can see them laughing, and then when I see them upstairs in line waiting to get back their shoes they treat me as if I'm a stranger.

So I go to these dances not really expecting anything and always being very careful if I dance with one of the pretty suburban girls. Most of the time I just hang around with the guys in the far corner, and we talk and talk some more, and whenever one of their boys walks by us in his silly lumber jacket we make noises with our mouths and call him sissy, jerk, fairy, queer, and every now and then in the bathroom there's a fight, like there was earlier tonight —a group of greasers beat up a dooper, or maybe it was the other way around. Blood's red regardless. I go into the brightly lit bathroom for a leak and see a smear of watered-down blood in the sink, and there's blood splashed all over the urinals and up on the wall and on the floor, and then when I come back out I hear the talk of a fight after the dance in the park.

This big greaser comes up to me and says that some dooper had gone out with this girl who was going steady with a guy who's in one of the local gangs, and then he promises there'd be a big mess after the dance tonight. I say, "Sure." He says, "We'll stomp their damn heads." I say, "Of course we will." He says, "It's us against them," and then he slaps me hard on my shoulder, and I nod and he shakes my hand as he walks away. I begin my circles around the dance floor, looking for that pretty long-haired girl.

My socks are wet and cold from all the snow people have tracked in from outside. The guys in the far corner stand around me joking, talking about tonight's fight. I don't remind them that Chicago's finest are always outside, sipping coffee in their squad cars. The guys know this. All of us know this. The big rumble's just talk. The only thing that's real is the blood in the bathroom, and who really cares about it if it isn't yours, if you aren't the one bleeding in the ambulance or the back of the squad car. I want to say all of this to the guys around me but I don't. I'm tired of talk tonight. So I tell the guys instead that I think I'll take a rain check on the extracurriculars and go home early, get a little sleep or maybe just sit around and watch something on TV.

The street outside has that special quiet that only a heavy snowfall gives the city. Everything is muffled and softly edged. As soon as I am out in the air I feel better, stronger. I walk directly toward Irving Park. My shoes sink quietly into the deep snow. Normally I'd head south so as to walk past Lane Tech and Riverview, but it being winter the amusement park is closed for the season. Its bright lights are unlit. I walk, not really thinking about anything, and now I see the lights of what seem to be squad cars, and I move slower, wondering what's happened in the park.

A policeman calls to me. "Hey, you," he shouts. "Stop."

I turn. A policeman is running toward me in the snow. Behind him are more squad cars. I hear the wail of sirens in the distance.

"Freeze," the policeman says, and I smile, thinking I don't need a cop to tell me it's cold out. I slow and turn, and the cop grabs my arms and throws me to the ground. He calls me a punk and kicks my side. I hold my stomach and draw my knees up to my face. The other policeman takes his club out and shouts for me to put my hands behind my back and stand. As I do, he shoves me toward one of the squad cars. The cops push me against the warm front grill.

"Hands on the hood," the cops holler. "Spread your legs."

My heart pounds. I look at my breath hanging before me in the air. The cops unbutton my jacket and frisk me down, then jerk my arms behind my back and cuff my wrists.

There's someone inside the squad car. The first policeman opens the door, then leans inside and talks. I try to look at him but the other cop pulls me over to the opposite side of the squad car, and then someone rolls down the back window.

It's the girl of my dreams, the one who picks me. She leans forward in the backseat and looks at me. Her white coat is splattered with blood. Beside her is the guy who must be her boyfriend. He's crouched down, his hands covering his face, the bright red of his blood pouring between his fingers.

"Is he the one?" the cop behind me asks. He pulls down hard on my wrists, and when I say it hurts he kicks my leg and tells me to shut up. The other policeman shines his flashlight on me.

"Is he the one?" the cop says again.

The boyfriend leans back and groans, then starts to throw up. His vomit comes out from between the fingers of his hands, splashing against the back of the front seat and then down onto his legs and his red-and-white lumber jacket.

"I don't know," the girl is saying. She's really really pretty but she looks so scared. Blood shines in her long, straight, blonde hair. "I think so. He could be." She bites her bottom lip. "Yeah, it's him. I'm sure of it. He's wearing the same jacket."

The cop behind me pulls back on my wrists again and pushes me away from the car.

The sirens are nearly upon us. All I think of is Riverview, its darkened towers and lights.

TONY ARDIZZONE

As Children Together

Under the sloped snow
pinned all winter with Christmas
lights, we waited for your father
to whittle his soap cakes
away, finish the whisky,
your mother to carry her coffee
from room to room closing lights
cubed in the snow at our feet.
Holding each other's
coat sleeves we slid down
the roads in our tight
black dresses, past
crystal swamps and the death
face of each dark house,
over the golden ice
of tobacco spit, the blue
quiet of ponds, with town
glowing behind the blind

white hills and a scant
snow ticking in the stars.
You hummed *blanche comme*
la neige and spoke of Montreal
where a *québecoise* could sing,
take any man's face
to her unfastened blouse
and wake to wine
on the bedside table.
I always believed this,
Victoria, that there might
be a way to get out.

You were ashamed of that house,
its round tins of surplus flour,
chipped beef and white beans,
relief checks and winter trips
that always ended in deer
tied stiff to the car rack,
the accordion breath of your uncles
down from the north, and what
you called the stupidity
of the Michigan French.

Your mirror grew ringed
with photos of servicemen
who had taken your breasts
in their hands, the buttons
of your blouses in their teeth,
who had given you the silk
tassles of their graduation,
jackets embroidered with dragons
from the Far East. You kept
the corks that had fired
from bottles over their beds,
their letters with each city
blackened, envelopes of hair
from their shaved heads.

I am going to have it, you said.
Flowers wrapped in paper from carts
in Montreal, a plane lifting out

of Detroit, a satin bed, a table
cluttered with bottles of scent.

So standing in a platter of ice
outside a Catholic dance hall
you took their collars
in your fine chilled hands
and lied your age to adulthood.

I did not then have breasts of my own,
nor any letters from bootcamp
and when one of the men who had
gathered around you took my mouth
to his own there was nothing
other than the dance hall music
rising to the arms of iced trees.

I don't know where you are now, Victoria.
They say you have children, a trailer
in the snow near our town,
and the husband you found as a girl
returned from the Far East broken
cursing holy blood at the table
where nightly a pile of white shavings
is paid from the edge of his knife.

If you read this poem, write to me.
I have been to Paris since we parted.

CAROLYN FORCHÉ

The Silence That Widened

I.

Bobby ruled fifth grade when I moved into it.
"Yeah, I flunked last year,"
he said more than once. "So what?"
By mid-winter he had beaten every boy
worthy of combat except one, and he had beaten them
well within the fifteen minutes of recess.
On my afternoon Bobby leapt for my head
and rode me like a rodeo steer to the ice of the playground.

He hugged me to his chest in the headlock
that made every boy give up. Bobby dug his bony wrist
into his opponent's temple, a pain focused, arrow-sharp,
shooting through the brain until the inside of the nose stung.

When we slammed to the ice, I landed on top of Bobby,
squirming fast to guard my temple from his killing wrist bone.
We struggled under bloodthirsty shouts of circled boys
and, minutes later, their quiet disappointment
when they learned the grim, silent, slowness of the fight.
Freezing wind whipped down our necks
as Bobby and I lay panting and straining
through the tardy bell and silence that widened between
the school buildings when the last screaming
recessor fled the playground.
"We'd better go in," I said.
"Does that mean you give?"
It didn't.

II.

Bobby and I became fast friends after that.
We shared a locker, chose each other first for teams,
vandalized wantonly at Halloween, stole outside Christmas
lights in December, drove the new music teacher
of seventh grade to such distraction she banished
us to study hall, where we sat triumphantly bored.

That same year the phys ed teacher pitted
Bobby and me against each other in wrestling.
We each scored a takedown and drew. By ninth grade,
interests, ambitions, and school-sanctioned testing
drove us apart, rockets speeding in different directions.
In the general track, Bobby never failed again.
One June we found ourselves in Washington, D.C.,
on a senior class trip. We took a midnight cab
to Georgetown, went to a disco, sat in a dark corner,
drank beer, didn't dance, and were startled
when two girls appeared at our table.
We told them about the rural Midwest
and bought them three rounds of whiskey sours
before they picked up their purses and excused
themselves to the rest room ten minutes before closing.

That fall I learned about existentialism, behaviorism,
and prose stylists of the twentieth century.
Bobby forged gun barrels in a steel mill, working
so fast the union steward sat him down
for double-time breaks to make the job last.
In three months Bobby was drafted into the army.
Less than a year from the night we looked at each other
in that Georgetown bar, the lights flickering,
and knew the girls weren't returning,
Bobby was missing in action. A month later
his body was found on a steaming jungle slope.

Bobby's father and brother went to Deckman's Funeral Home.
"I wouldn't look," warned Mr. Deckman.
Bobby's father insisted. Mr. Deckman opened the casket.
Bobby's brother, the one who had taught him bloodless
victory through the deadly headlock, fainted.

III.
On that winter afternoon in 1959 Bobby and I
tried to find out who was better, but he couldn't
adjust the headlock and I couldn't break it.
The principal burst through the schoolhouse doors,
bellowing commands neither Bobby nor I could obey.
Mr. Daggart's tie flapped over his shoulder;
his sport coat caught the wind, billowing behind him
like a madman's cape. He snatched our collars
in large hands, yanked us to attention, choked us
into the building, down the long hallway, where he drew
his paddle and whacked us five times each.

Before the principal banged the schoolhouse doors aside,
the playground was ice-quiet, waiting as Bobby
and I strained and sweat inside our clothing.
Pressed between Bobby's back and the ice-coated asphalt
my ungloved hand burned. My butch haircut brushed
Bobby's chin, my face crushed against his corduroy coat.
Breaking loose would have been the biggest mistake.
Bobby held me so fast, so close, so safe.

TOM ROMANO

Caroline

In eighth grade, we teased that girl
as much as we could, mocking

her clothes, her stringy hair,
her flat, pallid face that revealed

little protest. Used to being
the one white girl in our class

of blacks, Hispanics, she endured
our taunts on her lack of rhythm,

on her stiff, flat-butted walk.
How we pitied her—brown hair

parted straight, pulled back
in a dull ponytail, her jeans

or corduroy pants in washed-out
shades of gray or blue,

her homework neatly done
in pained, legible print.

How weak it was to be white,
we thought, not able to dance

or run fast, to have skin
that peeled from too much sun.

We never let Caroline forget
that she was white and we

were black, that we could
swing our hips and snap

our fingers without trying,
privy to street-slang rhythms.

But she was our white girl,
and if anyone else dared

to touch her or call her names,
we'd be on them in a second,

calling them ugly right back,
slapping offenders if necessary.

With one of us by her side,
she could walk the school

safely, knowing she was ours
even if we didn't let her in

all the way, even if we laughed
at her white speech, thin lips.

ALLISON JOSEPH

Poem for Anthony, Otherwise Known as Head

Anthony had the biggest Afro
In the neighborhood, one of those fros
That bounced atop his head
Like a Buddha's belly.
When he played ball
We used to joke
That he could dunk
If his hair had hands.
And it was rumored
His mother had a special
James Bond electro-slide
Sunroof installed
In her '73 Cadillac
Just so he could ride
With his hair *uncompromised*,
Though none of us had actually
Seen this, we could imagine that
Ballet of black curls
Balanced on top of his five
Foot eleven frame ovaling

Out the roof, down the highway;
But the amazing part's
No one ever saw Anthony
Proffer a pick—
Like his fro was borned
Full of bounce—
An imperfect globe
Flowed from his scalp
Night & day, from dirt lot
To junior high school gym
Class chase, a graceful dance
Of follicles in the face
Of every hair-weave, plait,
Or braid the decades have to offer.

SEAN THOMAS DOUGHERTY

from Personal and Impersonal Landscapes

II. Wakoski's Petunias

Ruffled skirts

How we applauded
Sylvia Estrada's flamenco dancing
in Southern California
8th grade.
          She
was not a Mexican
they said,
          but Spanish/ her father
owned an
orange grove.
Childhood bigotry/ all
we knew,
that some were better than us,
and a few not.
How important those last few,
as we sat on
the sagging screened porch
knowing we had nothing
but our whiteness

and the bank
did not even give credit for that.
I was plump and tired
at 13,
but Sylvia Estrada was a thin hot wire
of brown magnetism. Like a
stick
in her ruffled skirts
and rhythm, thinness, make-up, curls,
money
I would never have.

How we applauded.
I still think longingly
of the flamenco clatter and pistol fire
on the old Washington School
Auditorium floor.

DIANE WAKOSKI

The Dance at St. Gabriel's

for Louis Otto

We were the smart kids of the neighborhood
where, after high school, no one went to school,
you NYU and I CCNY.
We eyed each other at St. Gabriel's
on Friday nights, and eyed each other's girls.
You were the cute, proverbial good catch
—just think of it, nineteen—and so was I,
but all we had was moonlight on our minds.
This made us cagey; we would meet outside
to figure how to dump our dates, go cruising.
In those hag-ridden and race-conscious times
we wanted to be known as anti-fascists,
and thus get over our Italian names.
When the war came, you volunteered, while I
backed in by not applying for deferment,
for which my loving family named me Fool.
Once, furloughs overlapping, we met up,
the Flight Lieutenant and the PFC;
we joked about the pair we made, and sauntered.

That Father Murray took one look at us,
and said our Air Force wings were the only wings
we'd ever earn. We lofted up our beers.
Ah, Louis, what good times we two have missed.
Your first time up and out the Germans had you,
and for your golden wings they blew you down.

FELIX STEFANILE

Yellow Roses

pinned on stiff tulle,
glowed in the painted
high school moonlight.
Mario Lanza's *"Oh my
Love, my darling"*
over the basketball
floor. When Doug
dipped, I smelled
Clearasil. Hours in
the tub dreaming of
Dick Wood's fingers
cutting in, sweeping
me close. I wouldn't
care if the stuck
pin on the roses
went thru me,
the yellow musk
would be a wreath
on the grave of that
awful dance where
Louise and I sat
pretending we didn't
care, our socks fat
with bells and fuzzy
ribbons, bloated and
silly as we felt. I
wanted to be home,
wanted the locked
bathroom to cry in,
knew some part of me
would never stop

waiting to be
asked to dance.

LYN LIFSHIN

High School Reunion

The troublemaker has become a monk.
No longer able to push the puny boys down the stairs,
torture the wearers of glasses and braces
or set fire to anyone's locker,
he says an invocation before our meal.
It's been ten years
and none of the cheerleaders are as fat
as we had hoped, but pretty Suzy is skinnier
than we could have imagined.
One of her arms is covered
by the long sleeve of her sequined gown,
and the other is bare—cavewoman-style.
Suzy's perfect teeth seem to have grown yellow and pointed.
It is rumored that her track-star-husband beats her.
The locals say his name has been in the paper, more than once,
for drugs. I imagine him asking her
which shoulder will be hidden in her asymmetrical dress,
where else he can safely punch. The troublemaker monk
might hear the track-star's confession,
then say, sadly, he understands.
Suzy dances like it's not very fun,
with none of the energy she used
to scoot to the top of a pyramid of other girls,
her saddle shoes firmly planted on the backs
of their maroon and gold uniforms.
Her legs barely shook and her arms belted out
as though she were singing an opera.
When her husband says she doesn't deserve any dessert,
we feel the guilt of wishing her those extra pounds,
of wishing Suzy any harm at all.

DENISE DUHAMEL

The Story of My Life

It was my fate to help Billy Redanz learn how to read;
the bully king of second grade, left back three times,
head like a cinder block, with a dirty cowlick
and dirty nails he dug into the book
he pinned between us, torturing each word.

"So the Jews drink children's blood."
His eyes on mine were flat and bright. I drew back,
kicking a line of dirt across his shin,
and dragged him to the principal
who tightened her lipsticked mouth at me,
asked Billy to apologize. I saw in a flash how it was.

He showed up years later, holding a monkey wrench
—muscled, greasy, polite—to fix my father's car.
When I came to the door he grabbed me,
grinning, pressing his lips against my throat.
"So you remember me?" he cried,
"You were so patient, so good, like a little nun."
He kissed my mouth, then off he went with his shining toolbox,
a last touch of his delicate broad fingers in my palm.
All day his cool, his bird-like whistle haunted the driveway,
that old conspiracy of kindness after me again,
another sweetness.

LIZ ROSENBERG

Wearing of the Green

"Wearing green will honor one of Holy Mother Church's greatest
saints, boys and girls." Sister Bernadette, fingering olive-black rosaries, sprayed a fine mist out over the first row as she spoke. Nearing her middle sixties and sporting several wild gray hairs over a
collapsed upper lip, she continued in a patient voice.

"And *everyone* should wear green to show their respect for him
on his feastday. Is that understood?"

"Yes, Sister!" we answered.

It was the week before St. Patrick's Day, 1957. Most of the thirty-
eight kids in my eighth-grade class were Irish and the nun had

spent part of the previous month talking about the importance of observing St. Patrick's Day.

As one of nine Italian kids—six boys, three girls—in the class, I joined the rest of the class in the chorus of "Yes, Sister."

But later in the schoolyard during recess, I asked Nunzio Esposito if he was going to wear green. Nunzio was a five-foot, two-hundred-pound "chooch," a lad whose girth and perpetual look of befuddlement caused everyone to boss him around, even kids in the lower grades.

"What, you nuts?" he said, a pained expression on his face. "You want me killed? Hah?" A safe dropped from the sky could not kill Nunzio.

Just then, Concetta Sporcachini, the class bombshell, whose breasts were the obsession of every boy in the sixth, seventh, and eighth grades, appeared behind Nunzio and slid her arms underneath his, making him look, for a moment, like an oriental deity with undulating arms.

Looking directly at me she said, "Why, mister rebel, you're not wearing green on St. Patrick's?" Her husky voice was unsettling. I was speechless at first, transfixed by her breasts and her ever darkening mustache, which, to my shame, I envied.

"But we're not Irish, Concetta. We're Italian," I said, trying hard not to get caught staring at her chest.

"So?" she replied, hands on her hips, a full head taller than me. "You seen enough?"

God, I thought, my face reddening, not only is she hairier but she had to be taller, too.

"No. Yes. I mean . . . look, maybe just the Irish should wear green, it's their holiday, not ours," I said, noticing to my discomfort a small crowd gathering.

Now a crowd usually gathered wherever Concetta stood or, more accurately, radiated. With her full lips, heavy makeup, and brazen attitude—like the fiery Italian actress Anna Mangani—she exerted a gravitational pull on male hormones for blocks around. But this time the attention was on me.

"Yeah, you should all wear greaseball outfits," shouted Matthew Cornelius O'Brien, whom the nuns always called by his three names. It was rumored he had knocked out a high school kid the previous week in a dispute over baseball cards. At five feet six inches and shaving regularly, he was the toughest kid in Catholicism. He had the face of a perplexed longshoreman.

The dozen or so of us in the group froze, eyes downward, not wanting to chance even a glimpse of his fearsome gaze.

"Why don't you scrub off those tans you all got so you look like you're in the human race!" laughed his older brother Thomas, making his second try at eighth grade. He too towered over us, a thin, wiry kid in clothes too large for him. His induction into the neighborhood hall of fame came the previous summer when, on a dare, he french-kissed a German shepherd. Thomas had the look of a kid destined for a career with the carnival.

Only the miraculous appearance of Sister Bernadette saved me from possible hospitalization at the hands of the O'Briens. "And what is going on here, boys and girls? Is there a problem that Sister should know about?"

We answered, "No, Sister."

"Then return to class at once," she said.

At afternoon dismissal, Nunzio and I, certain we were marked for a beating, burst through the schoolyard gates, twisting and turning down sidestreets and alleys to elude Patrick and Thomas. Puffing as we sprinted for cover behind the neighborhood taproom, Nunzio said "Those guys'll kill you and me for being with you."

I knew they would. As I lay flat on my stomach in an alley strewn with discarded seafood, praying they weren't following us, I turned to Nunzio and said, "They're just bullies, you have to stand up to them."

"My god, what smells?" said my sister Madeline when I walked into the house, my clothes reeking of the afternoon's escape.

"You smell like garbage but that's an improvement for you," chimed in my other sister, Marie.

"That's enough from all of you. Wash up—it's time to eat," called my mother from the kitchen. "Hurry up, go change your shirt and pants, Anthony, and tell your Uncle Nick it's time to eat."

"Not Uncle Nick, mom," cried Madeline, "him and his crazy stories; Daddy says he should be locked up." We all laughed, causing my mother to strike that awful cobra-like stare she used when anyone talked about her oldest brother.

"Your father talks too much in front of you kids. Nick's a genius, nobody understands him," she said.

"He's a genius alright," said my father, appearing at the kitchen door, a folded newspaper under his arm, "a genius who told the Secret Service he wanted to have an affair with Eleanor Roosevelt. How come nobody understands Nick should be in the bughouse?"

My father never forgave Nick for a drunken outburst in a local tavern during World War II in which Nick proclaimed, to the horror of more sober patrons, his desire to molest Eleanor Roosevelt, an episode that led to a visit from the Secret Service, bringing utter shame to the family.

My mother's forehead flushed a deep purple, a prelude to the explosion we called the Madam Butterfly, whom Nick said she resembled; just then Nick walked in, gesturing with his right hand like the Pope greeting an audience. Nearing his mid-thirties, he had thick hair that stood straight up, in a style reminiscent of Leon Trotsky; his flannel shirt was buttoned at the collar and offset by a previously owned silk tie. He smiled at us and said, "So how's everybody, how's school, Anthony?"

"Sit, Nick, come on, everybody sit, the macaroni'll get cold," my mother said, ladling out spoonfuls of steaming pasta drenched in gravy laced with hot sausage. We leaped into our places, save for my father who took his seat deliberately, almost in slow-motion, trying to send a cold stare into Nick's eyes. But Nick purposely turned his head away and asked me again, "So how's school, Anthony?"

"It's OK, Uncle Nick, boring, same stuff everyday," I said, between mouthfuls of Italian bread. "St. Patrick's Day's coming, the nun wants us to wear green."

Nick looked up quickly, his face, like ours, dripping with perspiration from the sausage, and said, "Even the Italians? You see what an Irish church this is? All of them, nuns and priests, all Irish, telling the Italians what to wear, what to believe, Ma Fa, but what is this!?"

"Take it easy, Nick," my mother cautioned, "you want more wine? Dom, give my brother more wine."

My father shot another murderous stare at Nick, who pretended not to notice and continued, "So you have to wear green for some fairy Irish saint?"

"That's enough, Nick," hollered my mother.

"So St. Patrick's a fairy, is that it?" said my father, in a low, quivering voice, his eyes widening. Though not a religious man, he took whatever opinion was opposite to Nick's.

"Stop it, both of you! These kids remember everything they hear," said my mother.

"Say more, Uncle Nick," I said, warming to the topic, remembering that Concetta had called me "Mr. Rebel." I was seized with delight at the prospect of an effeminate St. Patrick and the expressions on the faces of the O'Briens and Sister Bernadette when they found out.

Taking a deep breath like a trained orator, Nick said, "The Irish invent things that make them look religious, they make all the rules, they think Italians are pagans, you watch, Anthony, they'll make you feel dirty and ashamed you don't have blue eyes and freckles." Drinking more wine, he now looked at my father, who sat, ashen, mouth half open.

"No more, Nick," said my mother without conviction, staring at Nick with her head tilted slightly, wearing the expression of an affluent coed titillated at hearing about Marxism for the first time.

"How many Italian kids in your class, Anthony, five, six?" he asked, not waiting for an answer. "You wear something special for St. Anthony's feastday, do they make you dress up like an Italian? No. But they're the priests and the nuns and the cops and the politicians, they're the white people in this country." Nick slowly lit up a Pall Mall, pushed his chair from the table, leaned his head back, exhaled smoke with a theatrical flourish, and finished his wine. "So you have to wear green," he said, triumphantly, like a Jesuit who had just demolished some heresy with unassailable logic.

Taking this as a cue, my mother leaped up and said, "Let's clear the table, Marie, put out dessert, Madeline, give your father and uncle coffee."

Marie protested, "How come Anthony just sits there, like a bigshot?"

"Because he's your brother; boys don't do the dishes," said my mother.

As they cleared, Nick quietly said, "Anthony, come up to my room in five minutes, I want to tell you something," and made his way to the small back bedroom he used between bouts of employment. His previous job as a locker attendant in a public pool had ended precipitously when he refused to return the clothes of a ten-year-old who had belched in his face. Nick felt it was a matter of honor and, when the kid refused to apologize, Nick set the kid's clothes on fire before four other attendants wrestled my uncle to the ground.

Five minutes later I tapped lightly on the door of his room and went in. Nick sat on the end of the bed, his mouth pursed in concentration, carefully clipping his toenails with what happened to be industrial-strength scissors.

"You see, Anthony," he said, not looking up, "you have to put these in jars under your bed to protect yourself from *malocchio*, the evil eye."

"Does it work?" I said, struck by the yellowness of his feet and the piles of newspapers in every corner, realizing why no one, except for my mother, ever came into this room. It looked, I realized years later, like the room of an assassin.

"Sure it works, you think people put the horns on me, never, not with these under the bed. Listen, you want to fix those Irish on St. Patrick's?" he said, gathering the clippings and carefully inserting them in one of the glass jars he kept on a bureau.

"I don't want to fix them, I just feel funny wearing green when it's for them," I said.

"Here's what you do. Wear something orange on St. Patrick's," he said, stretching back on the bed, his hands folded underneath his head.

"Why orange?"

"It'll bother them, that's why. I forget if it's Protestants that wear orange and Catholics wear green, I don't remember, some Irish guy told me years ago it'll drive them nuts."

"I don't know, uncle Nick, I mean the nun's wild about green," I said.

"You want to be a chooch like all the other Italians who go along with this Irish crap?" he snapped, looking over at me now for the first time, his huge brown eyes locking into mine.

"I'm no chooch, you know I'm not."

"I know, I know, it's just I'm upset when I hear stuff they do to kids in Irish schools, that's all." His voice trailed off. He closed his eyes and fell asleep.

I ran down the stairs and out the door, shouting to my mother I had to go to Nunzio's house to get homework. He was on the front step baby-sitting his little sister Guiseppina, a rotund seven-year-old trying out her mother's high heels.

"Nunz, we have to wear orange on St. Patrick's Day!" I said.

"No, you have to wear orange, I'm wearing green," he said.

"Listen, Nunz, listen, we have to stand up for Italians, not be chooches for the Irish."

"Where'd you get orange?" he asked.

"It bothers them, like when you put red in front of a bull, they don't like it," I said, pleased with my inventiveness.

"I'm not waving nothing at the nun, at Matthew O'Brien, at Thomas O'Brien, I want to live to graduate from eighth grade, we have three months to go," said Nunzio. He didn't notice Guiseppina had climbed on top of a parked Ford sedan, still in high heels.

"We don't wave, we don't holler, we just sit there in orange, come on Nunz. And don't think Concetta won't notice either."

"Notice what?" he asked, as Guiseppina fell backwards, bounced off the trunk, and landed on both feet, smiling, but leaving a huge dent in the Ford.

"That we stood up, that we're Italian guys, that maybe she should let us feel her up sometime." I was sure I had him now.

"Who else we got?" he said and I ticked off the other four Italians. I began to perspire heavily.

"Let's call them now, right now," I said, and we went into Nunzio's house.

"Where's Guiseppina?" said his mother excitedly.

"On the step, I watched her," he said, annoyed, as his mother bolted past us, out the front door, screaming, "My baby, my baby!"

So after two hours on the phone, pleading and cajoling, assuring physical protection and inventing convoluted explanations of how we wouldn't wind up in serious trouble, the six Italian guys in Sister Bernadette's eighth grade agreed to wear orange instead of green on St. Patrick's Day.

The night before, I found a bright red tie in Uncle Nick's closet and thought it came close enough to orange. My heart pounded through the night as I half dreamed and half imagined the O'Briens pursuing me on horseback, like crazed Cassocks, wielding huge swords, Sister Bernadette behind them holding a St. Patrick's banner, a deep sadness on her face.

I wore a green tie at breakfast.

"Oh, that's right, it's St. Patrick's Day today, it's nice you're wearing green, Anthony," said my mother. The red tie was folded inside my schoolbag, like an explosive, and I wondered if she could sense it.

A half hour later the six of us gathered, like Roman conspirators, in one corner of the schoolyard before the first bell. Everyone showed their green ties then their "Italian" ties, none of which were exactly orange, but all of which were colors far enough away from green to make the point.

After the morning prayer, which especially acknowledged this as St. Patrick's Day, I leaned partially under my desk, as planned, removed the green tie and put on Uncle Nick's red tie, looking around to see if the others had made the change.

They had, and at first, no one noticed; most heads were bent in recitation of arithmetic drills. Then I saw Sister Bernadette's face register astonishment as she glanced at Nunzio's tie.

"Mr. Esposito, Mr. Esposito, Mr. Esposito?!" she said in a rising crescendo of shouts, "what is . . . where's your . . . what does this *mean*?!" She screamed the last word, sending a shock wave through the class.

Nunzio sat there like a captured felon.

"I asked you why you're wearing that tie, Mr. Esposito," she said, her face crimson, mouth askew, sitting at her desk, rocking slightly from side to side. "ANSWER ME, YOU HEATHEN," she screamed, as Nunzio sunk lower, trying to disappear.

She was on her feet now, walking slowly toward him, and stopped short, now seeing that others wore forbidden colors. She hissed, "Boys and girls, it seems some of your classmates saw fit to dishonor—yes *dishonor*—one of Holy Mother Church's greatest saints. They will pay for their blasphemy, God will see to it."

Her face soaked in agitation, her breathing labored, she said, "Matthew Cornelius O'Brien, go tell Mother Superior I'm coming to see her with this bunch of savages!"

O'Brien shot up, gleefully, I thought, and vanished through the door.

I wanted to leap up and explain that this was a harmless act of rebellion, a tiny blip on the screen of grade-school history, a small statement of ethnic assertion, but panic riveted me to my chair.

We stood, one by one, and walked to the front for the death march to Mother Superior's Office. The Italian girls sat with their heads bowed, the Irish kids hosed us down with venomous grimaces. Thomas O'Brien balled up his fists and motioned to me, silently mouthing the words, "You're a dead man."

As we formed a single file, Nunzio suddenly fell to one knee, extending both arms out like some guy in an opera, and shouted, "Bruno made us do this, I'm innocent!"

I felt a sharp crack to the side of my head, a popping sound that came from far away, and fell into the blackboard in time to see it was Sister Bernadette, flailing both arms at me, connecting with several more blows, as the others scrambled out of her way. She pulled up, hands still raised, and called to the others, "Take your seats, you spineless jellyfish," and they did, shuffling remorsefully.

Turning to me, she said, "We shall see, Mister Wiseacre, we shall see," and punched my face with surprising power. I tried to stand still, to strike some dignified pose in front of classmates whose faces were awash in the horror of my rebellion. I remember watching Concetta's breasts press out against her uniform, though I couldn't be certain because by now I was entangled in Bernadette's rosaries.

"Remember this day, children, remember the wickedness and evil of this St. Patrick's Day," she said before throwing the overhand right that floored me. "Get up," she shouted, and pulled me by one ear down the corridor to Mother Superior's office.

As I stood facing a corner, the nuns talked in hurried whispers, then telephoned the pastor, Father Hoolihan, an athletic-looking man in his early fifties, who breezed in minutes later and sat at the desk, flanked by Sister Bernadette and Mother Superior, all of them now whispering urgently.

A half hour later my mother and father came, clutching one another, looking small, my mother in a smock, my father wearing a stained shirt.

As they approached the religious tribunal, the priest straightening up, the nuns raising their heads expectantly, I knew I would forgive Nunzio's treachery, but I wasn't sure about my own, having rekindled a level of family humiliation last reached fourteen years before when the Secret Service questioned Uncle Nick about Eleanor Roosevelt.

The proceedings were very brief. Father Hoolihan announced I would not be suspended, though he thought that was the most appropriate punishment. Instead, I was to sweep and mop the convent floors for the remainder of the school year. When he said this, my mother threw what I called her fake punch at me, the one she used on me in public to impress whoever happened to be standing there. I also had to write a thousand-word composition on St. Patrick's life.

We left the office and walked the six blocks home in silence. I felt a curious relief, warmed by the late afternoon sun, several steps ahead of my parents, wondering if Concetta would ever let me touch her breasts.

ANTHONY F. BRUNO

The Boy Without a Flag

To Ms. Linda Falcón, wherever she is

Swirls of dust danced in the beams of sunlight that came through the tall windows, the buzz of voices resounding in the stuffy auditorium. Mr. Rios stood by our Miss Colon, hovering as if waiting to catch her if she fell. His pale mouse features looked solemnly dutiful. He was a versatile man, doubling as English teacher and gym coach. He was only there because of Miss Colon's legs. She was wearing her neon pink nylons. Our favorite.

We tossed suspicious looks at the two of them. Miss Colon would smirk at Edwin and me, saying, "Hey, face front," but Mr. Rios would glare. I think he knew that we knew what he was after. We knew, because on Fridays, during our free period when we'd get to play records and eat stale pretzel sticks, we would see her way in the back by the tall windows, sitting up on a radiator like a schoolgirl. There would be a strange pinkness on her high cheekbones, and there was Mr. Rios, sitting beside her, playing with her hand. Her face, so thin and girlish, would blush. From then on, her eyes, very close together like a cartoon rendition of a beaver's, would avoid us.

Miss Colon was hardly discreet about her affairs. Edwin had first tipped me off about her love life after one of his lunchtime jaunts through the empty hallways. He would chase girls and toss wet bathroom napkins into classrooms where kids in the lower grades sat, trapped. He claimed to have seen Miss Colon slip into a steward's closet with Mr. Rios and to have heard all manner of sounds through the thick wooden door, which was locked (he tried it). He had told half the class before the day was out, the boys sniggering behind grimy hands, the girls shocked because Miss Colon was married, so married that she even brought the poor unfortunate in one morning as a kind of show-and-tell guest. He was an untidy dark-skinned Puerto Rican type in a colorful dashiki. He carried a paper bag that smelled like glue. His eyes seemed sleepy, his Afro an uncombed Brillo pad. He talked about protest marches, the sixties, the importance of an education. Then he embarrassed Miss Colon greatly by disappearing into the coat closet and falling asleep there. The girls, remembering him, softened their attitude toward her indiscretions, defending her violently. "Face it," one of them blurted out when Edwin began a new series of Miss Colon tales, "she married a bum and needs to find true love."

"She's a slut, and I'm gonna draw a comic book about her," Edwin said, hushing when she walked in through the door. That afternoon, he showed me the first sketches of what would later become a very popular comic book entitled "Slut at the Head of the Class." Edwin could draw really well, but his stories were terrible, so I volunteered to do the writing. In no time at all, we had three issues circulating under desks and hidden in notebooks all over the school. Edwin secretly ran off close to a hundred copies on a copy machine in the main office after school. It always amazed me how copies of our comic kept popping up in the unlikeliest places. I saw them on radiators in the auditorium, on benches in the gym, tacked up on bulletin boards. There were even some in the teachers' lounge, which I spotted one day while running an errand for Miss Colon. Seeing it, however, in the hands of Miss Marti, the pig-faced assistant principal, nearly made me puke up my lunch. Good thing our names weren't on it.

It was a miracle no one snitched on us during the ensuing investigation, since only a blind fool couldn't see our involvement in the thing. No bloody purge followed, but there was enough fear in both of us to kill the desire to continue our publishing venture. Miss Marti, a woman with a battlefield face and constant odor of Chiclets, made a forceful threat about finding the culprits while holding up the second issue, the one with the hand-colored cover. No one moved. The auditorium grew silent. We meditated on the sound of a small plane flying by, its engines rattling the windows. I think we wished we were on it.

It was in the auditorium that the trouble first began. We had all settled into our seats, fidgeting like tiny burrowing animals, when there was a general call for quiet. Miss Marti, up on stage, had a stare that could make any squirming fool sweat. She was a gruff, nasty woman who never smiled without seeming sadistic.

Mr. Rios was at his spot beside Miss Colon, his hands clasped behind his back as if he needed to restrain them. He seemed to whisper to her. Soft, mushy things. Edwin would watch them from his seat beside me, giving me the details, his shiny face looking worried. He always seemed sweaty, his fingers kind of damp.

"I toldju, I saw um holdin hands," he said. "An now lookit him, he's whispering sweet shits inta huh ear."

He quieted down when he noticed Miss Marti's evil eye sweeping over us like a prison-camp searchlight. There was silence. In her best military bark, Miss Marti ordered everyone to stand. Two lone, pathetic kids, dragooned by some unseen force, slowly came down the center aisle, each bearing a huge flag on a thick wooden pole. All I could make out was that great star-spangled unfurling, twitching thing that looked like it would fall as it approached over all those bored young heads. The Puerto Rican flag walked beside it, looking smaller and less confident. It clung to its pole.

"The Pledge," Miss Marti roared, putting her hand over the spot where her heart was rumored to be.

That's when I heard my father talking.

He was sitting on his bed, yelling about Chile, about what the CIA had done there. I was standing opposite him in my dingy Pro Keds. I knew about politics. I was eleven when I read William Shirer's book on Hitler. I was ready.

"All this country does is abuse Hispanic nations," my father said, turning a page of his *Post*, "tie them down, make them dependent. It says democracy with one hand while it protects and feeds fascist dictatorships with the other." His eyes blazed with a strange fire. I sat on the bed, on part of his *Post*, transfixed by his oratorical mastery. He had mentioned political things before, but not like this, not with such fiery conviction. I thought maybe it had to do with my reading Shirer. Maybe he had seen me reading that fat book and figured I was ready for real politics.

Using the knowledge I gained from the book, I defended the Americans. What fascism was he talking about, anyway? I knew we had stopped Hitler. That was a big deal, something to be proud of.

"Come out of fairy-tale land," he said scornfully. "Do you know what imperialism is?"

I didn't really, no.

"Well, why don't you read about that? Why don't you read about Juan Bosch and Allende, men who died fighting imperialism? They stood up against American big business. You should read about that instead of this crap about Hitler."

"But I like reading about Hitler," I said, feeling a little spurned. I didn't even mention that my fascination with Adolf led to my writing a biography of him, a book report one hundred and fifty pages long. It got an A-plus. Miss Colon stapled it to the bulletin board right outside the classroom, where it was promptly stolen.

"So, what makes you want to be a writer?" Miss Colon asked me quietly one day, when Edwin and I, always the helpful ones, volunteered to assist her in getting the classroom spiffed up for a Halloween party.

"I don't know. I guess my father," I replied, fiddling with plastic pumpkins self-consciously while images of my father began parading through my mind.

When I think back to my earliest image of my father, it is one of him sitting behind a huge rented typewriter, his fingers clacking away. He was a frustrated poet, radio announcer, and even stage actor. He had sent for diplomas from fly-by-night companies. He took acting lessons, went into broadcasting, even ended up on the ground floor of what is now Spanish radio, but his family talked him out of all of it. "You should find yourself real work, something substantial," they said, so he did. He dropped all those dreams that were never encouraged by anyone else and got a job at a Nedick's on Third Avenue. My pop the counterman.

Despite that, he kept writing. He recited his poetry into a huge reel-to-reel tape deck that he had, then he'd play it back and sit like a critic, brow furrowed, fingers stroking his lips. He would record strange sounds and play them back to me at outrageous speeds, until I believed that there were tiny people living inside the machine. I used to stand by him and watch him type, his black pompadour spilling over his forehead. There was energy pulsating all around him, and I wanted a part of it.

I was five years old when I first sat in his chair at the kitchen table and began pushing down keys, watching the letters magically appear on the page. I was entranced. My fascination with the typewriter began at that point. By the time I was ten, I was writing war stories, tales of pain and pathos culled from the piles of comic books I devoured. I wrote unreadable novels. With illustrations. My father wasn't impressed. I guess he was hard to impress. My terrific grades did not faze him, nor the fact that I was reading books as fat as milk crates. My unreadable novels piled up. I brought them to him at night to see if he would read them, but after a week of waiting I found them thrown in the bedroom closet, unread. I felt hurt and rejected, despite my mother's kind words. "He's just too busy to read them," she said to me one night when I mentioned it to her. He never brought them up, even when I quietly took them out of the closet one day or when he'd see me furiously hammering on one of his rented machines. I would tell him I wanted to be a writer, and he would smile sadly and pat my head, without a word.

"You have to find something serious to do with your life," he told me one night, after I had shown him my first play, eighty pages long. What was it I had read that got me into writing a play? Was it Arthur Miller? Oscar Wilde? I don't remember, but I recall my determination to write a truly marvelous play about combat because there didn't seem to be any around.

"This is fun as a hobby," my father said, "but you can't get serious about this." His demeanor spoke volumes, but I couldn't stop writing. Novels, I called them, starting a new one every three days. The world was a blank page waiting for my words to recreate it, while the real world remained cold and lonely. My schoolmates didn't undertand any of it, and because of the fat books I carried around, I was held in some fear. After all, what kid in his right mind would read a book if it wasn't assigned? I was sick of kids coming up to me and saying, "Gaw, lookit tha fat book. Ya teacha make ya read tha?" (No, I'm just reading it.) The kids would look at me as if I had just crawled out of a sewer. "Ya crazy, man." My father seemed to share that opinion. Only my teachers understood and encouraged my reading, but my father seemed to want something else from me.

Now, he treated me like an idiot for not knowing what imperialism was. He berated my books and one night handed me a copy of a book about Albizu Campos, the Puerto Rican revolutionary. I read it through in two sittings.

"Some of it seems true," I said.

"Some of it?" my father asked incredulously. "After what they did to him, you can sit there and act like a Yankee flag-waver?"

I watched the Yankee flag making its way up to the stage over indifferent heads, my father's scowling face haunting me, his words resounding in my head.

"Let me tell you something," my father sneered. "In school, all they do is talk about George Washington, right? The first president? The father of democracy? Well, he had slaves. We had our own Washington, and ours had real teeth."

As Old Glory reached the stage, a general clatter ensued.

"We had our own revolution," my father said, "and the United States crushed it with the flick of a pinkie."

Miss Marti barked her royal command. Everyone rose up to salute the flag.

Except me. I didn't get up. I sat in my creaking seat, hands on my knees. A girl behind me tapped me on the back. "Come on, stupid, get up." There was a trace of concern in her voice. I didn't move.

Miss Colon appeared. She leaned over, shaking me gently. "Are you sick? Are you okay?" Her soft hair fell over my neck like a blanket.

"No," I replied.

"What's wrong?" she asked, her face growing stern. I was beginning to feel claustrophic, what with everyone standing all around me, bodies like walls. My friend Edwin, hand on his heart, watched from the corner of his eye. He almost looked envious, as if he wished he had thought of it. Murmuring voices around me began

reciting the Pledge while Mr. Rios appeared, commandingly grab-
bing me by the shoulder and pulling me out of my seat into the
aisle. Miss Colon was beside him, looking a little apprehensive.

"What is wrong with you?" he asked angrily. "You know you're
supposed to stand up for the Pledge! Are you religious?"

"No," I said.

"Then what?"

"I'm not saluting that flag," I said.

"What?"

"I said, I'm not saluting that flag."

"Why the . . . ?" He calmed himself; a look of concern flashed
over Miss Colon's face. "Why not?"

"Because I'm Puerto Rican. I ain't no American. And I'm not
no Yankee flag-waver."

"You're supposed to salute the flag," he said angrily, shoving one
of his fat fingers in my face. "You're not supposed to make up your
own mind about it. You're supposed to do as you are told."

"I thought I was free," I said, looking at him and at Miss Colon.

"You are," Miss Colon said feebly. "That's why you should salute
the flag."

"But shouldn't I do what I feel is right?"

"You should do what you are told!" Mr. Rios yelled into my
face. "I'm not playing no games with you, mister. You hear that
music? That's the anthem. Now you go stand over there and put
your hand over your heart." He made as if to grab my hand, but
I pulled away.

"No!" I said sharply. "I'm not saluting that crummy flag! And
you can't make me, either. There's nothing you can do about it."

"Oh yeah?" Mr. Rios roared. "We'll see about that!"

"Have you gone crazy?" Miss Colon asked as he led me away
by the arm, down the hallway, where I could still hear the strains
of the anthem. He walked me briskly into the principal's office and
stuck me in a corner.

"You stand there for the rest of the day and see how you feel
about it," he said viciously. "Don't even think of moving from that
spot!"

I stood there for close to two hours or so. The principal came
and went, not even saying hi or hey or anything, as if finding kids
in the corners of his office was a common occurrence. I could hear
him talking on the phone, scribbling on pads, talking to his secretary. At one point I heard Mr. Rios outside in the main office.

"Some smart-ass. I stuck him in the corner. Thinks he can pull that shit. The kid's got no respect, man. I should get the chance to teach him some."

"Children today have no respect," I heard Miss Marti's reptile voice say as she approached, heels clacking like gunshots. "It has to be forced upon them."

She was in the room. She didn't say a word to the principal, who was on the phone. She walked right over to me. I could hear my heart beating in my ears as her shadow fell over me. Godzilla over Tokyo.

"Well, have you learned your lesson yet?" she asked, turning me from the wall with a finger on my shoulder. I stared at her without replying. My face burned, red hot. I hated it.

"You think you're pretty important, don't you? Well, let me tell you, you're nothing. You're not worth a damn. You're just a snotty-nosed little kid with a lot of stupid ideas." Her eyes bored holes through me, searing my flesh. I felt as if I were going to cry. I fought the urge. Tears rolled down my face anyway. They made her smile, her chapped lips twisting upwards like the mouth of a lizard.

"See? You're a little baby. You don't know anything, but you'd better learn your place." She pointed a finger in my face. "You do as you're told if you don't want big trouble. Now go back to class."

Her eyes continued to stab at me. I looked past her and saw Edwin waiting by the office door for me. I walked past her, wiping at my face. I could feel her eyes on me still, even as we walked up the stairs to the classroom. It was close to three already, and the skies outside the grated windows were cloudy.

"Man," Edwin said to me as we reached our floor, "I think you're crazy."

The classroom was abuzz with activity when I got there. Kids were chattering, getting their windbreakers from the closet, slamming their chairs up on their desks, filled with the euphoria of soon-home. I walked quietly over to my desk and took out my books. The other kids looked at me as if I were a ghost.

I went through the motions like a robot. When we got downstairs to the door, Miss Colon, dismissing the class, pulled me aside, her face compassionate and warm. She squeezed my hand.

"Are you okay?"

I nodded.

"That was a really crazy stunt there. Where did you get such an idea?"

I stared at her black flats. She was wearing tan panty hose and a black miniskirt. I saw Mr. Rios approaching with his class.

"I have to go," I said, and split, running into the frigid breezes and the silver sunshine.

At home, I lay on the floor of our living room, tapping my open notebook with the tip of my pen while the Beatles blared from my father's stereo. I felt humiliated and alone. Miss Marti's reptile face kept appearing in my notebook, her voice intoning, "Let me tell you, you're nothing." Yeah, right. Just what horrible hole did she crawl out of? Were those people really Puerto Ricans? Why should a Puerto Rican salute an American flag?

I put the question to my father, strolling into his bedroom, a tiny M-1 rifle that belonged to my G.I. Joe strapped to my thumb.

"Why?" he asked, loosening the reading glasses that were perched on his nose, his newspaper sprawled open on the bed before him, his cigarette streaming blue smoke. "Because we are owned, like cattle. And because nobody has any pride in their culture to stand up for it."

I pondered those words, feeling as if I were being encouraged, but I didn't dare tell him. I wanted to believe what I had done was a brave and noble thing, but somehow I feared his reaction. I never could impress him with my grades, or my writing. This flag thing would probably upset him. Maybe he, too, would think I was crazy, disrespectful, a "smart-ass" who didn't know his place. I feared that, feared my father saying to me, in a reptile voice, "Let me tell you, you're nothing."

I suited up my G.I. Joe for combat, slipping on his helmet, strapping on his field pack. I fixed the bayonet to his rifle, sticking it in his clutching hands so he seemed ready to fire. "A man's gotta do what a man's gotta do." Was that John Wayne? I don't know who it was, but I did what I had to do, still not telling my father. The following week, in the auditorium, I did it again. This time, everyone noticed. The whole place fell into a weird hush as Mr. Rios screamed at me.

I ended up in my corner again, this time getting a prolonged, pensive stare from the principal before I was made to stare at the wall for two more hours. My mind zoomed past my surroundings. In one strange vision, I saw my crony Edwin climbing up Miss Colon's curvy legs, giving me every detail of what he saw.

"Why?" Miss Colon asked frantically. "This time you don't leave until you tell me why." She was holding me by the arm, masses of kids flying by, happy blurs that faded into the sunlight outside the door.

"Because I'm Puerto Rican, not American," I blurted out in a weary torrent. "That makes sense, don't it?"

"So am I," she said, "but we're in America!" She smiled. "Don't you think you could make some kind of compromise?" She tilted her head to one side and said, "Aw, c'mon," in a little-girl whisper.

"What about standing up for what you believe in? Doesn't that matter? You used to talk to us about Kent State and protesting. You said those kids died because they believed in freedom, right? Well, I feel like them now. I wanna make a stand."

She sighed with evident aggravation. She caressed my hair. For a moment, I thought she was going to kiss me. She was going to say something, but just as her pretty lips parted, I caught Mr. Rios approaching.

"I don't wanna see him," I said, pulling away.

"No, wait," she said gently.

"He's gonna deck me," I said to her.

"No, he's not," Miss Colon said, as if challenging him, her eyes taking him in as he stood beside her.

"No, I'm not," he said. "Listen here. Miss Colon was talking to me about you, and I agree with her." He looked like a nervous little boy in front of the class, making his report. "You have a lot of guts. Still, there are rules here. I'm willing to make a deal with you. You go home and think about this. Tomorrow I'll come see you." I looked at him skeptically, and he added, "to talk."

"I'm not changing my mind," I said. Miss Colon exhaled painfully.

"If you don't, it's out of my hands." He frowned and looked at her. She shook her head, as if she were upset with him.

I reread the book about Albizu. I didn't sleep a wink that night. I didn't tell my father a word, even though I almost burst from the effort. At night, alone in my bed, images attacked me. I saw Miss Marti and Mr. Rios debating Albizu Campos. I saw him in a wheelchair with a flag draped over his body like a holy robe. They would not do that to me. They were bound to break me the way Albizu was broken, not by young smiling American troops bearing chocolate bars, but by conniving, double-dealing, self-serving Puerto Rican landowners and their ilk, who dared say they were the future. They spoke of dignity and democracy while teaching Puerto Ricans how to cling to the great coat of that powerful northern neighbor.

Puerto Rico, the shining star, the great lapdog of the Caribbean. I saw my father, the Nationlist hero, screaming from his podium, his great oration stirring everyone around him to acts of bravery. There was a shining arrogance in his eyes as he stared out over the sea of faces mouthing his name, a sparkling audacity that invited and incited. There didn't seem to be fear anywhere in him, only the urge to rush to the attack, with his armband and revolutionary tunic. I stared up at him, transfixed. I stood by the podium, his personal adjutant, while his voice rang through the stadium. "We are not, nor will we ever be, Yankee flag-wavers!" The roar that followed drowned out the whole world.

The following day, I sat in my seat, ignoring Miss Collon as she neatly drew triangles on the board with the help of plastic stencils. She was using colored chalk, her favorite. Edwin, sitting beside me, was beaning girls with spitballs that he fired through his hollowed-out Bic pen. They didn't cry out. They simply enlisted the help of a girl named Gloria who sat a few desks behind him. She very skillfully nailed him with a thick wad of gum. It stayed in his hair until Edwin finally went running to Miss Colon. She used her huge teacher's scissors. I couldn't stand it. They all seemed trapped in a world of trivial things, while I swam in a mire of oppression. I walked through lunch as if in a trance, a prisoner on death row waiting for the heavy steps of his executioners. I watched Edwin lick at his regulation cafeteria ice cream, sandwiched between two sheets of paper. I was once like him, laughing and joking, lining up for a stickball game in the yard without a care. Now it all seemed lost to me, as if my youth had been burned out of me by a book.

Shortly after lunch, Mr. Rios appeared. He talked to Miss Colon for a while by the door as the room filled with a bubbling murmur. Then, he motioned for me. I walked through the sudden silence as if in slow motion.

"Well," he said to me as I stood in the cool hallway, "have you thought about this?"

"Yeah," I said, once again seeing my father on the podium, his voice thundering.

"And?"

"I'm not saluting that flag."

Miss Colon fell against the doorjamb as if exhausted. Exasperation passed over Mr. Rios' rodent features.

"I thought you said you'd think about it," he thundered.

"I did. I decided I was right."

"*You* were right?" Mr. Rios was losing his patience. I stood calmly by the wall.

"I told you," Miss Colon whispered to him.

"Listen," he said, ignoring her, "have you heard the story of the man who had no country?"

I stared at him.

"Well? Have you?"

"No," I answered sharply; his mouse eyes almost crossed with anger at my insolence. "Some stupid fairy tale ain't gonna change my mind anyway. You're treating me like I'm stupid, and I'm not."

"Stop acting like you're some mature adult! You're not. You're just a puny kid."

"Well, this puny kid still ain't gonna salute that flag."

"You were born here," Miss Colon interjected patiently, trying to calm us both down. "Don't you think you at least owe this country some respect? At least?"

"I had no choice about where I was born. And I was born poor."

"So what?" Mr. Rios screamed. "There are plenty of poor people who respect the flag. Look around you, dammit! You see any rich people here? I'm not rich either!" He tugged on my arm. "This country takes care of Puerto Rico, don't you see that? Don't you know anything about politics?"

"Do you know what imperialism is?"

The two of them stared at each other.

"I don't believe you," Mr. Rios murmured.

"Puerto Rico is a colony," I said, a direct quote of Albizu's. "Why I gotta respect that?"

Miss Colon stared at me with her black saucer eyes, a slight trace of a grin on her features. It encouraged me. In that one moment, I felt strong, suddenly aware of my territory and my knowledge of it. I no longer felt like a boy but some kind of soldier, my bayonet stained with the blood of my enemy. There was no doubt about it. Mr. Rios was the enemy, and I was beating him. The more he tried to treat me like a child, the more defiant I became, his arguments falling like twisted armor. He shut his eyes and pressed the bridge of his nose.

"You're out of my hands," he said.

Miss Colon gave me a sympathetic look before she vanished into the classroom again. Mr. Rios led me downstairs without another word. His face was completely red. I expected to be put in my corner again, but this time Mr. Rios sat me down in the leather chair facing the principal's desk. He stepped outside, and I could hear the familiar clack-clack that could only belong to Miss Marti's reptile legs. They were talking in whispers. I expected her to come in at any moment, but the principal walked in instead. He came in quietly, holding a folder in his hand. His soft brown eyes and beard made him look compassionate, rounded cheeks making him seem friendly. His desk plate solemnly stated: Mr. Sepulveda, PRIN-CIPAL. He fell into his seat rather unceremoniously, opened the folder, and crossed his hands over it.

"Well, well, well," he said softly, with a tight-lipped grin. "You've created quite a stir, young man." It sounded to me like movie dialogue.

"First of all, let me say I know about you. I have your record right here, and everything in it is very impressive. Good grades, good attitude, your teachers all have adored you. But I wonder if maybe this hasn't gone to your head? Because everything is going for you here, and you're throwing it all away."

He leaned back in his chair. "We have rules, all of us. There are rules even I must live by. People who don't obey them get disci-plined. This will all go on your record, and a pretty good one you've had so far. Why ruin it? This'll follow you for life. You don't want to end up losing a good job opportunity in government or in the armed forces because as a child you indulged your imagination and refused to salute the flag? I know you can't see how childish it all is now, but you must see it, and because you're smarter than most, I'll put it to you in terms you can understand.

"To me, this is a simple case of rules and regulations. Someday, when you're older," he paused here, obviously amused by the sound of his own voice, "you can go to rallies and protest marches and express your rebellious tendencies. But right now, you are a minor, under this school's jurisdiction. That means you follow the rules, no matter what you think of them. You can join the Young Lords later."

I stared at him, overwhelmed by his huge desk, his pompous mannerisms and status. I would agree with everything, I felt, and then, the following week, I would refuse once again. I would fight him then, even though he hadn't tried to humiliate me or insult my intelligence. I would continue to fight, until I . . .

"I spoke with your father," he said.

I started. "My father?" Vague images and hopes flared through my mind briefly.

"Yes. I talked to him at length. He agrees with me that you've gotten a little out of hand."

My blood reversed direction in my veins. I felt as if I were going to collapse. I gripped the armrests of my chair. There was no way this could be true, no way at all! My father was supposed to ride in like the cavalry, not abandon me to the enemy! I pressed my wet eyes with my fingers. It must be a lie.

"He blames himself for your behavior," the principal said. "He's already here," Mr. Rios said from the door, motioning my father inside. Seeing him wearing his black weather-beaten trench coat almost asphyxiated me. His eyes, red with concern, pulled at me painfully. He came over to me first while the principal rose slightly, as if greeting a head of state. There was a look of dread on my father's face as he looked at me. He seemed utterly lost.

"Mr. Sepulveda," he said, "I never thought a thing like this could happen. My wife and I try to bring him up right. We encourage him to read and write and everything. But you know, this is a shock."

"It's not that terrible, Mr. Rodriguez. You've done very well with him, he's an intelligent boy. He just needs to learn how important obedience is."

"Yes," my father said, turning to me, "yes, you have to obey the rules. You can't do this. It's wrong." He looked at me grimly, as if working on a math problem. One of his hands caressed my head.

There were more words, in Spanish now, but I didn't hear them. I felt like I was falling down a hole. My father, my creator, renouncing his creation, repentant. Not an ounce of him seemed prepared to stand up for me, to shield me from attack. My tears made all the faces around me melt.

"So you see," the principal said to me as I rose, my father clutching me to him, "if you ever do this again, you will be hurting your father as well as yourself."

I hated myself. I wiped at my face desperately, trying not to make a spectacle of myself. I was just a kid, a tiny kid. Who in the hell did I think I was? I'd have to wait until I was older, like my father, in order to have "convictions."

"I don't want to see you in here again, okay?" the principal said sternly. I nodded dumbly, my father's arm around me as he escorted me through the front office to the door that led to the hallway, where a multitude of children's voices echoed up and down its length like tolling bells.

"Are you crazy?" my father half whispered to me in Spanish as we stood there. "Do you know how embarrassing this all is? I didn't think you were this stupid. Don't you know anything about dignity, about respect? How could you make a spectacle of yourself? Now you make us all look stupid."

He quieted down as Mr. Rios came over to take me back to class. My father gave me a squeeze and told me he'd see me at home. Then, I walked with a somber Mr. Rios, who oddly wrapped an arm around me all the way back to the classroom.

"Here you go," he said softly as I entered the classroom, and everything fell quiet. I stepped in and walked to my seat without looking at anyone. My cheeks were still damp, my eyes red. I looked like I had been tortured. Edwin stared at me, then he pressed my hand under the table.

"I thought you were dead," he whispered.

Miss Colon threw me worried glances all through the remainder of the class. I wasn't paying attention. I took out my notebook, but my strength ebbed away. I just put my head on the desk and shut my eyes, reliving my father's betrayal. If what I did was so bad, why did I feel more ashamed of him than I did of myself? His words, once so rich and vibrant, now fell to the floor, leaves from a dead tree.

At the end of the class, Miss Colon ordered me to stay after school. She got Mr. Rios to take the class down along with his, and she stayed with me in the darkened room. She shut the door on all the exuberant hallway noise and sat down on Edwin's desk, beside me, her black pumps on his seat.

"Are you okay?" she asked softly, grasping my arm. I told her everything, especially about my father's betrayal. I thought he would be the cavalry, but he was just a coward.

"Tss. Don't be so hard on your father," she said. "He's only trying to do what's best for you."

"And how's this the best for me?" I asked, my voice growing hoarse with hurt.

"I know it's hard for you to understand, but he really was trying to take care of you."

I stared at the blackboard.

"He doesn't understand me," I said, wiping my eyes.

"You'll forget," she whispered.

"No, I won't. I'll remember every time I see that flag. I'll see it and think, 'My father doesn't understand me.' "

Miss Colon sighed deeply. Her fingers were warm on my head, stroking my hair. She gave me a kiss on the cheek. She walked me downstairs, pausing by the doorway. Scores of screaming, laughing kids brushed past us.

"If it's any consolation, I'm on your side," she said, squeezing my arm. I smiled at her, warmth spreading through me. "Go home and listen to the Beatles," she added with a grin.

I stepped out into the sunshine, came down the white stone steps, and stood on the sidewalk. I stared at the towering school building, white and perfect in the sun, indomitable. Across the street, the dingy row of tattered uneven tenements where I lived. I thought of my father. Her words made me feel sorry for him, but I felt sorrier for myself. I couldn't understand back then about a father's love and what a father might give to insure his son safe transit. He had already navigated treacherous waters and now couldn't have me rock the boat. I still had to learn that he had made peace with The Enemy, that The Enemy was already in us. Like the flag I must salute, we were inseparable, yet his compromise made me feel ashamed and defeated. Then I knew I had to find my own peace, away from the bondage of obedience. I had to accept that flag, and my father, someone I would love forever, even if at times to my young, feeble mind he seemed a little imperfect.

ABRAHAM RODRIGUEZ JR.

Early Snow

(for my mother)

Smoking, wearing high heels and lipstick
 at thirteen
 because you're tall and have
as your step-mother says, "a big mouth"
the older kids take you to the dance
where you dance with all the high-school stars
 the actor, football player
 the comic, the scholar and
 the brother of your sixteen
 year old husband to be
 then because you get cornered
 by a wise-guy who's been
 drinking, presses into you
you look for your step-brother, wriggle away
 find him and his girl
 (you think it's she) in the parking lot

but don't care to interrupt
so you sit on the running board
of someone's car for a smoke
while "Wonder where my baby is tonight"
is squeezed out of a sax and
think about this new world, part of the same
world's October snow you'll run through
pregnant, fifteen
and late for school.

DONA LUONGO STEIN

Butch Traynor

The best I can remember, it was April.
I was in Miss Vaughn's second grade.
She was old and wrinkled
and I did not like her.

We were doing math and the room
was very quiet because
that was the rule.

Then an unpleasant odor.
It lingered and got worse.
Miss Vaughn opened the outside door
and we all began to look at Butch.

Finally Miss Vaughn announced
what we already knew:
"Someone has done something and needs
to go to the bathroom," she said.
No one moved. No one said a word.

A few pointed silently at Butch,
But he wasn't talking.
He wasn't turning red either.
I think he was beyond that,
busily wishing himself dead.

And here's what I can't figure:
Everyone knew it was Butch,

Miss Vaughn must have known, too,
but out of some rarely shown
sense of human decency,
she must have decided,
as she began to carry out her threat
to check each of our pants,
to begin the inspection
on the other side of the room.

To me, this meant that she
was going to get
to my desk before she got to Butch,
and I was not, I thought,
going to let her feel my pants.

The closer she got, the more I worried.
How would I refuse her? And if I did,
what would the others think?

I remembered the time in the hospital
when I swore to myself that I'd make the nurse
put my toy train back together before I let her
give me another shot. But I had chickened out
and silently rolled over when she came to stick me.

I was worried that I would do that again.
Chicken out.

I was mad at Butch and mad at Miss Vaughn,
but mostly, I think, I was mad at myself
because I didn't know what to do.

I didn't know about angels back then, but now
I think there must have been one in that room
because when Miss Vaughn was just two desks away
from mine, Butch stood up and said, "It's me."
And he walked out of the room.

And Miss Vaughn was saying something,
but I didn't hear a word because
I was sitting there, astonished,

wondering where he found the guts to do that,
wondering if I would have had such guts
had Miss Vaughn kept coming toward me.

MICHAEL S. GLASER

The Weird Kid

Charlie was the weird kid—there's always one in every class, and even if I've forgotten his last name, I haven't forgotten that it was in fifth grade with a teacher none of us liked very much. And I still remember him every time I see a ball-point smudge, for Charlie was one long streak of smeared ink. He seemed to ooze ink, and cowlicks, and ripped seams, and tardy slips. He was the suicidal one who perfected the head-first slide in baseball—on a gravel playground. He was the kid whose homework was never done, who always smelled funny and had fuzzy teeth, who tracked in mud from the school yard and got sent back to clean his shoes three or four times till he got it right.

Charlie was the only kid I ever knew who dared to let farts during the flag salute. He was the only kid who was crazy enough to dip Mary Kay's braids in an ink bottle; she was the one beautiful girl in the fifth grade, and Charlie must have known that five or six of the hulking types would be waiting for him after school to pulverize him for Mary Kay's honor and their pleasure. And it was Charlie who told me my first really filthy joke—in fact, he told the whole class, one day when the teacher decided to indulge us all with a new kind of fun called "Joke Sharing Hour," which, thanks to Charlie, lasted only about five minutes and was never held again, not even on the best of days.

And long after all the beautiful Mary Kays were married off and manufacturing beautiful children, long after the Wallys and Steves had packed away their baseball gear forever, long after the Geralds and Dianas had won full scholarships to the graduate schools of their choice, Charlie is the one I still wonder about. He's probably a bartender or a race car driver or a deck hand—whatever it is, he's not very good at it, still sweating out a lifetime of principals' offices. But I wish I had him here right now—maybe to thank him, to tell him that even if all of us were embarrassed about him and really didn't like him very much, he was a kind of martyr we could always count on to take the heat off everyone else. I'd at least

like to show him what I've written about him, to show him the
way I still smudge my own ink, and tell him that sometimes now
I'm even able to admit it.

MARK VINZ

Sterling Williams' Nosebleed

Sterling Williams has a nosebleed.
Sterling Williams of the cow's tail.
Miss Alidyce called him the cow's tail,
the cow's tail after eight forty-five A.M.
Sterling Williams with the incredible swagger.
Sterling Williams who'd flush the toilet
in the boy's room at P.S. 24 over and over
until clean water began to pour
over the edge of the bowl.
Sterling Williams who'd drink that water on a dare
and prove we were all "chickenshit."
Sterling Williams has a nosebleed.
Sterling Williams who could turn his eyelids inside out
and leave them that way forever.
Sterling Williams the black kid.
Sterling Williams who knew everything worth knowing.
Sterling Williams who could gouge your spinning top
squinting one eye on the throw.
Sterling Williams has a nosebleed.
Sterling Williams with brown clay
rolled into a foot-long snake
dangling out of his unzipped pants.
Sterling Williams who could swagger
swaying the dangling clay back and forth.
Sterling Williams has a nosebleed.
Sterling Williams from the wrong side of Hudson Boulevard,
the wrong side of Bergen Avenue,
the wrong side of Jackson Avenue,
the wrong side of the world beyond Jackson Avenue.
Sterling Williams has a nosebleed.
Sterling Williams who drank watercolor rinse water
to prove it was nontoxic.
Sterling Williams who seized every second
Miss Alidyce was somewhere else.

Sterling Williams who knew the score early on.
Sterling Williams who taught me how
to make my armpits fart.
Sterling Williams has a nosebleed.

Sterling Williams has a nosebleed—
the blood pours out
all over his white shirt.
Sterling Williams whose parents
have to meet with Miss Alidyce
and Mr. Benway the principal.
Drops of Sterling's blood fall
on the smooth yellow third-grade desk.
Miss Alidyce runs for the wet rag.
Miss Alidyce holds Sterling's head way back.
Miss Alidyce who has jewelry
and a brown leather cover for the attendance book.
Sterling Williams has a nosebleed.
Sterling's blood flecks the floor.
Sterling's blood blossoms in the wet white rag.
Sterling's blood drips from Miss Alidyce's bracelet.
Sterling's blood drips from Miss Alidyce's elbow.
Sterling Williams shows us he knows how to bleed.
Miss Alidyce has to go for ice.
Sterling on the verge of tears.
Sterling who has found Miss Alidyce's last straw.
Sterling gives us a sidelong glance.
Sterling shrugs his shoulders and fakes a smile.
Sterling Williams the scapegoat
condemned to act out for the class.
Sterling Williams has a nosebleed.
The tragic suspended and resuspended
Sterling Williams who could make me laugh uncontrollably
even in front of Miss Alidyce.
Sterling Williams who never had a chance.
Sterling Williams.

DAVID CHIN

Losing Faith

In second grade I had the braids
the name and faith
to play the mother of Christ
Instead they gave the part to white Patty
and meant to appease me
with "conductor of the ho-ho-ho choir"

I scraped and bowed the verses
in a party dress that rose and fell
with applause and laughter
Even my mother and sister saw the joke
inside a saggy pair of bloomers

Who among them understood
how the role of "Mary"
suited me better
How it still does
thirty years later
with only a name
to recommend me

MARY McLAUGHLIN SLECHTA

Altar Boy

my feet tread marbled aisles in a cloud
of incense and forgiveness was a saturday night
ritual of ashes to ashes promises of glory loud
though I prayed in candlelight
lit for the poor for the sick for the lame
for my spotted soul my knees bent
to the almighty my heart a sack of guilt I came
into the world branded I knew and went
through motions of repentance holy days
of obligation penance and communion
dreaded hellfire among my fellow third grade

fallen angels one step up from pagan
babies and others unanointed whose only sin
was being born

CHARLES ROSSITER

School of Night

Sister Madeline greets me when I ring the bell. She seems cleaner than other women, scrubbed until her face is flaked and powdery; her clothes without seam or wrinkle. She smiles, and it is as if her smile is everywhere, a smile walking through the holy darkness made of Protestant frugality and Catholic self-abnegation, a smile that glints like the instruments of torture hung on a nail. The sisters fast on Friday, all day, and give their food to the poor. Now, like the needy, I follow her rubber-soled footsteps through the dark oak halls. We pass windows framed into the doors of classrooms that are also frames of light. I pity the children in there, their bodies like rags caught on the hook of her smile; its teeth over every head, every classroom, over the bare roof naked to heaven—before we can get to God, we must walk through that smile. We climb to the top of the world, the third floor, where, in one classroom, the windows flash a sky so bright and whole, I stumble toward it, dizzy. The whole building threatens to topple and fall through that opening into chaos. I nail my feet to the floor. But my body streams out like a vivid cloth.

TOI DERRICOTTE

No Consolation

I'm not the lucky type, I always say,
I never won a thing in my life. But
that's not quite true. Once, young,
I won something at a Saturday matinee
at Schine's Waller Theater in Laurel,
Delaware. Kids packed the theater for
the drawing, popcorn littered the floor.
Noisily we sat through previews
of coming attractions, newsreels, cartoons,
a Hopalong Cassidy, and a Gene Autry.

Finally the house lights came up
and Mr. Kopf, the theater manager,
ambled onstage, blinking like an owl
behind wire-rim spectacles. He wore
white-buck shoes and chewed gum.
Now, he announced, now was the moment
we all had been waiting for. Now
he would produce a slip of paper
from the goldfish bowl and proclaim
the winner of the brand-new Schwinn

bicycle. From the wings he wheeled
it onstage. It stood propped
on its kickstand: shiny, coveted,
and red. I didn't have a bike;
at twelve I was the only kid I knew
who didn't. Was our family too large,
too poor? Hadn't I begged hard enough?
I don't know. But I remember imagining
me Schwinning my way about town,
a red blur, happy as a boy can be.

Mr. Kopf drew the piece of paper.
It had Billy Prettyman's name on it.
(Billy was the town dentist's son.
An only child, he had two bicycles.)
Kids began to hiss and boo. Billy
didn't mind. He ran down the aisle,
up carpeted stairs to claim what he
believed he deserved. (I never knew
what he did with his other two bikes.
Kept them, I assume—a collection.)

Then Mr. Kopf looked mischievous,
announced the drawing wasn't over.
There was to be a Consolation Prize.
From the wings he produced a sack
of potatoes. Everyone laughed, but
not so hard as when my name was called.
I walked down that aisle as if toward

the guillotine. When he handed me
"the prize," laughter began again.
From orchestra to balcony, derision.

Then I carried that hateful sack home.
It grew heavier with every block,
the potatoes reeked of dirt. I thought
of Jesus writhing on the tree
while Barabbas was set free. I considered
throwing the sack away. But my parents
would hear that I had "won," and I knew
that we could use those potatoes. Sunday
Mother cooked some in an Irish stew.
It stuck to the roof of my mouth like glue.

ROBERT PHILLIPS

The Way of the Cross

When Sister said God was unknowable
     and unknown,
that only silence could express
     His Nothingness,
we hushed for a few seconds
in that sixth grade class,
Joey McGraw, up front, white shirt,
     tie, pants pressed,
nodding his head, as though he could
     hear Him,
and Leslie Stiles, tall, blond girl with
     pimples
who carried the nuns' lunch from the
     convent,
sitting with her mouth open as though
     waiting
for God to soundlessly enter, Richie
     Freeman and Donald Wilcox
cocking their ears as they bet
     on an ant
that crawled past their desks,
Richie stomping down when it turned
     back,

making me laugh even as Sister wafted
    up the aisle
with the three-edged brass ruler, tapping
    heads as she went,
Good, Good, Good, she said till she got
    to where
I sat, then hissed *Bad, Bad,* and whacked
    till I bled,
the rosary beads on her belt clicking
    between
her knees, the silver cross on her chest
    thumping
whle she shouted, *This is what happens*
    to sinners,
stumbling her way back to the front of the class
where she wrote *The Way of the Cross* with red chalk,
    told us
we must lift our crosses *up, up,*
so the sinner among us *might, might,* she whispered,
    get into heaven,
making us stand to do it that very second,
twenty-two eleven-year-olds lifting heavy crosses
    of air onto our shoulders,
balancing them there as we staggered around
    the empty seats,
some bumping into the scarred desks,
some easing them from shoulder to shoulder,
some stopping to kneel and catch their breath,
no one daring to put down the crossed weights
    or whisper a joke
as we circled each other for a silent hour
    that gray, darkening December day.

LEN ROBERTS

VI. 〜

LEARNING BY ROTE

Reading and writing and 'rithmetic,

Taught to the tune of a hickory stick

Teaching English from an
Old Composition Book

My chalk is no larger than a chip of fingernail,
Chip by which I must explain this Monday
Night the verbs "to get," "to wear," "to cut."
I'm not given much, these tired students,
Knuckle-wrapped from work as roofers,
Sour from scrubbing toilets and pedestal sinks.
I'm given this room with five windows,
A coffee machine, a piano with busted strings,
The music of how we feel as the sun falls,
Exhausted from keeping up.

                                        I stand at
The blackboard. The chip is worn to a hangnail,
Nearly gone, the dust of some educational bone.
By and by I'm Cantinflas, the comic
Busy body in front. I say, "I want the coffee."
I pick up a coffee cup and sip.
I clip my heels and say, "I wear my shoes."
I bring an invisible fork to my mouth
And say, "I eat the chicken."
Suddenly the class is alive—
Each one putting on hats and shoes,
Drinking sodas and beers, cutting flowers
And steaks—a pantomime of sumptuous living.

At break I pass out cookies.
Augustine, the Guatemalan, asks in Spanish,
"Teacher, what is 'tally-ho'?"
I look at the word in the composition book.
I raise my face to the bare bulb for a blind answer.
I stutter, then say, "It's like *adelante*."
Augustine smiles, then nudges a friend
In the next desk, now smarter by one word.
After the cookies are eaten,
We move ahead to prepositions—
"Under," "over," and "between,"
Useful words when *la migra* opens the doors

Of their idling vans.
At ten to nine, I'm tired of acting,
And they're tired of their roles.
When class ends, I clap my hands of chalk dust,
And two students applaud, thinking it's a new verb.
I tell them *adelante,*
And they pick up their old books.
They smile and, in return, cry, "Tally-ho"
As they head for the door.

GARY SOTO

Among Children

I walk among the rows of bowed heads—
the children are sleeping through fourth grade
so as to be ready for what is ahead,
the momumental boredom of junior high
and the rush forward tearing their wings
loose and turning their eyes forever inward.
These are the children of Flint, their fathers
work at the spark plug factory or truck
bottled water in 5 gallon sea-blue jugs
to the widows of the suburbs. You can see
already how their backs have thickened,
how their small hands, soiled by pig iron,
leap and stutter even in dreams. I would like
to sit down among them and read slowly
from *The Book of Job* until the windows
pale and the teacher rises out of a milky sea
of industrial scum, her gowns streaming
with light, her foolish words transformed
into song, I would like to arm each one
with a quiver of arrows so that they might
rush like wind there where no battle rages
shouting among the trumpets, Ha! Ha!
How dear the gift of laughter in the face
of the 8 hour day, the cold winter mornings
without coffee and oranges, the long lines
of mothers in old coats waiting silently

where the gates have closed. Ten years ago
I went among these same children, just born,
in the bright ward of the Sacred Heart and leaned
down to hear their breaths delivered that day,
burning with joy. There was such wonder
in their sleep, such purpose in their eyes
closed against autumn, in their damp heads
blurred with the hair of ponds, and not one
turned against me or the light, not one
said, I am sick, I am tired, I will go home,
not one complained or drifted alone,
unloved, on the hardest day of their lives.
Eleven years from now they will become
the men and women of Flint or Paradise,
the majors of a minor town, and I
will be gone into smoke or memory,
so I bow to them here and whisper
all I know, all I will never know.

PHILIP LEVINE

Our Room

I tell the children in school sometimes
why I hate alcoholics: my father was one.
"Alcohol" and "disease" I use, and shun
the word "drunk" or even "drinking," since one time
the kids burst out laughing when I told them.
I felt as though they were laughing at me.
I waited for them, wounded, remembering how I imagined they'd howl at me
when I was in grade 5. Acting drunk
is a guaranteed screamer, especially
for boys. I'm quiet when I sort the junk
of my childhood for them, quiet so we
will all be quiet, and they can ask what
questions they have to and tell about what
happened to them, too. The classroom becomes
oddly lonely when we talk about our homes.

MOLLY PEACOCK

Chinese in Academia

Away from the streaky windows'
venetian blinds, the sun pours
from cold sky on beaten grass. Shadows
move past afternoon. I walk down
and up the speckled tile floor.
Cinderblocks glisten bluish-bright
under fluorescent banks. There will
always be a person staying till
the last for a two-hour exam.
The wall-clock drips its seconds. She
is pink-cheeked and wants an A for
the accounting test. She doesn't know
I am twenty years older,
that shadows have moved past noon.
It is quiet here but not silent.
The blushing bulbs hiss like bees
feeding their queen. I am queen of fluorescent
lighting. Shoes scuff. Outside the corridor
is full of vanishing people.
They've been tested and have come through.
I have picked up two pens, two broken pencils,
a stack of squared sheets on which I write . . .
My life is a square of others' tests.
She bends over the computer paper,
soft stomach creased above dungarees.
I am reminded of myself, young girl
facing a two-hour exam, locking
thighs against the wish to urinate
while my pen scratches a future.
History is crammed with exam fever.
I look at the young woman fated
to make her fortune. I am afraid
I have studied far too long,
the day of reckoning is here and
I know nothing. Knowledge is security.
Frightened, I wait for the examiner.
I know only my life will always be
what it is, powerless, ignorant.
There will always be exams

I cannot pass. Chinese mandarins
learned of universal failure,
and I am learning that well, bent
over my watch, proctoring shadows
walking down and down the academic lawns.

SHIRLEY GEOK-LIN LIM

For Sal Sanjamino: On His Retirement

He sits back in his chair
behind his desk,
cigarette in hand,
tip glowing,
smoke swirling,
thoughts back
to a family
in a little town
not far from Rome.

He sits in front
of the cathedral
in the town square,
peeling his fruit
with a paring knife,
cutting a slice
and a piece
of semolina bread
to fill his mouth,
washing it down
with a glass of local wine
so cold—for a moment—
it cools even the summer sun.

He sits in the Sicilian fields,
where his family
plants and picks the grapes—
migration even closer to the sun.
While "all roads lead away from the south,
no roads return,"
his family—Ciancimino—works its way
even more south than Orvieto,

down to Trinacria, the three-pointed isle,
where cattle of the sun god
graze quietly in the mythic fields.

He sits on the deck
of the ship journeying
to America! America!—
a passage of time and place
past the portals to the paradise
of imagined glories!
He becomes more American than America.

He sits on the stoop
of the two-family walk-up,
his nose in a library book
about the rise and fall
of ancient empires
he snuck past the other kids
playing stickball.

He sits in front of the classroom,
opening another history book,
rubbing his pepper-and-salt mustache,
patiently explaining how and why
things came to be as they are . . . now.
How things could be, should be!

To his students,
to the teachers,
to all the principals
he taught so well.

STANLEY H. BARKAN

Poem on the First Day of School

All night the priestesses of wisdom have been practicing
the orders I remember of obedience,
silence and devotion to their measured tones,
index fingers hushed across their lips.
Consequently, it is pointless to inform them, half-asleep
as I appear, arriving with my son,

how tiny I am in my own eyes, giving him up
to their language, a guide through fifth grade.
Now he must learn to mouth it as if it were a tongue
by which the world is formed. And he must take a second one
from such images as boys his age barter among themselves
that his words assume their sounds, therefore his own.
I remember. This is how it's done.
This is how I was given to the world.

PETER COOLEY

Big World, Little Man

"Some things it is wrong to think of,"
my mother said. "Don't think of them."
She was adjusting my scarf, sending me
off to school through the snow.

On the schoolground Orville would have me look up
and then he would hit me in the throat.
The flakes would look dark and come down
graceful and soft toward my eyes.

In the classroom after the bell
Miss Doherty always brought us in a circle
for reading, and I sat by Emily,
while outside the snow brushed past windows.

All of that comes meandering along,
even crowding into today—
falling in a long slant from the sky.
I stand here still, ready for then, for now.

Many things I do not think of.

WILLIAM STAFFORD

A Long Way

Red, my schoolmates' "Red-Indian"-red, I crayon-cartooned myself,
curved like a clown-grin moon snuggled between awkwardly em-

bracing, scarlet stars, the time, the time, the time Dad murmured to Mother, "Sweetheart, let's us . . ."

My mind, that summer, my fifth, was like honey-hued flypaper, spiraling, a gilded miniature stair, from the livingroom's pipe-smoke-clouded heavens. Darkening, as it accumulated the weight of fatal appetites, the golden spiral became a dust devil blacker than Dad's cowboy hat, hovering like a crow above bald-spot oval as an egg, seemingly settling to brooding but actually about to take flight.

"He draws quite nicely, for never having had kindergarten," remarked the teacher, glancing at captive wings crayoned as vivid as Mother's first husband's Purple Heart Medal ribbon, wings those of the violet butterflies, which, having survived scorched July by skimming cool cow-pee puddled in hoof-prints, must have seen the flypaper's gleaming amber as a fresh stream.

Finishing writing me down for first grade in autumn—awe-tomb—the pretty lady explained that in "German"—in-jure-man —"kindergarten," the word for what I would not be able to get, out here in "the wilderness," simply meant "child-garden." Wasn't it "nice a whole nation"—a-hole-nay-shun—thought of children as "flower-buds or"—staring at my perennially grimy, ranch-kid's, Indian-brown hand—"vegetables." It was "almost unbelievable" that "Hitler"—hit-lure—"had been a German"—a germ-man. "Germany"—germ-man-knee—had "produced" great artists. "Would you like to be a painter?"

Though thinking of houses and ladders, not butterfly wings stuck in goo, with spiders swinging down to enticingly helpless fluttering, I nodded, tickled pink at the lilac-smelling lady's praise, but Mother scolded: "My husband *and* my first son's dad both fought Nazis. Fooling around with paint's not my idea of man's work, and I won't have this boy encouraged in"—in-courage-din—"sissydom."

Years from following precedents of manliness, I'd teeter on baby-brother's high chair—risking wrecking this rickety survivor from Mother's own childhood, a fall, a spanking, *and* sissy-dumb—gently prying at desperate flutterings, trying to free me my own pretty pet to imprison in glass-jar, the result, always, jig-saw-puzzle pieces; then, after I licked sticky poison off skin and spit-slicked fingers to ease loose, whole, a delicate prize, it only spread, a purple-ink-stain stigmata, on its savior's palm.

I flared fist and blew the fragile corpse into sky. It flew, escaping—due to my dumb tantrum—then died a second death, as breath died.

Mother's voice I hear, through the years, and through six feet of Sacred Earth, is quiet and welcoming, as Dad's rough, scarred, huge hand seizes her soft, smooth, slender, his voice, his singing voice, murmuring, "Sweetheart, let's us have us . . ."

All spring and summer, my little sister and I had to pester for stories, which had lulled us in winter, and, after we'd been dumped into our hot bed, whose dried-cornshuck-stuffed-tick-crackled like flames, Dad's banjo would sound, like his stories' ghost-people's mournful wailing, from the cool front porch, where he sat with Mother, his singing beautiful and vibrant with longing, I realize now, though then I only drowsily dreamed myself the hero of his tales of animals and hunters and war.

"Sweetheart, let's us have us a look to see will our corn reach knee-high by the Fourth of July," was what Dad had murmured, but this was August, frost and first-grade threatening, and they'd passed the last, head-high to them, corn, without a glance, as I, almost six and no longer a sissy but a military scout, stealthily followed, dawdling along, taking my time, stomping to make puff-balls spurt army-color smoke, while waiting for my chance to run up and grab their hands—conveniently, and somewhat surprisingly, holding on to each other—and yell "BOO!"

Dad's hat now a perch-seeking crow gliding, ever more distant, over bushes hiding flashes of creek, tired, sweaty, hot, itchy and discouraged, I started to turn back, but couldn't see the rusted, rooster-shape weather-vane atop our barn beyond the tall corn; and, even though my guiding crow had shrunk to blackbird, at least it was still visible over every bush that wasn't taller than Dad, so I kept on punishing my short legs to pound feet blistered by new, white-crescent-moon-toed black tennis shoes hard against brown earth—packed by decades of wheels and by hoofs long ago turned into glue, possibly for flypaper—frantic to catch up.

When my half-brother's father was, maybe, five, like me, like me, he had followed a Spirit Bird into the forest—"Deep, deep into the forest"—only he hadn't known that it was a Spirit Bird and kept on following it just because its head was red, its body gold.

"He was just a little boy, like you, little Lackey," Mother murmured, and, "no," she didn't know exactly how old but little; and he was supposed to be resting where his parents had left him while they were gathering mushrooms or nuts or something or maybe hunting a grouse or a rabbit, but he got—"pondering" was how my mother put it—he got to pondering, and he thought he'd just walk a little further, and a little further, along a deer-trail and, then, a little further still, all because he had got to pondering what might be beyond bushes, which were so much the same they'd got to seem nothing at all.

"And after he'd gone further than he should and was going to turn back because now there were almost more cross trails than he could remember—right then, this beautiful gold and crimson bird, like he'd never seen before, flew out of a tall tamarack ahead of him and landed, just out of sight, only a short way beyond.

"Oh, and he was such a lovable little boy, pinched face all solemn, and shining black eyes about to jump right out at you."

His picture, on my half-brother's book-case, showed a solemn soldier, either sepia-toned or *born* more Indian-dark than my dad, and in the same frame, under glass, like the lilac-fragrant-teacher's butterfly collection, was a beautiful purple ribbon, "because of being killed in Germany." Injure-man-knee.

"And he was so scared, so-o scared, because night was starting to fall, and when the sun had gone down, the bird had vanished, just like—just like an ordinary bird, and he was—reluctant, you see, reluctant to shout, because he knew he hadn't minded his father and mother and hadn't stayed where he was supposed to stay; and it's like they say, it's like they always say, as soon as you do one thing wrong, one thing leads to another and there you'll be, you'll find yourself doing a second wrong thing before you know it. So the second wrong thing he did was he didn't start yelling for all he was worth before it got dark; and no doubt his poor parents were looking for him everywhere, just everywhere, all frantic because there were snakes and wolverines and bears and all sorts of wild things in the Northwoods, where he grew up, and not to mention falling off one of those high—'bluffs,' they call them back home, white limestone, teachers said used to be under the ocean, there, all long ago—or drown in the river.

"But he was brave, he was brave, and he volunteered, as men and boys would do in that war, because it was to save the little Jew babies and women and freedom and voting and all. Not your dad. He'd seen the National Guard kill his own dad in a coal mine strike, and he held back till he was drafted. But your brother's father"—which was what she always called her first husband—"he volunteered—and once, at a dance, these two men, they made a mistake, you see, because I am quite light-skinned, being half white—but even though they were taller and heavier, and none of our people daring to help, he whipped those two bullies, he whipped them both.

"Such a brave little fellow, even if he shouldn't have disobeyed his parents—but it was this Spirit Bird, he believed—he always said it turned out to be a Spirit Bird, even after someone showed us a photograph of a Western Tanager."

Foe-toe-graph, I thought. Tan-uh-jur, I thought, and saw jungles and scarlet and golden birds and cats as big as bulls.

"Because Western were different, you see, little Lackey, from Tanagers up in the Northwoods. And it led him on and on and him just a little fellow and not knowing any better but full—full of the Spirit Presence of those wings glimmering in shadows and glowing out into sun—a very pretty sight, he'd always say, in spite of how things turned out.

"And how things turned out was he was lost all night, his little body shivering in cold and shaking with fear of—of badgers and wildcats and so on and, also, feeling the Other World, he said, just as our people had long ago—and wolves howling not far distant, and the moon by now like a golden bird, itself, all feathery and sharp-winged, and ghostly, the way it gets in the mists of autumn." Awe-tomb.

"His poor mother was worried out of her mind, I should think —and his dad, too, probably, though the dad was a kind of Med- icine Man, as close as anybody can maybe come to being one in our time; and the father maybe had him some notion of what was going on with his son.

"Terrified out of his wits, of course, little as he was—but he slept, as children must, no matter what, no matter where."

Like me, at a lovey-dovey movie my older brother had picked, my drowsy head dropping against an arm, big like my dad's but smelling of cigarettes and soap, not pipe-tobacco and sweat.

"Chill air slipping around his little ankles, the world still all dark under leaves he'd piled over him, he felt something warm and wet touch him between his sock and his pants cuff. He was too scared to move—and a good thing, little Lackey, a good thing, because, if he had moved, he might have waked still in the Beyond and never got back, to grow up, and be your brother's father—and die, all brave, in war.

"He never remembered, for certain, how; but, whether in his mind or with his two little eyes, he saw a giant, fiery, golden bear—which the bird had become—glowing in glowing dawn; and then it slipped deeper into Spirit Dream or into forest shadows or was hidden by leaves settling in the pile, or by eyelids slipping back down."

My Spirit Bird was a black cowboy hat, which seemed to me to put my half-white dad on the winning-team in tv cowboy-and-Indian shoot-out competitions. I must have known I could just trudge back along the lane and get home safe; but, only five—still slave to sight, sound, touch, smell, taste—I kept on panting air into aching lungs, and jolting sore feet faster and harder against hard earth, terrified I'd be lost forever—certain my parents would come if only I called out—and afraid they would not be able to hear me if I put it to the test—terrified of deep—deeper-than-deep—truths: that no one ever hears anyone—that the man in the movie will always get up, shoving one's drowsy head against one's brother's bony shoulder, causing a sharp elbow-dig into ribs—that a call might bring not my Good Dad concerned for his little son but my Bad Dad mad as hell he'd been tracked to the woods, where his whisky-still boiled silver creek water flypaper-amber-bad.

"Don't let him see you!"

I've been comforting myself, by thinking only of her, and, as usual, in terms of eggs fried just right for me—flat—and pancakes—and butter melting—and syrup descending, as golden as glowing flypaper-ribbon but tasting the way new-fallen maple-leaves smelled.

"Don't let him see you!"

Her warning, from laurel-leaves, which glittered like moss-scabbarded daggers in the County Court House War Memorial, always meant I should hide my "nigger-in-the-woodpile" face, re-minder of my half-brother, darker, even, than myself, reminder of my mother's first husband, a reminder to my dad that love had betrayed him into marrying "colored"—into marrying and losing the life of a light-skinned traveling-musician and bootlegger, the life of his youth, his youth, his youth—reminder of his own dad, who'd died Indian and proud and young. "Don't let him see you," always meant hide from Dad, whisky had again turned as crazy as a bed-bug, hide till he sobered.

"Don't let him—" The words were her warning, but her tone was one I'd only previously heard just before my parents' bedroom door slipped gently shut.

In time, in time, I'd hear the tone again, and again the exact words, coming from the bathroom, in which my sister was primping for her first date.

"Don't—" But words cannot hold back anything if it must come, come into mind, come into being.

In time, in time, taking a short-cut across the football field at the end of the day, I'd see red panties lying like a referee's handkerchief signaling a penalty—see, as I sidled around empty bleacher-benches, two classmates, a boy and a girl—a girl—see, as our know-it-all, high school-jock-stud idiom put it, "everything."

And, then, even then, some French businessmen and some American businessmen were discussing—diz-cuss-sing—with some Vietnamese businessmen, and, in time, in time, in time, somebody appeared on tv and there was some voting and somebody was sent to war, then came home, or did not.

Familiar and strange—as familiar and as taken for granted as my own breath—as strange, as mysteriously, completely and utterly strange as my own Medicine, own future, own doom—loved and feared, Dad strides, and strides again, from the Sacred Earth, and again and again, from behind laurel-leaves shining like World-War-One-Memorial Greco-Roman daggers, his Indian-tan, English-misnomered-"red" torso bared, as if for battle, to defend his honor, his Medicine, his tribe, though his cowboy-hat is a wide-winged bird black as his night-patrol, egg-shape helmet in the World War Two, War Department—depart-meant—foe-toe-graph.

A little male child, understanding nothing—nothing—trembles because it seems that, though he has done nothing, nothing, nothing, his drunk dad's fumbling to unfasten the wide cowboy-belt to employ it as he has not long since employed his wide razor-strop.

The labor-and-age-stiffened trigger-finger of a practiced killer works with terrible deliberation and at last succeeds in guiding sweat-tarnished tongue of silvery buckle into the last possible—and, this year, strained—wrinkle-surrounded hole and tucks the belt end into the loop, where it belongs.

All the Italians and Germans—as young, as young as Dad was then—rise from his stories of blood, drenching Old Country earth.

A solemn, sepia-faced father, as young, as young as the Italians and Germans, takes good aim at his rival, whose only—only—

advantages are somewhat lighter skin and his having lived longer. The handsome volunteer kills again—and again—as he must and falters back into grave, into memory, into honoring, grieving, loving words—as he must—fulfilling again and again a destiny he cannot—and no one, no one—can ever—ever—escape.

"If Thunder's sons' words had been heeded, there would be no Death; but, now—Sun's daughter alive only in Redbird's sad, beautiful song—when our loved ones die, we can never bring them back."

It is years, it is years, and—become, through my mother's stories, the black-eyed, solemn little boy, become the solemn dead bridegroom, father and hero—I must—must—come home, once more, once more, from a war not Dad's, not Dad's at all, at all, but "mine"—though only in words—and in an "Old Country" partly "mine," migration theories tell me—in Asia, "in-country," yes, in "Indian-Country," so called by white buddies—war lost, lost, like my Indian people's and my white people's "Indian Wars"—like all wars, from Cain to Nuclear-Winter, lost; and a Good Dad—more loved, more loved, because it had seemed he might be bad—hoists his exhausted little boy up onto a bare shoulder, whose sweat, whose unashamed, healthy worker's—and lover's, and lover's—sweat is his own and smells like no one else's in the world—in the whole World—which men have named two wars for, while planning the next—and, from the black cowboy-hat, falls phantom odor of pipe-tobacco, the portrait on its tin that of an Indian-Conqueror poet, Sir Walter Raleigh—rewarded by his sovereign by being beheaded—his ghost become smoke from flakes brown as "Red-Indian"-skin—as brown as last season's maple leaves, as fragrant as green beginning to crimson.

"You come you a long ways, little Lack," my father says; and, as my mother joins us, smoothing her nice blue dress; and, as they hold me, hugging each other and hugging me between them, I hear him say again—and again—"Sweetheart, we got us a brave little feller here."

"Yes," she responds, sharing his laughter, their secret knowledge, their love for each other and for me—for me—at that moment become—though not ever, ever, again, to be—a miracle-child blessed by gold bird and destined for beautiful, heroic death—all of us loved, probably, more than we can know, more than we can bear to know. "Yes, he came a long way, a long way, all by himself."

She is holding Dad's hand in the hand that is not helping to hold me hugged—little moon curved like a crimson clown-grin between big bright stars—and laughing together—together—they carry me home.

RALPH SALISBURY

The First Day

In an otherwise unremarkable September morning, long before I learned to be ashamed of my mother, she takes my hand and we set off down New Jersey Avenue to begin my very first day of school. I am wearing a checkeredlike blue-and-green cotton dress, and scattered about these colors are bits of yellow and white and brown. My mother has uncharacteristically spent nearly an hour on my hair that morning, plaiting and replaiting so that now my scalp tingles. Whenever I turn my head quickly, my nose fills with the faint smell of Dixie Peach hair grease. The smell is somehow a soothing one now and I will reach for it time and time again before the morning ends. All the plaits, each with a blue barrette near the tip and each twisted into an uncommon sturdiness, will last until I go to bed that night, something that has never happened before. My stomach is full of milk and oatmeal sweetened with brown sugar. Like everything else I have on, my pale green slip and underwear are new, the underwear having come three to a plastic package with a little girl on the front who appears to be dancing. Behind my ears, my mother, to stop my whining, has dabbed the stingiest bit of her gardenia perfume, the last present my father gave her before he disappeared into memory. Because I cannot smell it, I have only her word that the perfume is there. I am also wearing yellow socks trimmed with thin lines of black and white around the tops. My shoes are my greatest joy, black patent-leather miracles, and when one is nicked at the toe later that morning in class, my heart will break

I am carrying a pencil, a pencil sharpener, and a small ten-cent tablet with a black-and-white speckled cover. My mother does not believe that a girl in kindergarten needs such things, so I am taking them only because of my insistent whining and because they are presents from our neighbors, Mary Keith and Blondelle Harris.

Miss Mary and Miss Blondelle are watching my two younger sisters until my mother returns. The women are as precious to me as my mother and sisters. Out playing one day, I have overheard an older child, speaking to another child, call Miss Mary and Miss Blondelle a word that is brand new to me. This is my mother: When I say the word in fun to one of my sisters, my mother slaps me across the mouth and the word is lost for years and years.

All the way down New Jersey Avenue, the sidewalks are teeming with children. In my neighborhood, I have many friends, but I see none of them as my mother and I walk. We cross New York Avenue, we cross Pierce Street, and we cross L and K, and still I see no one who knows my name. At I Street, between New Jersey Avenue and Third Street, we enter Seaton Elementary School, a timeworn, sad-faced building across the street from my mother's church, Mt. Carmel Baptist.

Just inside the front door, women out of the advertisements in *Ebony* are greeting other parents and children. The woman who greets us has pearls thick as jumbo marbles that come down almost to her navel, and she acts as if she had known me all my life, touching my shoulder, cupping her hand under my chin. She is enveloped in a perfume that I only know is not gardenia. When, in answer to her question, my mother tells her that we live at 1227 New Jersey Avenue, the woman first seems to be picturing in her head where we live. Then she shakes her head and says that we are at the wrong school, that we should be at Walker-Jones.

My mother shakes her head vigorously. "I want her to go here," my mother says. "If I'da wanted her someplace else, I'da took her there." The woman continues to act as if she has known me all my life, but she tells my mother that we live beyond the area that Seaton serves. My mother is not convinced and for several more minutes she questions the woman about why I cannot attend Seaton. For as many Sundays as I can remember, perhaps even Sundays when I was in her womb, my mother has pointed across I Street to Seaton as we come and go to Mt. Carmel. "You gonna go there and learn about the whole world." But one of the guardians of that place is saying no, and no again. I am learning this about my mother: The higher up on the scale of respectability a person is— and teachers are rather high up in her eyes—the less she is liable to let them push her around. But finally, I see in her eyes the closing gate, and she takes my hand and we leave the building. On the steps, she stops as people move past us on either side.

"Mama, I can't go to school?"

She says nothing at first, then takes my hand again and we are down the steps quickly and nearing New Jersey Avenue before I can blink. This is my mother: She says, "One monkey don't stop no show."

Walker-Jones is a larger, newer school and I immediately like it because of that. But it is not across the street from my mother's church, her rock, one of her connections to God, and I sense her doubts as she absently rubs her thumb over the back of her hand. We find our way to the crowded auditorium where gray metal chairs are set up in the middle of the room. Along the wall to the left are tables and other chairs. Every chair seems occupied by a child or adult. Somewhere in the room a child is crying, a cry that rises above the buzz-talk of so many people. Strewn about the floor are dozens and dozens of pieces of white paper, and people are walking over them without any thought of picking them up. And seeing this lack of concern, I am all of a sudden afraid.

"Is this where they register for school?" my mother asks a woman at one of the tables.

The woman looks up slowly as if she has heard this question once too often. She nods. She is tiny, almost as small as the girl standing beside her. The woman's hair is set in a mass of curlers and all of those curlers are made of paper money, here a dollar bill, there a five-dollar bill. The girl's hair is arrayed in curls, but some of them are beginning to droop and this makes me happy. On the table beside the woman's pocketbook is a large notebook, worthy of someone in high school, and looking at me looking at the notebook, the girl places her hand possessively on it. In her other hand she holds several pencils with thick crowns of additional erasers.

"These the forms you gotta use?" my mother asks the woman, picking up a few pieces of the paper from the table. "Is this what you have to fill out?"

The woman tells her yes, but that she need fill out only one.

"I see," my mother says, looking about the room. Then: "Would you help me with this form? That is, if you don't mind."

The woman asks my mother what she means.

"This form. Would you mind helpin me fill it out?"

The woman still seems not to understand.

"I can't read it. I don't know how to read or write, and I'm askin you to help me." My mother looks at me, then looks away. I know almost all of her looks, but this one is brand new to me. "Would you help me, then?"

The woman says Why sure, and suddenly she appears happier,

so much more satisfied with everything. She finishes the form for her daughter and my mother and I step aside to wait for her. We find two chairs nearby and sit. My mother is now diseased, according to the girl's eyes, and until the moment her mother takes her and the form to the front of the auditorium, the girl never stops looking at my mother. I stare back at her. "Don't stare," my mother says to me. "You know better than that."

Another woman out of the *Ebony* ads takes the woman's child away. Now, the woman says upon returning, let's see what we can do for you two.

My mother answers the questions the woman reads off the form. They start with my last name, and then on to the first and middle names. This is school, I think. This is going to school. My mother slowly enunciates each word of my name. This is my mother: As the questions go on, she takes from her pocketbook document after document, as if they will support my right to attend school, as if she has been saving them up for just this moment. Indeed, she takes out more papers than I have ever seen her do in other places: my birth certificate, my baptismal record, a doctor's letter concerning my bout with chicken pox, rent receipts, records of immunization, a letter about our public assistance payments, even her marriage license—every single paper that has anything even remotely to do with my five-year-old life. Few of the papers are needed here, but it does not matter and my mother continues to pull out the documents with the purposefulness of a magician pulling out a long string of scarves. She has learned that money is the beginning and end of everything in this world, and when the woman finishes, my mother offers her fifty cents, and the woman accepts it without hesitation. My mother and I are just about the last parent and child in the room.

My mother presents the form to a woman sitting in front of the stage, and the woman looks at it and writes something on a white card, which she gives to my mother. Before long, the woman who has taken the girl with the drooping curls appears from behind us, speaks to the sitting woman, and introduces herself to my mother and me. She's to be my teacher, she tells my mother. My mother stares.

We go into the hall, where my mother kneels down to me. Her lips are quivering. "I'll be back to pick you up at twelve o'clock. I don't want you to go nowhere. You just wait right here. And listen to every word she say." I touch her lips and press them together.

It is an old, old game between us. She puts my hand down at my side, which is not part of the game. She stands and looks a second at the teacher, then she turns and walks away. I see where she has darned one of her socks the night before. Her shoes make loud sounds in the hall. She passes through the doors and I can still hear the loud sounds of her shoes. And even when the teacher turns me toward the classrooms and I hear what must be the singing and talking of all the children in the world, I can still hear my mother's footsteps above it all.

EDWARD P. JONES

Pennies

Grampa paid me a penny a hundred
for killing flies,
a penny a bushel for picking string beans.

And that money was not much, even then.
We children got more for the scrap
found on the hill, sold

to the junkman who came around in his truck.
But it was recognition—
and a penny from my grandfather's hand,

the approval I could see in his eyes
as he gave it, meant much that year—
for we were not held so precious by those

who left us there on Grampa's farm
to serve in such ways. That autumn
Sis and I walked two miles on red earth

to the crossroads schoolhouse.
And what magic we had left was taken,
beginning with the teacher yanking

the penny pencil out of my left hand,
cramming it into my right,
saying that was the only way, the right way.

She would slap my left hand every time
I forgot, threatened to cut it off,
paced between desks, swinging her paddle

to oversee the miserable work, children
hunched over, trying to hide their scrawls
from that teacher, not provoke her scorn.

And yet I had killed plenty of flies,
picked plenty of green beans
with that left hand, and kept my pennies to prove it.

DAVID RAY

Going to School

In knickers that came to our knees
we boys were herded on one side
of the street and the girls on the other
in their uniform pinafores, hair

all bobbed the same. Anyone passing
could see that to our shame we were kids
from the orphanage, trudging toward school,
guarded as if we might try to escape.

The brown corduroys, blue ribbons, tags
pinned in our caps, made it clear
where we should be brought back to
if we ran away and were captured.

There were no chains rattling at ankles
or ropes looped around necks and yet
we trudged along with leaden feet, as if
they were tugging, restraining our steps—

joyless, apologetic, crossing the tarmac
in rain of a weekday morning. If a car
at the corner came to a halt, we paused
before it and were honked at, stumbled

into by the orphan behind us. I would search
through rain and fogged windshield
for the face that might be my father's
or mother's. The true orphan stumbled,

knowing the dead never drove cars.
In Europe, we learned later, others
were treated far worse than we were.
And thereafter we marveled that the heart

could bear yet more and sometimes survive,
though there would always be the slow trudge
and the stooping as if chains and ropes
were still at our ankles and necks

and for life we were sentenced that year—
—to shame as if green tattoos still stain
our arms. And to hot blushes on the face because
even on Sundays we were mistaken for orphans.

DAVID RAY

Shame

I washed
my arms
scrubbed
my face

powdered
soap
fell from
my hands

but
my skin
only got
redder

I was
just

another
itching

brown
boy
getting
ready

for school

FRANCISCO X. ALARCÓN

Disc 'n Dat

"Mr. McCall / is not tall" we'd say—but not so he could hear us. This isn't the reason he hated me. The real reason, I never knew. But one thing he *couldn't* take away in eighth-grade English, is that I could use words. The better I got, the madder he'd get.

When the school paper came around, naturally it was under him, and I wanted to write. Anything. Just give me an assignment. Music. How about music. My grandmother had a juke box in The Venice, her restaurant on South Broad. How many hours I spent there each week, waiting for my mother to finish taking cash— well, I could be a four-star musicologist. I knew every tune, lyric and artist on those hard plastic 78s.

I didn't approach Mr. McCall the next day. It was an especially hard day, one where—while I say working at my desk—he'd stare at me, until my eyes filled with tears from not blinking. I just kept my face down toward my paper, while he fixed his look.

But I specifically remember it was the following day, because Nilda and Jan had each wanted to sit next to me and I chose Nilda, because her mother was divorced and always going out with other men, and Nilda stayed alone so much in her apartment. Jan had a nice big Irish family with a house and a porch, and lots of stew and bread you dunked. So I chose Nilda. I remember that day precisely because Jan slapped my face in the girl's room and I just put my hand up there on my cheek for a moment before the bell rang.

That is when I told Mr. McCall I'd like to write for the paper. I knew he'd sneer as always. But I held on to the underside of his desk and added "Music. I can do a music column." Torn by passion and will, I figured out that nobody had asked for that yet, and I stood a chance. At least he couldn't say "Oh, no, Larry already had . . ."

Triumphantly, he found his ground. "You don't have a title! You have to have a title." There. He had me. I didn't have a title for the column. How could I? I hardly had feet that worked or legs which could stop shaking.

"I'll bring one in from home tomorrow. I'll think of one tonight." Time. I needed time.

That's when I did it. Sabotaged myself. Because he didn't do it for me. "I'll get my father to write it." Anything for a laugh. And I had won. He relaxed. In admitting my weakness, inferiority, submission, obedience, respect for a man's brain, I'd finally won him over. He smiled. For one moment, he forgot that I was the dark-haired girl wild with ambition and heat, the one who attracted the other kids—gregarious, energetic, and somewhat irresistible to life. But he was not afraid. I'd admitted defeat.

My father of course didn't make up a title, and wouldn't if I had asked. This and that. "Disc 'n Dat." Obviously too much Amos and Andy heard on my radio, but the imagination does not make distinctions; there were censors enough outside of me, I didn't need more within.

"Disc 'n Dat," hmmm. Mr. McCall liked it. He said my father did a good job. This was my chance to take what was mine. "He didn't do it. I did," I blurted. But too late. I'd sold myself the day before to earn a moment's kindness. And now he loved me all the more—a weasel, who'd even lie to get a moment of glory away from a poor beleaguered father who probably came home tired and had to put aside his supper to help with homework. Mr. McCall raised his eyebrows and looked down his long nose with pity and contempt. Or maybe they're the same.

The column came out that next week. I thought I'd like to see my name in print. But there was that title . . . which hung so heavy over it. Like the phenolic records themselves. Thick, dark, after the music had gone. I didn't write the next one. I guess Larry did.

But I finally think I know why Mr. McCall would never be tall. Not in this life or the next. Because words have power. And he wanted to be sure whom he allowed that.

GRACE CAVALIERI

The Captain of the Safeties

Sister Euphrasia, the eighth-grade teacher,
said Italians were irresponsible
  but I was an exception

She counted on me
  to run errands
  tabulate grades
  do her roll book
  handle money

Sister Euphrasia said I was
different than most Italians
  who were dishonest
different than my Italian classmates
  who were lazy

I was smart, responsible
I was the Captain of the Safeties

I had a red book
with all the safety patrol members' names
I put a mark against their names
  if they were not at their posts
  if they did not have their badges on straight
  if they forgot an item of the regulation uniforms
  white shirts, blue tie, blue pants for boys
  white blouse, blue jumper, blue beanie for girls

Sister Euphrasia said
the beanie symbolized a girl's modesty
the safeties must set an example
most of the marks against the girl safeties
were for beanie violations

I secured my beanie tight with bobby pins
so even the strongest winds did not blow it off the head
of the Captain of the Safeties

One day my beanie disappeared
maybe it was stolen
maybe it was lost
but it was a disaster

at home I cried and cried
my mother gave me money for another
I cried harder
I would have to buy a new beanie
from Sister Euphrasia
who then would know that
even the Captain of the Safeties
was an irresponsible Italian

My grandmother, a seamstress,
told me not to cry
she knew how to make a beanie
my grandfather gave her
his best blue work pants for material
she worked all night
fashioning a hat
that fit me perfectly and
looked exactly like a regulation beanie
except for the inside where
my grandmother placed a thick cloth hatband
not the regulation leather band

The next day and everyday
until the end of the school year
I wore my imposter beanie

The Captain of the Safeties
was determined
that nobody
would ever see the inside of the beanie

Sister Euphrasia
would never know
that I, too, was an irresponsible Italian.

MARIA FAMA

Senior Will

Maria sat in the last row by the windows, the fourth seat back just where there was a crack in the linoleum, a camel-shaped hole peeled open and dark amber-colored, revealing ancient adhesive now as smooth and as polished as the rest of the gray and beige checkerboard floor. Mr. Staples had let them pick their own seats on the first day of class and Maria chose her usual one, not in the back where the black boys and the real troublemakers sat, but a few seats up from there and off to the side where it was unlikely she would ever be called on, or noticed at all, as far as that went. All the seniors had to take an elective English class. You could pick from Rhetoric, Advanced Composition, The Contemporary Novel, or just plain Senior English. Which was her choice. Those other courses were for college types. They were known to be a lot of work and all Maria wanted was the credit. Mr. Staples was focusing on American junk.

No one had ever called her a prize student. Many teachers at South High made it clear to her that academics did not seem to be her strong suit. They called her lazy and unmotivated, wrote her scolding notes on the backs of her papers which accused her of not using the mind with which she was gifted. She'd do much better work, they said, if she spent more time paying attention to the lesson and less time watching the clock. As a matter of fact she did choose her seat not only so she could be inconspicuous, but also because from there you could always get the best look at the clock, located on the wall opposite the window. She remembers how while Mr. Staples droned on and on about some silly story, which maybe had a ghost in it and maybe did not, the second hand on the clock above the chalkboard hardly moved at all. It was so slow that she finally had to stop watching it and put her head down on her desk.

Staples was an odd character, she always thought. Old-fashioned, like something out of one of those foreign movies, or like one of those fussy men on those English comedy shows they put on Channel Two during the late news. But he was black. He always wore a suit—a nice suit—and he would walk up and down the aisles often, almost as if he were on patrol, hands behind his back, delivering his sermons about this or that. She didn't follow the words, only the soothing sound of that voice, which resonated as if he were built like a massive organ, rather than slight and narrow, as he was.

She would ride the rhythms of his speech, her heart keeping time, calming her to just this side of sleep.

Behind her, her boyfriend Josh, who back then was just a big goofy-looking kid with sandy blond hair down to his shoulders and buck teeth (which she loved), sat bolt upright in his desk. He balled up bits of paper in his fingers and flicked them so they dropped down the neck of her blouse. She picked them away and swatted at him, trying to ignore the nasty-sounding laughs from the boys across the way. He looked so innocent back there, Josh did. That was his cover, really. Dumb as the day was long, and he knew it and she knew it and so did Mr. Staples and all the other teachers. The deal seemed to be that as long as he sat quiet and made at least some effort to get the work done, they would give him D+s and C−s, and at the end of his required time at South, he would walk across the stage with everyone else, be handed a diploma and be gone. She'd wanted to tell him to lay off the paper wads, but she had been afraid to call attention to him, had not wanted to get him into trouble. In twenty minutes it would be noon, their lunch hour, and he would be done for the day and off to his DECA job at a garage over on University Avenue. Any behavior notes might threaten his status in the program, so she turned toward the window with her head still down and adjusted her body in such a way that she could catch his eye. She gave him an evil look, and he looked back at her, his yellow-green eyes smoldering in the way they had done all last summer when they'd sneak away to a secluded part of the beach out at Fort Snelling State Park. He raised his eyebrows in a way she thought was nasty and silly and sexy all at the same time. He would stop now, she knew, and she eased herself back around facing front.

"Miss Bonner," Mr. Staples said to her from his desk after the bell. "A minute of your time, if you will."

Josh stood in the door, waiting.

"To your next class, Mr. Jessup," Mr. Staples said.

"Hurry," he mouthed at Maria, and he walked away, but not before directing at the teacher, who was a bit shorter than him, a look full of benign disdain.

"Have a seat," he offered.

"I got lunch," she said, nervous. It was October and this was the first indication she had that he even knew who she was.

"It's my lunch, as well, and I'll only take a minute of your time. You may sit, if you like," he repeated. She stood. He fished through a stack of papers and pulled out one on which she recognized her own handwriting. The assignment had been to write about some poem by some woman named Emily something.

"I put a D on this," he said.

She shrugged.

"You don't care?"

"Not really," she lied. She shrugged again.

"You can do it over if you want. I can move you up at least to a B."

"Why?"

Mr. Staples had laughed. "Because you want a better grade? Because you want to do your best? You tell me."

"I don't have a reason. I'm not interested in that poetry junk."

"You surprise me, Maria. I guess I read you wrong. I expected you to be more ambitious."

"Well, I'm not," she said. And though she remembers it being hard, she had stared him down. He was a black man with intense dark eyes that sparkled almost as if he were laughing even when he was not. He did not blink and did not look away.

"What will you do with yourself, then?" he asked.

"What do you mean?"

"When you graduate. What will you make of yourself? You seem to be fairly carefree."

"I never said that. I said I didn't care about this stupid assignment." She had smirked when she said this and had tried to sound as tough as she could.

"Fair enough," he nodded. "Pick your own topic. Write about something you are interested in."

Maria remembers feeling boxed in when he said that. She remembers that what she really wanted was just to be done with the whole damn episode, but with his fast talk he had backed her into a corner where now she had to do what he wanted—which was more work—or look like a fool. "I don't have anything to write about," she said.

"Write about your honey back there," he'd said. He had been packing his briefcase, tossing in criss-crossed piles of papers as if they were bricks.

She flushed and dropped her eyes at the mention of Josh.

"That's your boy, am I right? That Josh?"

She nodded, still avoiding his eyes.

"No shame. Do me a little paper of some kind about him. However it suits you. A poem. A story. A song. I guarantee you a C," he said. He clicked the briefcase closed and offered her the door, which he locked behind them as they stepped into the corridor.

"Unless it's too hard for you," he said, over his shoulder, walking away.

Maria finds the essay folded into the same page of her South High School yearbook which has Josh's senior portrait on it. His hair in the photo cascades to his shoulders in golden waves the way the boys wore it back then. Meeting the camera, his bright eyes shine out from smooth skin that predicts none of the ravages of fifteen years of alcohol and slave wage scut work beneath every worn-out beater in the city. The essay is handwritten in the neat Palmer-method script she had learned so well with Ms. Anderson hovering over her shoulder back at Groveland School in the third grade. Across the page the cross strokes on the Ts line up as perfectly as soldiers marching across a field, the loops of the Ls and Bs and Ds rise off the line, each a proud standardized whorl. This is what she remembers most about the essay—the pleasure she had had sitting there at the kitchen table in the apartment on Minnehaha Avenue crafting the final draft in her very best hand, and how she had tolerated not one blemish, cross out, or noticeably uneven stroke. The trash can next to the loud old refrigerator had been heaped with balls of wadded up paper so it looked like a pile of snowballs ready to be thrown. She doesn't remember that she wrote all of this.

Josh: A One of a Kind Person

Not every girl is lucky enough to meet a guy like Josh Jessup. I was one of the lucky ones, I guess. I will tell you about how we met and a little about why he is so special. I can't tell you all the reasons he is because I would be writing forever.

I met Josh when we were sophomores and we had a class together. The class was Science and the teacher was Mr. French. For one class we had to go to the lab and work on experiments. We had to mix stuff together and if it was blue it meant one thing and if it was red it meant something else. Mr. French gave everybody a partner and so I ended up with Josh. I had seen him before and thought he was kind of goofy looking but I didn't really know him. We mixed the stuff together and wrote down the answers. He made me read the instructions and write in the workbook, but he did all the mixing and pouring. We talked a lot and it turned out he was pretty friendly. We would see each other in class, and then he asked me out and we have been together ever since.

What makes Josh special is he is a kind person. He does not say mean things or hurtful things about anyone, and when he seen little kids in trouble in the street he stops to help them. He has a sick grandma on the East Side and he is forever going over there to check in on her and see does she need anything. He is not the sort of guy who when he is going with you is also chasing after every other girl in school. I would not put up with that, so it means we have a good relationship. He does not do too well in school, but he comes everyday and tries hard. I help him with things he cannot do too well and try to encourage him. Even though he has trouble in school he is good with his hands and is learning a trade. He is very proud of his work and will have no trouble getting a job because he is good at what he does.

I cannot wait until we are finished with school. We are planning to get married and spend the rest of our lives together. We will live in Saint Paul and I plan to work for a while until we start our family. Josh loves kids and would like to have as many as we can afford.

To summarize, I feel privileged to have a boyfriend as kind and as loving as Josh. I only wish that all girls could be as lucky as me.

She smooths the paper against the edge of the yearbook. She rolls her eyes and snickers at her own optimism.

"Didn't you hear the bell on the damn microwave," he shouts down the hall.

She lays the yearbook on the closet shelf and goes to dish up the casserole for Josh and their two little boys.

She had handed the essay to Mr. Staples a week after he approached her about doing it. He hadn't spoken to her again about the assignment—nor about anything else, for that matter—but he did look at her more often now when he stood at his desk lecturing or when walking the aisles during discussions. At least it seemed to her he was looking at her more. Maybe he had always been watching her and maybe she had been so busy watching the clock that she hadn't noticed. Whatever. Now he would catch her with those twinkling eyes and somehow the hour went by faster. It seemed easier to pay attention and to follow where he was going, to figure out what all these old-timey stories and poems were about.

He gave her a B on the essay, and he wrote her a note. He told her that despite the sentimentality, he could tell she had put a lot of herself and a lot of her time into the piece.

She should have looked up sentimentality. She really didn't know what it meant, whether it was a bad thing or just something he didn't like. She did not look it up because she was sidetracked by the last sentence on the page. In parentheses he had written: *Are you sure you want to marry this guy?*

He handed her the essay in class just after he gave them an assignment to read a story about some guy who murdered his girl-friend and buried her in the floor. She had read his response and then, in her shock, had folded it quickly and stuck it in her notebook.

"What's that?" Josh asked. No one else had been handed anything.

"Nothing," she said. She had planned on reading him that essay on their way to the homecoming dance. It would have been perfect. She would read it and he would know how much she loved him, and why, and they would have a perfect romantic evening. Now, there was this ugly question scrawled in bright red ink across the bottom of her beautiful writing.

"Some extra credit," she said.

"Do some for me," he whispered, his voice husky with innuendo. And then he began to complain about how hard the words in the story were. Mr. Staples signaled for him to be quiet.

"Wait for me at the lockers," she told him at the end of class. She waited at her desk until the rest of the class had exited, then approached Mr. Staples.

"Why did you write that on my paper?" she asked.

"The B? You worked hard. That's worth something in my book."

"About me marrying him. That ain't your business." She stared him in the eye and pushed down the emotion in her voice.

The teacher pursed his lips, prissily she remembers. "I'm sorry," he said. "You are absolutely correct. None of my business at all. Please forgive me." His eyes were lit up in a way that felt to her like a challenge.

Even so, she relaxed. She had expected him to be harder than this, more confrontational. She felt brazen.

"What's wrong with him?" she asked.

He stopped packing up, got a sly smile on his face. "I thought we just agreed that was none of my business."

"You already put your nose in it. I want to know."

"Fair enough," he said. "You may consider my query as a thought provoker. Nothing more."

"Think about what?"

He nodded toward the door, picked up the briefcase, and started with her down the corridor.

"If this is really what you want. That's all."

"What's wrong with him?" she asked, dogging him, stepping around in front of him, persisting. "What gives you the right to judge a person?" she asked.

He stared at her for a minute. "My question was for you, Maria. It wasn't my intention to criticize your young man. He's . . ." and here the man had hesitated. "He's like a lot of the young men around here. Seems like a decent sort. Good enough and hard-working. You young women come through here and so many of you, the only thing you think about is catching one of these guys as if that's all you were put on earth for. You all sound as if life was always going to be happily ever after. Then you come back ten, fifteen years later full of regret. I always wonder if anyone ever asked: Are you sure? Is this really what you want? And I wonder if it would have made any difference. So I'm asking you: Are you sure you want to marry this guy?"

"Yes," she said. "Yes I am." And she walked away toward Josh, waiting as faithful as a big pup, down the hall by their lockers.

After supper, after she has washed and put away all the dishes, made the sack lunches for tomorrow, and while Josh is sprawled on the couch with his six-pack and the boys are in bed, she pulls down the yearbook and turns to the teacher page. There is Mr. Staples, looking much the way she sees him in her head. Well dressed, a shit-eating, no-teeth-visible smile dominating the picture. She wonders if he is still the same—if he is even there anymore. On the dresser is the invitation to the fifteenth reunion of her South High class. She can go back and see if she wants to. She turns to her own picture. Then she stands in front of the mirror. She is not the same, but not so bad, really. She's long since cut all the wings off of her hair, and her face is certainly fuller. And she would never get into that scoop-neck dress again. But she could walk into that Radisson and feel pretty good about herself. She goes out to show the invitation to Josh.

"We got our reunion coming up," she says.

He belches. He is watching the cop show with the fat guy and the thin guy. She doesn't know if they make it anymore or if this is just a rerun.

"I think I'm gonna go," she says.

He pops open another can of beer.

"Should I put your name down?"

He gets up and pushes past her to the bathroom. Finished, he saunters out around her, zipping himself up, suppressing some disgusting digestive noise, letting the sound sputter from his lips.

"You're serious about this crap?" he asks. He scans the flier and tosses it on the floor. "Fifteen bucks. Shees."

She retrieves it. "I'd like to see some of the old crowd. I think I'm gonna go."

"Such as? Who you gonna see that you don't see in line over at Rainbow?"

"Some people left town, maybe. I haven't heard from Sherri in a while. Some of the old teachers even."

"Yeah, right." He sucks down most of a beer. "Look, spend your money if you want. Me, I don't need to go down to some hotel to have a bunch of folks look down on me."

"We got nothing to be ashamed of."

"Yeah, a damn grease monkey and you're a grocery store checkout girl. We're living real high."

"There's people worse off than us."

"And they'll have the good sense to stay home, too." He dismisses her with his hands and goes back to the show.

Maria was pleased that, despite her standing up to him, Mr. Staples still showed her respect. He still caught her eye, still made it a point to try to get her engaged in the discussion. In the spring they read this play by some guy with a state for a name about some girl who never left her house and finally got one pathetic date who didn't even like her. This was just after Josh finally got her a ring, a real ring, one that told everyone—even people like Staples—just how special he thought she was.

"Your reaction, Miss Bonner. To the play," Mr. Staples prompted.

Maria had been lost in a reverie, staring at her ring, imagining the ideal Como Park wedding, with a dozen bridesmaids and a train on her wedding gown a hundred feet long. This diamond might be small, but it was real and it meant she was getting married, and because he loved her, too, not because they had to. It was the real thing.

"I . . . uh," she began. "I thought it was sad. That poor girl stuck up there all alone without a life."

"The poor girl's name, Miss Bonner?"

She had no idea. She had been letting what little studying she did slip as of late, ever since he gave her the ring on Easter, and though she had skimmed most of the words, she remembered nothing much about the play, certainly none of the names.

"Rose, isn't it?" she says. She remembers something about roses. There was some snickering in the room.

"If you wish," Mr. Staples smirked. "Is it this Rose's fault what happens to her? Her isolation. Her loneliness?"

"Who else's fault would it be? My stepdad says you make your luck."

Mr. Staples had laughed, she remembers, and had moved the discussion on elsewhere.

"Nice ring, Rose," he said to her, on her way out of the room at the end of the period. Josh had already run out ahead. Since he'd given her the ring he seemed to have the need to put some space between them, to not always be around her, hovering. She remembers not minding.

"Is that the chick's name, or what?" she asked.

"Look it up," he said, nodding toward the textbook. He grabbed her hand and hoisted it. "So, this is the rock I've heard tell of."

She stretched her fingers daintily.

"I'm blinded," he said.

"It's what we can afford." The cash had actually come from the sick grandmother on the East Side, or at least a hundred dollars of it had. The other four hundred was financed at the jewelry store.

"When's the big date?"

"This summer. We're keeping it simple."

"Still got a few months to change your mind, then."

And she had laughed. "You don't give up," she said.

"My dear Rose: I've been in this business fifteen years. Every year they show up with the rings and the babies and the eyes full of hope. And then every year just as many show up again, five years down the line, after the Love Boat's sailed, fat and miserable and trying to figure out what comes next."

"There's no baby here," she said, patting her perfectly flat stomach.

"A blessing, to say the least." He looked her over as if he were a car shopper about to make an offer on last year's model. "I'll make you a promise," he said. "When I'm an old man and I run into you in Dayton's and you've long since left this guy in the dust, I promise I won't gloat."

She shook her head and walked towards lunch. Gloat? He'd never get the chance.

Josh snores beside her in the bed. He is warm tonight. Sweaty. She wonders if beer can get into your sweat, because if it can, it has. That's just how he smells. He isn't a bad man. Not like some. He worked everyday. Worked till he dropped, but he did not like it, she knew. And there was so much they wanted from life that was so far out of their reach. Their boys, nine and eleven: They couldn't imagine there would be a way for them to go past high school. Jeremy, the youngest, she could see had begun to figure that out, had already developed this cool, why-bother attitude toward his studies—that same attitude she had worked so hard herself to cultivate. The oldest, Joshua, was smart enough, but so many other kids had the advantages. Books that she could not afford, and trips, and camps, and educational toys. And, and, and. If he stayed with it he just might make it, might get that scholarship and make something of his life. Thinking of that breaks her heart a little, because she wonders if he should be so lucky, will he walk away from them, turn up his nose at them because they were ignorant and poor and hadn't done better for themselves.

She takes down the yearbook again and pages through the pictures of the young men and women they knew so well. Mostly alive, she believes, because there has been no war to erase them. This one is a carpenter and that one is a nurse. That woman works construction now—she's been seen out on I-94 in her orange vest, tanned and bulky. There are plumbers and teacher's assistants, and many of them, like her, are still checking at the grocery store, or on the line at some job they got while still in high school. Look at them all: so earnest, so proud. "You have not failed," she tells the faces. "You done good!"

On Saturday she will wear her gray and white striped dress, a very tailored one she bought just for a special parent's night at school so her boys would be proud. A hundred and fifty dollars— a half week's salary—and it was worth it because the boys had clung to her all night like she was a queen.

She turns to the back of the yearbook to the "Senior Wills." Recorded there, all the hopes and fears that her class left to the ones coming up behind them. A quarter is fixed to the page, under a yellowed piece of cellophane tape. Mr. Marvin Staples has signed his name right underneath it. She's almost forgotten why, until she finds above it, faded and smeared, the cryptic will, buried amongst the hundreds of others. "To Rose," it says. "I leave twenty-five cents for the call when it's time to get out. M.S." She peels the quarter from the page and drops it in her purse.

More have turned out for the reunion than she expected. Packed in the ballroom it is as if she is wearing fun house glasses—every face is fatter or fuller or thinner or has changed shape, and they are all smiling and they hug her and tell her how she hasn't changed one bit.

"Neither have you," she says, and she giggles at each little fib.

There is Ronald Alsop whom she had that terrible crush on in junior high. He is a little round around the middle these days, and is still smoking, just as he was out on the corner during eighth grade. That stuck up Cindy Stevenson has put on weight. Serves her right, but she is happy and shameless. She gives Maria one of those phony Hollywood embraces people do on TV, complete with the smacks in the air by each ear.

She spots him over with the teachers. He is talking with some younger men she has never seen. His trimmed tight head of hair is now peppered with gray, and he looks a bit stoop-shouldered. She approaches him.

"Mr. Staples?" she asks, her voice weak, tentative. "Do you remember me?" She covers her name tag with her hand.

"Is it Rose?" he asks, and she can tell he really believes that this is her name.

"You called me that," she says, surprised at how pleased she feels that he has remembered her at least in some way. She drops her hand revealing her names—maiden and married—written in different colors of pastel marker.

"Oh, Maria," he says, shaking his head, dramatically. He extends his hand to her. "It's good to see you again. How are you?"

"I brought you this," she says. She has already fished the quarter from her handbag. She drops it in his hand. "We're still married," she says.

His eyes look away as if he is searching for someone. Then they come back to her face. He takes her hands between his and shakes them. "Well, yes, of course, darling," he says. "Of course you are."

DAVID HAYNES

VII. ～

OUR BODIES, OURSELVES

I was your girl in calico,

You were my bashful, barefoot beau

My Father's Love Letters

On Fridays he'd open a can of Jax
After coming home from the mill,
& ask me to write a letter to my mother
Who sent postcards of desert flowers
Taller than men. He would beg,
Promising to never beat her
Again. Somehow I was happy
She had gone, & sometimes wanted
To slip in a reminder, how Mary Lou
Williams' "Polka Dots & Moonbeams"
Never made the swelling go down.
His carpenter's apron always bulged
With old nails, a claw hammer
Looped at his side & extension cords
Coiled around his feet.
Words rolled from under the pressure
Of my ballpoint: Love,
Baby, Honey, Please.
We sat in the quiet brutality
Of voltage meters & pipe threaders,
Lost between sentences . . .
The gleam of a five-pound wedge
On the concrete floor
Pulled a sunset
Through the doorway of his toolshed.
I wondered if she laughed
& held them over a gas burner.
My father could only sign
His name, but he'd look at blueprints
& say how many bricks
Formed each wall. This man,
Who stole roses & hyacinth
For his yard, would stand there
With eyes closed & fists balled,
Laboring over a simple word, almost
Redeemed by what he tried to say.

YUSEF KOMUNYAKAA

Mortal Sins

Aldo Palmieri straddles
the back seat of the schoolbus,
chainsmokes Luckys like a cowboy.
I'm fifteen.
I love his pathos, his acne,
his yellow-stained fingers.
JFK dies during study hall.
Jane Murphy gets pregnant, leaves
school. I take phenobarbital daily
for my nerves.

At sixteen my face falls into place
around my nose.
I meet Harvey Brotman underwater
at the Jones Beach pool.
We share whoppers with cheese in Franklin Square.
His parents say: "One date with a Catholic
girl is too much."
I think Harvey is making this up.

I'm seventeen:
long hair, brace-less teeth.
I worship Kevin Duffy, boast
his fraternity pin
on my Peter Pan collar.
I think kissing is a mortal sin.
I think holding hands is possibly
a mortal sin.
Father Reilly says: "Watch out! Holding hands
is a venial that could easily lead
to a mortal."
Kevin drops me for a "Popover Girl" from Patricia Murphy's
who giggles whenever a car with one headlight
passes by.

I meet my husband-to-be at the Ship Ahoy
in New Rochelle, acquire a taste for scotch;
at eighteen, trade eternity

for a good french kiss.
I learn to cook Thanksgiving dinner
for twenty in-laws, put on weight,
take it off, put it on, learn
my husband prefers blondes.

I'm thirty-one:
the year of designer jeans.
My ass is finally "in."
I get my ears double-pierced,
cut six inches off my hair, let it grow
on my legs, under my arms.
I take my daughter to the Twin Towers.
We look down, say "Wow."
She holds my face in her baby hands,
says: "You're so pretty, Mommy."
I laugh.
She tells me again & again
until one day, I am.

MAUREEN SEATON

Training Bra

When I was eleven, I wore white cotton undershirts,
serviceable and plain. All winter
I wore one under my school blouse; in summer,
I wore one as my only garment,
tucked into shorts with elastic around the waist.
One day, I came running in from playing tag on 19th street,
and my mother said, "You can't wear that shirt outside anymore."
The next day she took me to Jacobs Department Store
to buy a training bra. I was proud of it,
a symbol that I was growing up.

"I got her a training bra," my mother whispered to my aunt,
and asked me to lift my shirt to show it off. They both smiled
and exchanged a look I could not read, half proud, half exultant.
"You're a woman now," my aunt said and when she said it, I knew
some petty meanness in her was glad that I was caught too
as she had been caught in the life of a woman, the training bra
the beginning of constrictions, all the snaps and hooks

designed to train us to accept the boundaries
of the women we would become.

MARIA MAZZIOTTI GILLAN

The One Girl at the Boys' Party

When I take my girl to the swimming party
I set her down among the boys. They tower and
bristle, she stands there smooth and sleek,
her math scores unfolding in the air around her.
They will strip to their suits, her body hard and
indivisible as a prime number,
they'll plunge in the deep end, she'll subtract
her height from ten feet, divide it into
hundreds of gallons of water, the numbers
bouncing in her mind like molecules of chlorine
in the bright blue pool. When they climb out,
her ponytail will hang its pencil lead
down her back, her narrow silk suit
with hamburgers and french fries printed on it
will glisten in the brilliant air, and they will
see her sweet face, solemn and
sealed, a factor of one, and she will
see their eyes, two each,
their legs, two each, and the curves of their sexes,
one each, and in her head she'll be doing her
wild multiplying, as the drops
sparkle and fall to the power of a thousand from her body.

SHARON OLDS

The Boy

My older brother is walking down the sidewalk into the suburban
   summer night:
white T-shirt, blue jeans—to the field at the end of the street.

Hangers Hideout the boys called it, an undeveloped plot, a pit
   overgrown
with weeds, some old furniture thrown down there,

and some metal hangers clinking in the trees like wind chimes.
He's running away from home because our father wants to cut his
    hair.

And in two more days our father will convince me to go to him—
    you know
where he is—and talk to him: No reprisals. He promised. A small
    parade of kids

in feet pajamas will accompany me, their voices like the first peepers
    in spring.
And my brother will walk ahead of us home, and my father

will shave his head bald, and my brother will not speak to anyone
    the next
month, not a word, not *pass the milk,* nothing.

What happened in our house taught my brothers how to leave,
    how to walk
down a sidewalk without looking back.

I was the girl. What happened taught me to follow him, whoever
    he was,
calling and calling his name.

MARIE HOWE

Practicing

I want to write a love poem for the girls I kissed in seventh grade,
a song for what we did on the floor in the basement

of somebody's parents' house, a hymn for what we didn't say but
    thought:
That feels good or *I like that,* when we learned how to open each
    other's mouths

how to move our tongues to make somebody moan. We called it
    practicing, and
one was the boy, and we paired off—maybe six or eight girls—and
    turned out

the lights and kissed and kissed until we were stoned on kisses, and
    lifted our
nightgowns or let the straps drop, and, Now you be the boy:

concrete floor, sleeping bag or couch, playroom, game room, train
    room, laundry.
Linda's basement was like a boat with booths and portholes

instead of windows. Gloria's father had a bar downstairs with stools
    that spun,
plush carpeting. We kissed each other's throats.

We sucked each other's breasts, and we left marks, and never spoke
    of it upstairs
outdoors, in daylight, not once. We did it, and it was

practicing, and slept, sprawled so our legs still locked or crossed, a
    hand still lost
in someone's hair . . . and we grew up and hardly mentioned who

the first kiss really was—a girl like us, still sticky with moisturizer
    we'd
shared in the bathroom. I want to write a song

for that thick silence in the dark, and the first pure thrill of
    unreluctant desire
just before we made ourselves stop.

MARIE HOWE

from Drops of This Story

To the flow of a beat box, dripped from leaky faucets into rusted
sinks. Spread like government cheese on Goya crackers, and swallowed down with malta. In school, we mixed them into the Vaseline we slathered on our faces before fights. The slickness on our
young faces would make it hard for an opponent with a blade to
do much damage. Schoolyard fights were decided on during lunch,
and by three, your earrings and chains were being held by friends.
The only jewelry worn were the name rings that clawed two or
three fingers into a weapon. Hair was pulled back with the ghetto's
barrette, a rubber band. I know now that all them fights can make

you stronger, but I wish there was some other nourishment to give
our kids. Too bad we have to remember Vaseline and blood as the
cocktails of our youth.

Pumped out of the bottles of curl sheen. Use the colorful words to
polish nails. Spread the meaning of this madness across lips, shinier
than any gloss. Don't need blush, even on sallow days. Line eyes
with the lines of these pages, ink as kohl. This beauty is of earth,
ain't no plastic here.

Kneaded into the skin of beautiful tired women, this wet tried
to reduce the visible signs of aging. Smile lines after years of forcing
pleasant faces to a world that hated them. Told their value lay in
their looks, were sold face creams and youth lotions, as though they
were blessings. Selling their souls, these women bought up these
prayers in a bottle with food stamps and welfare checks. Bleaching
their hides to reach an impossible shade of porcelain. Arab, Latina,
and African women compared each other's progress in the fight
against their own natural faces.

The story about the acceptance of tired, sad beauty that radiates
with the love of mothers and grandmothers. Tired and sad beauty
that's more genuine than any poison in any bottle. It don't sell itself,
or buy others. These drops travel down the cheeks of women who
have forgotten that God held each of their noses in divine hands
and shaped them into perfection. This drop falls on to the tips of
Semitic noses and quivers, then joins the ink on the page. I write
this love song in the name of our mothers' beauty, to let them
remind themselves that we were beautiful before there was Revlon.

SUHEIR HAMMAD

Playing with Dolls

Every weekend morning, I'd sneak downstairs to play
with my sisters' Barbie dolls. They had all
of them: Barbie, Ken, Allan, Midge, Skipper and
Skooter. They even had the little freckled boy,
Ricky ("Skipper's Friend"), and Francie, "Barbie's
'MOD'ern cousin." Quietly, I'd set the dolls

in front of their wardrobe cases, take the dolls'
clothes off miniature plastic hangers, and play
until my father woke up. There were several Barbies—

blonde ponytail, black bubble, brunette flip—all
with the same pointed tits, which (odd for a boy)
didn't interest me as much as the dresses and

accessories. I'd finger each glove and hat and
necklace and high heel, then put them on the dolls.
Then I'd invent elaborate stories. A "creative" boy,
I could entertain myself for hours. I liked to play
secretly like that, though I often got caught. All
my father's tirades ("Boys don't play with Barbies!

It isn't *normal!*") faded as I slipped Barbie's
perfect figure into her stunning ice blue and
sea green satin and tulle formal gown. All
her outfits had names like "Fab Fashion," "Doll's
Dream" and "Golden Evening"; Ken's were called "Play
Ball!," "Tennis Pro," "Campus Hero" and "Fountain Boy,"

which came with two tiny sodas and spoons. Model boy
that he was, Ken hunted, fished, hit home runs. Barbie's
world revolved around garden parties, dances, play
and movie dates. A girl with bracelets and scarves and
sunglasses and fur stoles. . . . "Boys don't play with dolls!"
My parents were arguing in the living room. "All

boys do." As always, my mother defended me. "All
sissies!" snarled my father. "He's a creative boy,"
my mother responded. I stuffed all the dresses and dolls
and shoes back into the black cases that said "Barbie's
Wonderful World" in swirling pink letters and
clasped them shut. My sisters, awake now, wanted to play

with me. "I can't play," I said, "Dad's upset." All
day, he stayed upset. Finally, my mother came upstairs
    and said: "You're a boy,
David. Forget about Barbies. Stop playing with dolls."

DAVID TRINIDAD

Rice and Beans

We're cooking rice and beans. It's women's work.
My mother married, learned the recipe—
Got angry chopping onions, gossiping
And hissing over quickly frying pork.
I try to teach it to my daughter, but
It isn't women's work to her, it's not
A culture anymore; she hasn't got
A grandmother whose Cuban appetite
To serve her husband rice and beans each night,
Dependably for years, was more like starving.
She almost made my mother Cuban, carving
Roasts, serving Spanish *tortas*, taking bites
As if she weren't hungry to this day.
My daughter is a vegetarian,
Or so she claims. I want to feed her beans
To fatten her. I know this single way.

RAFAEL CAMPO

Defining Us

No knowledge is more powerful
Than knowing love, than knowing how
To love despite a world so full

Of the intent to hate. I know
Of others who are like me now.
I've seen us on *Arsenio*;

I've seen us march on Washington,
The love I felt so deep I feared
It was a dream. But one in ten

Of us, supposedly, got stunned
In utero with something queer,
A sort of poison laser gun

(A hormone gone berserk, some say,
While others tout a faulty gene).
All that I know is this: I'm gay,

And knowledge is less powerful
Than love, and that whatever dream
I have, in him it is fulfilled.

RAFAEL CAMPO

Imagining Drag

I think that illness is a form of drag:
The body dresses in the gossamer
Of death, as thin as fog upon a moor,
The cemetery's moon a kind of drug
That makes forgetting possible. I think
That writing poetry is just as queer:
Adorning language with a rhyme as clear
As diamonds dangled from the ear. The link
Is not as tenuous as it might seem.
To die, to write in artificial meter,
To wear beneath a suit a silken girdle—
Each has everything to do with dreams,
Their loss and their attainment equally
Ungainly, equally too fanciful.
Perimeters are what the fingers feel,
Where what the eyes can touch is all we see.

RAFAEL CAMPO

Choice in Colored Rain

a dozen gold bracelets
weigh on my arms
quietly cutting into the flesh
            as they did to my mother
                  and my mother's mother
wedding guests press against me
            offering red envelopes stuffed with money
                  gold characters on paper for good luck
they congratulate my parents in this finest moment

i touch my face, sweet remembering, now guilt remembering
the way he moved, deliberate and steady
his hazel eyes, wide and deep
strawberry blonde hair familiar to me
    what am i to do with this—
           bury it in rice and colored rain

i serve dragonwell tea on a tray to my in-laws
my face powdered and eyes framed in liquid liner

don't cry on your wedding day—it is bad luck

i wear red, pink, then emerald green
with bright embroidered phoenix and feathers rising up
past my thighs, my sex, my stomach, my breasts, to my neck
where the collar of mother's silk dress wraps securely
    no gap of air shows between that and my skin
a family of jade pendants rests on my chest
    chunks of old jade in soft, solid gold from women long ago

i am alone to face my choices
i look into the eyes of my chosen husband
and see mine, the same color, even the same shade
it's better this way, they say
a guarantee of centuries

i kiss my bouquet good-bye
    champagne roses, fading from the hot lights
at last, i throw my youth
    a token to someone
        who barely knows me at all

LISA YUN

Graffiti

Any romantic ideas for a cheap date?
Buy a twenty dollar bottle of champagne;
make love by candlelight.
——WOMEN'S REST ROOM, UNIVERSITY OF CALIFORNIA, BERKELEY

Sex was on the sneak in 1964.
The few times I did it
it was fast on the living room couch.
Jane was the first girl I told.
She was the first to tell me.
We knew the others were liars.
There were more imaginary virgins
in a women's Catholic college
than anywhere else on the planet.

I remember another day.
She cried in her dormitory room.
On her birthday, no family calls.
Her father had sent one hundred dollars.
Unable to afford the dorm, I rode the subway home.
Her straight As, expensive clothes
did not take away her sadness. Making classmates laugh
crossing over the class line between resident
and commuter cliques did not take away mine.
We sought different kinds of comfort
for our different kinds of grief.

When I retrieve her pain and her privilege
understand that I am still stunned
that a college student would see
a twenty dollar bottle of champagne as cheap.
I heard she married well; has two kids

lives in a fancy suburb.
In the beginning, I hope she made
slow love by a long candle's light
that he remembers her birthday without a check.
We're all entitled to start off like that, at least.

MARGIE NORRIS

The Girls

for Margaret Atwood & Cathy Davidson

I never understood the girls
who had the sweaters
and the latest hairdos copied out of magazines
and who were not afraid of snakes.
They were the thin-hipped ones who looked good
in straight skirts, like exclamation points
behind phrases like "Wow," and "Gee Whiz."

I envied their lemon-scented hands
raised to answer almost as many questions
as I, the ugly duckling class brain, did,
with my fat ankles,
and ass as soft as a sofa pillow.
Valerie Twadell who was Miss La Habra
at our August Corn Festival
chased me with worms.

Cathy, with her Zelda-ish bob,
and slimness that even her sorority girl students envy
tells of a snake they ritually put in the 8th grade teacher's
    desk;
and now you, Peggy, as I heard someone nice
call you, slender and chic as Jane Fonda,
tell of your own simple connection with snakes,
wearing them as electric tight bracelets,
wound on a willow wrist,
the delight you took in scaring others,
even men, or women like me,
who would have died had we found even a harmless little
    black
fellow
curled in the grass.

I have never been
one of the girls:
smart without being labelled with derogatory titles like
        "the encyclopedia"
        "the brain,"

graceful without watching calories,
followed by men who adored me even when I turned them
    away,
slow-voiced,
quiet,
with ankles like colts,
and at complete ease with snakes.
I have never been
one of the girls.
At 47, I still envy your cool acceptance
of all these gifts.
                Some part of me
was denied
what all women have,
or are supposed to have, an ease
with the fatly coiled Python whose skin
is like milky underwear,
the thread-like green mamba who slips past
your fingers like mountain water,
the cobra who sits on the family radio
in Sri Lanka,
the cottonmouth who swims next to you all night
in muddy fertile loving water,
or the magic necklace Denise imagines
around her throat.

Men see me as the Medusa,
with vipers hissing around my hair.
How ironic/ I have always been so afraid
of snakes that when I was six
I couldn't turn to the S N A K E page
in my Golden Encyclopedia.

I have never been one of the girls,
comfortable wearing a blacksnake as a belt.
Had I been Lawrence,
near his well in Sicily,
I would have turned and run. He knew
snakes were
the Lords of Life,
but I know you pretty girl women,
who handle them like hula hoops,

or jump ropes,
or pet kittens,
are the real Gods, and your ease with snakes
is proof.
In your presence I am neither man
nor woman. I am simply the one
afraid of snakes; who knows
that in this life
it is the one thing
not allowed.

DIANE WAKOSKI

Aunt Dorothy

Aunt Dorothy used to bleach my cousin Freddy's hair
    platinum blond when he was six years old
    (and for years after that)
All the members of my family found this deeply disturbing
    although it was true Freddy was born a blond
But year by year his hair turned gradually darker
    until by first grade, it was a light brown
He was a handsome kid with his startling pale blue eyes
    (not to mention his pale hair) that seemed almost
    fluorescent not unlike fake blue contact lenses
    on a brown-eyed individual though we didn't know
    about contacts then
It was soon after Aunt Dorothy's husband Marty ran off with
    another woman that Aunt Dorothy started bleaching
    Freddy's hair
I remember how people would turn to stare at Freddy's platinum
    blond hair—sometimes with the darker roots growing in
Freddy was always a great athlete—even as a kid—
So there he would be at bat—hunched over, serious expression—
    platinum blond hair with dark roots showing
I don't know if kids teased him in school because my family
    and I made the trip only on Sundays to Brooklyn
    where my grandparents had an apartment a few blocks
    away from Aunt Dorothy and Freddy's tiny apartment
    but I know no one ever teased him on
    the neighborhood baseball lot; he was too respected a
    player

Sometimes his father would appear to take his only son,
        his only child to a Dodgers' game or swimming—
I never found out what his reaction was to his son's
        obvious bleach job
But it must have been hard on this navy veteran in
        the late 40s when male appearances
        were so rigidly defined
Perhaps it was my aunt's revenge on her husband who
        was living with some other woman
But I like to think Aunt Dorothy just wanted to hold
        on to something beautiful—
even if it were just hair

LAURA BOSS

Aunt Rose

As a little girl, I modeled myself after my Aunt Rose, not my mother. My Aunt Rose with her bright green high-heeled ankle-strapped shoes, her numerous bottles of perfumes, her dresser drawers filled with black silk lingerie. My mother wears sensible oxfords that she duplicates in child version for me; my mother teaches third graders, struggles with lesson plans and finances after suppers ending with canned fruit salad. My Aunt Rose is the hostess in a Manhattan theater district restaurant that her husband owns. (She met him when she was first working there.) She leads customers into a dining room with velvet chairs where they can have Nesselrode pie for dessert. She smells of Tabu and wears a large topaz ring. She has bleached platinum blond hair and is often mistaken for Ginger Rogers. She gives my photograph to a customer who is looking for a child actress; I lose to Margaret O'Brien. My aunt tells me I'm prettier. My aunt is charming and warm and diplomatic. My mother is critical—tells the truth though it hurts and you might not want to hear it. Years later, after my aunt's husband dies, she has a beau (a handsome lawyer) she travels to Europe with—at a time when such travels were considered avant-garde for single women. Men are always calling her up. She marries again—and after he dies, she still has at least five marriage proposals a year when she is in her sixties. Last week my mother tells me that to get to sleep my mother counts first, second and third cousins. She tells me my Aunt Rose gets to sleep by counting the men she's known. I always knew I took after my Aunt Rose.

LAURA BOSS

The Accordion

The day I came home to discover that Mamma had hocked my gold-and-white accordion was the same day I had decided, probably in a fit of confused sexuality, to practice for hours every day, until maybe I could get on *Ed Sullivan* or *Arthur Godfrey*, some new way to get rich and get out of the house on Trenton Avenue, away from my father's yelling in the night about money or work or me.

I had hated the accordion, hated the man who gave me lessons in a little cubicle at Corrie Music downtown Paterson. Most of the time, Pop dropped me off while he went and hung out with Uncle Marty Longo at the gas station, or sometimes he went down to the Buffalo Bar and Grill and talked with Rocco Bazzi about the numbers. Sometimes I took the bus and more often than not got vaguely sick from the smell of the fumes.

I wanted to be at the Paterson Public Library, where the smell of the old and musty books was exciting to me, like the smell of a parade, and where the librarians were mostly women who talked in soft tones, and had thoughtful-looking glasses, and whose hands, when they brushed mine as I checked out my books, felt soft, the kind of hands that used cold creme, or hand creme, which were magic words to me, never having used it, nor had my mother used it. Both of us had hands that were red, rough, and wrinkly looking, the hands of peasants working the fields in Sicily instead of packing meat at the A & P, which is what my mother did, or reading books or playing the accordion, which is what I did.

I was twelve when my mother hocked the accordion with its sparkly gold buttons. The C-button, with its smooth and pearly indentation, was what I missed most about it being gone. I remember that it was early spring, and as I walked the ten blocks home from school I could hear birds singing and I smelled the earth awakening. There was a boy named Rico with blazing eyes, and another, Mario, whom I had met at the Italian Social Club the Friday before. The following Sunday my mother made me take the accordion to my cousin Sammy's birthday party so I could play "Happy Birthday" while all the other cousins sang. "Happy Birthday" and "Drink to Me Only With Thine Eyes" were the only two songs I ever really learned to play.

I walked home thinking about Rico, Mario, and that little indented button on my accordion, and I guess I made the decision to put all my sexual feeling into making music, and walked into the house, my pants damp beneath the blue plaid skirt of St. Victory's School uniform. I could feel the wetness as I went to the closet to get the accordion.

Mamma looked at me funny the second I got in the house—I must have seemed so directed in my actions, walking in and heading straight for the closet. Usually I got something to eat, an orange or a peach, and talked to Mamma till it was time for *American Bandstand*. We always watched it together, and when it was over, Mamma would get up and get supper. This day I strode in full of purpose, and probably a little too passionate about the accordion, and Mamma's face took on a fearful kind of look, sort of like a bird or a small animal being threatened.

"Where's my accordion, Mamma?" The closet where I kept it had a big clean spot in the shape of the accordion case on the floor. "You haven't touch it in weeks," Mamma said, avoiding my eyes. "I know, but I'll be better from now on. Where is it?" I looked up at Mamma; she fidgeted with her pale blue housedress, ran her short rough fingers through her black hair.

She looked at me, her eyes nervous, and kind of sad too.

"It's gone, Maria."

"What do you mean, 'gone,' gone where? Did you loan it to Cousin Mickey?"

"I hocked it."

"What does that mean, Mamma?"

"It means I took it to a little store downtown to get some money to pay for your glasses."

"My accordion? Can we get it back?"

"Probably not. Don't tell your father."

Like I would. I had learned long ago there were certain things you didn't tell Pop; most things, in fact, because he had one of two reactions: scorn or rage. The night before I heard them having one of their whispered fights in the kitchen in the middle of the night. I heard the word "glasses" so I knew it was about me: The week before I had an argument with Pop, and he ended it with a backhand across my face, breaking my glasses. For the last few days I wore them taped across the bridge, but yesterday, Sister John Frances, the school nurse, called Mamma about them. I already hated her because once, in fourth grade, she asked everybody what they had for breakfast. I told her it depended on what we ate for supper the night before, a dish of macaroni, or maybe cabbage and noodles. Sometimes there was apple pie, and a lot of mornings we had Minute rice with butter and milk. The last two were my favorites. Sister John Frances came right to our house and talked to Mamma about our "eating habits." I remember Mamma's face as she listened to Sister John Frances; it looked sad and ashamed, the way it did today, when I asked her about the accordion.

In school today, Sister asked me how my new glasses were. "Fine," I had answered, proud that she saw them, new and untaped. Now, thinking about Sister, I wanted to punch her stomach, the soft part hidden under the brown habit.

I cried a little, thinking about the round little button, and the sparkling gold keys, and especially for Mamma having to hock one thing for another, and they both had to do with me. I could picture Mamma, by herself, lugging the huge, heavy accordion on the bus, walking into the store to get money for it, and coming back home, lighter but sadder somehow. I went outside in the small backyard where a few years earlier I tried to convince myself I had a religious call by seeing if I could fly off the sloped, tar-papered walls of the shed. I looked at it now and laughed: It was only three feet off the ground. I was glad that even as a little kid I hadn't wanted to risk such a short distance for any convent, any sacrifice that had to do with nuns like Sister John Frances.

Now I went off further back in the yard, where the tomatoes were staked, and sat for a second there, smelling them, before I got down on my hands and knees, still in my uniform, looking for something—some small, familiar indentation in the ground. I made one, a small pocket of earth near the tomatoes and basilico and scraped till I had it just the way I wanted it. I ran my middle finger over and over the small spot, chanting a kind of litany, promising I'd get the accordion back for Mamma, and for me. I swore I would someday get even with Sister John Frances. After about fifteen minutes, I stood up and felt holy, like a breeze of cleanliness had come up out of the little circle of earth I made, where my outrage was buried now, and where I could get back to it whenever I wanted to. I picked a handful of basilico and put it in my pocket, and on my way back inside I held my hands cupped under my nose, smelling the garden, the fresh Italian herb, the life I wanted.

I went back inside. It was Thursday, and we were having fusilli for supper. Mamma's sauce smelled good, familiar, like her smile after someone hurt my feelings. From my uniform pocket I took the handful of basilico I'd picked in the garden for Mamma to add to the sauce. I pushed my new glasses up on my sweat-shiny nose, and took two meatballs from the big pot, put them in one dish, got two forks from the silverware drawer. Then, Mamma and I went and watched them dance on *American Bandstand*, far away from accordions or hock shops, a place where people like Sister John Frances never went. But it was where Mamma and I went every day after I came home from school, knowing the dancing and the music belonged to us and nobody could shame either of us as we sat eating meatballs, side by side on the old mohair couch. There we held the scent of each other, like the little garden, between us, cupped in our hands and sacred.

RACHEL GUIDO DEVRIES

Uncle Earl and Guns

No one loved guns like Uncle Earl,
barrel-chested and eighty, too old for World War II.
He hated being alone, his mountain woods so quiet
he praised the wings of owls. His cabin was a mansion
of trophies, old heads of moose and rams,

four grizzlies he swore he killed with pistols.
He kept guns loaded for us, his summer nephews.
Mother warned us about his wandering
after Aunt Ethel's death in a car wreck,
his squandered fortune, his dozen jungle safaris.

But he told stories we wanted, wore bracelets of rattles,
a loop of fangs as an earring. Our mother frowned,
worried we'd follow, get shot and rot in a canyon.
He taught us to draw, that slap of leather
and wavering whine through a valley.

He taught us load and lock, how to survive
with only pistols and bedrolls, sipping bourbon
with Uncle Earl, his back to the campfire,
shouting, tossing rocks at the dark,
daring anything to strike.

WALT MCDONALD

Legacy

For the men in my family,
the rules were always easy:
quit school, marry young,
work in the steel mill, and die.

For thirty-eight years
my father poured steel
and hauled slag
without complaint,
dreaming of a life
without sweat or desire,
a heaven on earth
as sweet reward for his calluses,
the hard yellow hills
on my father's palms
I traced at night
with the still-soft tips
of my fingers.

But the wars that were fought
within him were lost,
and the glow of the blast furnace
seared a defeat
so permanent in his flesh
that where he walked
whole cities burned,
and when he died,
a child's life was forged.

CHRIS KENNEDY

The Politics of Buddy

I.
Buddy and I cruise the make-up
at Macys. I swipe a lipstick
tester across my mouth
Buddy does the same.
We try eyeshadow, mascara

two shades of blush
before a Macys matron
whose face would crack
a chisel shoos us away.
"Is it a crime for a boy
to wear make-up?" Buddy shouts
"Or is it a crime for a boy
to look so good in it?"

II.
Buddy and Guy saunter down the street
a few beats in front of me.
They do not touch
but their heads bent in boytalk
is enough to slow a car.
Ugly faces leer
"Hey, faggots," "Hey sissy boy,"
"Hey, you goddamn queers."
Buddy yells back, "We're homos.
We're as healthy as the milk you drink,"
then slaps a fat, juicy
kiss on Guy's lips
that no one could possibly argue with.

III.
I take Buddy to Gay Pride
wheeling him carefully through the streets.
A woman bounces up to us
"Where's your red ribbon?" she asks,
fishing out her supply.
Buddy says no thanks
and when she insists he pricks
his thumb with her safety pin.
A thin trickle of blood
oozes down his skin.
"Here's my ribbon.
Is it red enough for you?"
Buddy holds his fist high as I wheel him away.

LESLÉA NEWMAN

"You know what I'm saying?"

I was shy and tender as a 10 year old kid, you know what I'm
     saying?
Afraid people'd find me out in Eastside H. S. locker room you
     know what I'm saying?
Earl had beautiful hips & biceps when he took off his clothes to
     put on gym shorts you know what I'm saying?
His nose was too long, his face like a ferret but his white body
Proportioned thin, muscular definition thighs & breasts, with
     boy's nipples you know what I'm saying? uncircumsized
& strange, goyishe beauty you know what I'm saying, I was
     dumbstruck—
at Golden 50th H.S. Reunion I recognized him, bowed, &
     exchanged pleasant words, you know what I'm saying?
He was retired, wife on his arm, you know what I'm saying?
& Millie Peller "The Class Whore" warmest woman at our last
     Silver 25th Reunion alas had passed away
She was nice to me a scared gay kid at Eastside High, you know
     what I'm saying?

ALLEN GINSBERG

The Robe

Mama and her sisters
were dancing in the living room,
cackling, bending the floor.
I was downstairs in the tub,
scrubbing my knees with Ajax,
wondering where the black
came from, where it went.
I was afraid to cross
the living room sea of women
with their party, afraid of what
I did not know of women,
their delight in measuring
the sex of naked little boys.
They prophesied a boy's

potential to please a woman
by studying hairless pricks.
Afraid more of being late for bed
than of being seen, I put on
my yellow robe. I wrapped myself
like a fireman about to enter
a burning building, and I climbed
the stairs where my mother
stood with her mischievous smile.
I walked into this room of women
who loved me, and my mother
pulled off my robe for all to see
what kind of man I could be.
Shame cut me like a cleaver.
Once in a nightmare, I saw
my mother at the top of the stairs,
face raging, hair full like Medusa,
daring me to climb, daring me.

AFAA M. WEAVER

Acupuncture and Cleansing at Forty-eight

No longer eating meat or dairy
      products or refined sugar,
I lie on the acupuncturist's
      mat stuck with twenty
needles and know a little how
Saint Sebastian felt with those
      arrows
piercing him all over, his poster
tacked to the wall before my fourth-
      grade desk
as I bent over the addition and loss,
tried to find and name the five oceans,
      seven continents,
drops of blood with small windows of
      light strung
from each of his wounds, blood like
the blood on my mother's pad the day
      she hung

it before my face and said I was making
    her bleed to death,
blood like my brother's that day
he hung from the spiked barb
at the top of the fence,
a railroad track of stitches gleaming
for years on the soft inside of his arm,
blood like today when Dr. Ming extracts
    a needle and dabs
a speck of red away, one from my eyelid,
    one from my cheek,
the needles trying to open my channels
    of *chi*,
so I can sleep at night without choking,
so I don't have to fear waking my wife
    hawking the hardened mucus out,
so I don't have to lie there thinking
of those I hate, of those who have died,
    the needles
tapped into the kidney point, where
    memories reside,
tapped into the liver point, where
    poisons collect,
into the feet and hands, the three
    chakra of the chest
that split the body in half, my right
    healthy, my left in pain,
my old friend's betrayal lumped in my
    neck,
my old love walking away thirty years
    ago
stuck in my lower back, father's death
    mother's
lovelessness lodged in so many parts
it may take years, Dr. Ming whispers,
    to wash them out,
telling me to breathe deep, to breathe
    hard,
the body is nothing but a map of the
    heart.

LEN ROBERTS

VIII. ~

BEYOND DICK AND JANE

I am proud of my mother

all dressed in black,

proud of my father

with his broken tongue,

proud of the laughter

and the noise of our house.

Garden State

It used to be, farms,
stone houses on green lawns
a wooded hill to play Jungle Camp

asphalt roads thru Lincoln Park
The communists picnicked
amid spring's yellow forsythia
magnolia trees & apple blossoms, pale buds
breezy May, blue June.

Then came the mafia, alcohol
highways, garbage dumped in marshes, real
estate, World War II, money
flowed thru Nutley, bulldozers.

Einstein invented atom bombs
In Princeton, television antennae
sprung over West Orange—lobotomies
performed in Greystone State Hospital.

Old graveyards behind churches
on grassy knolls, Erie Railroad
bridges' Checkerboard underpass
signs, paint fading, remain.

Reminds me of a time pond's pure
water was green, drink or swim.
Traprock quarries embedded
with amethyst, quiet on Sunday.

I was afraid to talk to anyone
in Paterson, lest my sensitivity
to sex, music, the universe, be discovered &
I be laughed at, hit by colored boys.

"Mr. Professor" said the Dutchman
on Haledon Ave. "Stinky Jew" said
my friend black Joe, kinky haired.
Oldsmobiles past in front of my eyeglasses.

Greenhouses stood by the Passaic in the sun,
little cottages in Belmar by the sea.
I heard Hitler's voice on the radio.
I used to live on that hill up there.

They threw eggs at Norman Thomas the Socialist speaker
in Newark Military Park, the police
stood by & laughed. Used to murder
silk strikers on Mill St. in the twenties.

Now turn on your boob tube
They explain away the Harrisburg
hydrogen bubble, the Vietnam war,
They haven't reported the end of Jersey's gardens,

much less the end of the world.
Here in Boonton they made cannonballs
for Washington, had old iron mines,
spillways, coach houses—Trolleycars

ran thru Newark, gardeners dug front lawns.
Look for the News in your own backyard
over the whitewashed picket fence, fading sights
on upper stories of red brick factories.

The Data Terminal people stand on Route 40
now. Let's get our stuff together. Let's
go back Sundays & sing old springtime music
on Greystone State Mental Hospital Lawn.

ALLEN GINSBERG

Thelonious

for Laurie Schmidt

It's as if you are given the sky to carry,
lift it on your shoulders and take it to lunch,
sit in McDonald's with it weighing you down,
this business of being black, of staying black
until the darkness of some eternity kisses you.
Birth gives you something other folk thank
God for not having, or else they pray for it,

to have its gift of a body inclined to touch,
inclined to sing. Yet they will not give back
to God the paleness of being able to touch
absolute power. They envy only for so long,
as being black is being bound to danger.

Among us there are masters like Monk,
who understood the left hand stride
on a brick. In his rapturous dance beside
the piano, he was connected to silence.
He danced the disconnected steps to knowing
the scratch and slide of the shoes leaving
the ground, the shoes of the lynched men.
He carried this thing that we are,
as the mystic he was, reveling in its magic,
respectful of its anger, mute and unchanged
at the hate and envy surrounding us.

One day we learn there is no sky above
this trapped air around the earth.
The sky is but a puff of smoke from
this giant head smoking a Lucky Strike,
pretending not to know the truths.
We learn sometimes in this life,
sometimes in what comes after, where
there is really nothing but everything
we never knew. We learn in silence
the dance Monk knew. We find
secrets for pulling the million arrows
from our souls each time we move
to sleep, to forget that we are both
jewel and jetsam, wanted and unforgiven.

AFAA M. WEAVER

Robin's Nest

Mr. Rosen, my social studies teacher, is standing in front of the
blackboard and talking about the Vietnam War, which took place
in the nineteen sixties. Mr. Rosen is my favorite teacher this year.
For one thing, he has a red mustache, and I've loved red hair ever
since I was a little girl. Robin, my mother, has red hair. But Mr.

Rosen talks a lot, really fast, and Robin doesn't talk at all. Ever.

Mr. Rosen's hair isn't as beautiful as Robin's, though. Nobody has hair that beautiful. And I bet that if Robin could speak, her voice would be beautiful, too.

Ambrose, my boyfriend, also has red hair. Ambrose is in the sixth grade, like I am, but he goes to the Emerson School, which my dad says is too unstructured. I go to the Smythe-Durham School, which is very structured. I also like Mr. Rosen because he used to teach at the Emerson School, but I've never told my dad that. Right now, Mr. Rosen is saying that innocent people, even women and children, were killed during the war. I try to take notes while he speaks. But it's hard because I keep picturing the women and children, and they all start to look like me and Robin, and then I can't concentrate on his words. But I have to concentrate so that I can pass. I've been failing English since last year, and if I start to fail social studies too I don't know what my dad will do. It makes me nervous just thinking about it. So I start writing really fast, trying to copy down everything Mr. Rosen is saying. "President Johnson," I write down. "Amnesty for draft resisters," I write that down, too, but I'm not sure I know what amnesty means. Mr. Rosen must have said, but I guess I wasn't concentrating. Amnesty is a pretty word, though. I like the way it sounds. Maybe Ambrose and I can use it in Ooola, which is the private language he and I are inventing. Nobody in the whole world will know how to speak Ooola except me and Ambrose. But I can't think about Ooola now. I have to pay attention. Mr. Rosen is saying something about the draft resisters having to move to Canada. I know that my dad didn't like the draft resisters. My dad was an officer in the Marines in Vietnam, and he says that he lost close friends there, and that he and his friends were patriots, and that it was a good war. In Ooola, patriot means cappuccino. My dad says that the people who protested against the war were so self-indulgent and immature that they thought sex and rock 'n' roll were more important than freedom and honor. Or else they were crazy. He says that history will prove him right. Robin was a war protestor. Mr. Rosen is saying that he was a war protestor, too. "War protestor," I write down. I wonder if Robin and Mr. Rosen used to know each other during the nineteen sixties. Maybe Mr. Rosen even lived on Robin's commune with her.

Another thing I like about Mr. Rosen is that he talks about things I care about. For instance, last week he talked about the people in America who are so poor they have to live out on the streets, and how they get malnourished and freeze to death and other terrible stuff. He calls them "the homeless." I see them, these homeless people, every day, when I walk through the park on my way to and from Smythe-Durham. Sometimes I even see homeless mothers with homeless children. I shiver when I see them. My dad forbids me to give them dimes or quarters or anything. He says it could be dangerous because they're crazy. But I don't think most of them are crazy. And even the ones who are deserve some dimes and quarters. But Ambrose's father, who's a plastic surgeon like my dad, says that it's good to give them dimes and quarters, so Ambrose gives for both of us. Robin never carries money, but one day last winter, she and I were walking in the park and we passed a homeless woman who was only half dressed. Robin was wearing a big baggy black coat. She took it off and gave it to the woman. I bet my dad wouldn't have liked that if he'd been with us.

The bell rings. I close my notebook. Mr. Rosen says that the only homework we have tonight is to think about whether it's okay to disagree with your government. Or with your parents. He smiles. He has a nice smile.

Next I have my session with Ms. Ullman, the psychologist at Smythe-Durham. Last year when I started failing English, the headmaster, Dr. Prescott, who has almost no hair at all, called me into his office, which was filled with ships in bottles. He said, "Your reading scores are extremely high, young lady. You shouldn't be failing English." I didn't say anything. So he said that he was going to send me to see Ms. Ullman. He said my dad had called him and was very unhappy that I wasn't passing English. And he said he didn't want my dad to be unhappy.

I knock on Ms. Ullman's door and she says, "Come in, Rachel." Ms. Ullman's office is nice, much nicer than Dr. Prescott's office, and I like sitting in the big brown leather chair across from her. Above her desk there's a painting of a big red bird sitting on the branch of a tree. I once asked Ms. Ullman if the bird was a robin, and she said she didn't think so. She said it was more like a bird painted from the artist's imagination. I like to look up at the red bird when we talk because that bird's eyes are big and sad, like Robin's.

Ms. Ullman and I talk a lot about birds, because when I was little I used to think that Robin wasn't really my mother, but that she was some strange bird that had flown into our apartment. I figured that she had a broken wing and couldn't fly home. Sometimes I thought that she was a lost bird from another planet.

The thing is, Robin really does look more like a bird than a mother. At least, she doesn't look like the mothers of the other kids I know. And she doesn't act like them, either. Ambrose's mother, for example, is tall and she wears high heeled shoes which make her look taller and blouses with padded shoulders and she talks all the time. But Robin is very small, and she wears simple dresses that just slip over her head, and flat sandals. And she's always looking over her shoulder, like birds do. And she has those big sad bird eyes. Even sadder than the eyes of the real bird on Ms. Ullman's wall. And she has long hair that goes way past her waist, so that sometimes it looks like bright red feathers are growing down her back. Ms. Ullman thinks it's good that I've accepted that Robin really is my mother, and not a bird.

Ms. Ullman and I also talk a lot about my dad. My dad does nose jobs and face lifts and tummy tucks and breast enlargements. Sometimes he calls himself a "sculptor." He also calls himself "Pygmalion," which Ambrose says is the title of a play about a rich man who wants to make a poor woman act rich. Most of my dad's patients are women. They come from all over the world, he says, "because I speak their language, Rachel. They all want to be beautiful, and I speak the language of beauty." Sometimes he tells me and Robin stories about his patients, like the woman who had a nose like Jimmy Durante's, but wanted a nose like Marilyn Monroe's, or the woman who was flat-chested and had never had a boyfriend but after my dad gave her bigger breasts she had two boyfriends. "I gave her perfect breasts," he said, looking right at Robin who has really tiny breasts, almost no breasts at all, and what she has she hides completely underneath baggy dresses. Robin looks over her shoulder when he says things like that. But I say, "Really, Daddy?" and "Wow, Daddy," because I'm too scared not to act excited about his work. I'm scared that when I grow up he's going to want to do those jobs on me, too. Ambrose says I shouldn't be scared, that he won't let him. But I don't know. I'm afraid that if I don't grow up to be beautiful enough, he'll start sculpting me.

Since Ms. Ullman encourages me to talk to her about my fears, I've told her that lately I've noticed that my nose is starting to grow. "It's not a tiny pug nose anymore like it was when I was little, and I'm afraid my dad will notice it soon," I say.

"You have a lovely nose, Rachel," Ms. Ullman says. "Honestly."

I don't ever want my dad to meet Ms. Ullman. I'm afraid he'll want to do something to her nose, too. Ms. Ullman has short frizzy brown hair, but sometimes, when the sun shines through her office window, her hair looks almost red. And she has big thick eyebrows and a long hooked nose with a bump on it. Ambrose met her one Saturday morning when he and I were sitting on a bench in the park, practicing Ooola and counting out change to give to homeless people. Ms. Ullman walked by. She looked different in blue jeans and a sweatshirt. She came over and said, "How nice, that you both care so much about the less fortunate." "She's intense looking," Ambrose said after she left. But I don't think my dad would find intense beautiful.

The very first thing Ms. Ullman ever said to me during our very first session was, "So I hear you're having some trouble in your English class." But I just shrugged. I didn't want to talk about English class. I looked up at the painting of the red bird. "Is it okay if we forget the English class stuff today?" I asked. "Can I tell you something else instead?"

She didn't answer right away. And then she gave me a big smile and said, "Shoot!" So I took a deep breath, and I told her the story of how my dad met Robin and why Robin doesn't ever speak. I told it exactly the way my dad tells it to me. "Robin was in a hospital because she'd taken all this LSD during the nineteen sixties and it had made her stop speaking," I said. Ms. Ullman began taking notes. "My dad says that LSD is a drug that makes you see the world as though you're crazy. It ruins your mind like a . . ." But I had to stop there because my dad always says, "like a bump and a hook ruin a nose," and I didn't want to repeat that in front of Ms. Ullman. So I just said, "Anyway Robin had taken a lot of it. My dad was working in the hospital. He says that from the first moment he saw her, sitting on top of her bed in her hospital gown, staring over her shoulder, he knew what he wanted. 'I wanted to take her home, Rachel,' he says. 'To heal her, to make her whole again. I saw that there was something special about her. Her suffering had enriched her. It was my duty. I would be a plastic surgeon of the mind. Instead of a nose job, I would give your mother a mind job.' "

Ms. Ullman looked up from her notes. "A mind job?" she asked. "Those are your father's words?"

I nodded.

"Did he . . . smile when he said it?" she asked.

I shrugged. "I can't remember."

"Well . . . just what is a . . . mind job?"

"I'm not sure," I said. "I think he . . . talked to her a lot. About the things he wanted her to believe in. Things that would make her less crazy. Things for her . . . own good."

Ms. Ullman took a wrinkled handkerchief from her desk and blew her nose.

"Anyway, he took her home and married her. And he gave her the mind job. And then they had me." I didn't say anything else because I wasn't sure what else to say. That's where my dad always stops when he tells the story.

"A mind job," Ms. Ullman said again. She was writing really fast now.

"I'm afraid," I said.

"Afraid, Rachel?" Ms. Ullman put down her pen and leaned forward and looked into my eyes. "What are you afraid of?"

"I'm afraid that a mind job hurts."

"Oh," she said. "Well, has Robin . . . gotten better?"

"My dad says yes," I said. "He says that even though she doesn't speak she's not crazy or unhappy anymore and that she believes in all the right things and that she would never do the kinds of things she used to do like protest against the Vietnam War and take drugs and live in a commune and dance naked at hippie festivals and not buy from the military-industrial complex and not give money to taxes because the money is spent on weapons and things like that. . . ."

"And what do you think?"

"I don't know." And then I told her that when I used to think Robin was a bird from another planet I also believed that she was really speaking all the time, but that people on earth just couldn't hear her because her language was on a higher frequency than earth ears could hear. "Even though she doesn't say so, I know Robin loves me," I explained to Ms. Ullman. I told her that Robin takes me on long walks through the park and that when I have a fever she sits by my bedside for hours and holds my hand and puts wet towels on my forehead, and that she sometimes sits with me and Ambrose and we all eat tuna fish sandwiches together. Ms. Ullman said that Robin sounded like a very caring person, and I felt happy when she said that.

Sometimes Ms. Ullman doesn't say anything at the beginning of the session. She just lets me start talking about anything I want to. But other times she starts by asking me a question, and today the first thing she asks me to do is describe our apartment. "I'd like to have a sense of your home," she says. "Tell me about it, Rachel."

"It's very big," I tell her. "My dad has a bedroom and a study, and Robin and I each have a bedroom, and there's a living room and a kitchen and a dining room. And last year my dad put this white furniture all over the place. It's kind of like a hospital now, and he doesn't like it if there's the slightest bit of dirt on anything."

Ms. Ullman waits for me to say something else. But I don't have anything else to say about the white furniture.

"Any other thoughts about your home?" Ms. Ullman runs her hand through her frizzy hair.

So I tell her about how one day I told my dad that I felt guilty about how big our apartment was, because there are so many home-less people. I said maybe we had more than our fair share of space. He said that I shouldn't feel guilty, that most of the homeless people wouldn't know how to survive in an apartment building like ours anyway, that they wouldn't want the responsibilities of mortgages and coop board meetings and things like that, and that chopping a bedroom or two off of our apartment wouldn't solve the home-less problem. Ms. Ullman asks, "Did he smile when he said those things?" But I shrug. "I can't remember."

Then Ms. Ullman says, "You're a very caring girl, Rachel."

I'm glad that Ms. Ullman thinks I'm a caring girl. I also hope she thinks I'm pretty just the way I am. Sometimes my dad takes my face in his hands and looks at it from different angles and I get very scared.

"So," Ms. Ullman says, leaning back, "how's Ooola going?" Ms. Ullman asks me about Ooola a lot during our sessions. After I'd had a few sessions with her, I told her about it because I knew I could trust her. I told her that sometimes Ambrose and I invent brand new words to mean things, words which sound like nonsense to anyone else. And that other times we take words that already mean something in English but we make them mean something else, which is just as good as inventing a new word, and that we're going to have a whole Ooola dictionary some day which only we'll know how to read. And a grammar handbook, too.

"Ambrose found the word ablutions in the dictionary yesterday," I tell her. "It means a ceremonial washing of oneself." Ms. Ullman may know this already, but I can't be sure. "But in Ooola, it's going to mean sad." Sometimes I tell Ms. Ullman a few words in Ooola. Ambrose says it's okay, because even if I tell her a few words, she still won't know enough to speak it. "Today after school Ambrose and I are going to invent words for colors," I tell her. "Last week we invented words for the seasons. Cratoup means winter."

"Cratoup," she repeats, blowing her nose.

She puts away her handkerchief and looks serious for a minute. "Maybe, Rachel," she says softly, "the reason you're inventing Ooola has something to do with the reason you're not passing English. What do you think of the idea?"

I don't say anything. Ms. Ullman comes up with weird ideas like this all the time.

"Well, I'm afraid that our time is up for today," Ms. Ullman says, looking at her watch.

"Arugula," I say to her, which is Ooola for goodbye.

"Arugula," she says.

My next class is English. I dread it. This year I was put in a slow class, even though Dr. Prescott said my reading scores are so high. It's a punishment for failing, I guess. Ms. Buschel is my English teacher. She's got blonde hair and a tiny nose. She's the type, I think, that my dad has in mind when he fixes noses. I always sit in the back of the room, hoping that she won't remember I'm there. Today she tells us to write, stories about anything we want. I wish I could write my story in Ooola. But if I did that I'd be afraid Ms. Buschel would show it to Dr. Prescott and then they'd send me to a hospital like Robin was in. And then my dad would definitely want to do a mind job on me. I force myself to pick up my pen and write.

Ms. Buschel says, "Okay, that's enough writing time. Now we'll call on a few of you to share your stories. How about Carl first?" Carl walks to the front of the room. He licks his lips. His story is about a little boy who wants a donkey for Christmas more than anything else in the world, and then on Christmas morning Santa Claus gives him one. Everyone applauds. Ms. Buschel says, "Okay, everyone, let's give Carl some feedback." Annie raises her hand and says, "It made me feel good that he got the donkey." "Very perceptive, Annie. And thank you, Carl, for sharing your story," Ms. Buschel smiles.

I pray that Ms. Buschel doesn't call on me next. "Nancy," she says. Nancy walks to the front of the room. She holds the paper right in front of her face while she reads. Her story is about a little girl who wins a pie baking contest and starts a pie business and becomes a millionaire. Everyone applauds. Ms. Buschel asks for feedback. "It's good because she succeeds," Nicky says. "Very insightful, Nicky. And thank you, Nancy, for sharing that," Ms. Buschel says.

I pray again that Ms. Buschel doesn't call on me. But this time

I'm not so lucky. "Rachel," she says. I walk to the front of the room. I clear my throat and read. "There was a little girl whose mother was a beautiful silent bird from another planet. The little girl's father said the little girl's mother was crazy. So he gave her mother something he called a mind job. But a mind job hurts. It pushes words down into your brain. So the little girl started to speak a special, secret language that nobody else would understand. That way nobody could ever give her a mind job." Nobody applauds. Nobody gives feedback. Ms. Buschel doesn't thank me for sharing my story. So I sit down and some other students get up and read their stories, but I don't pay any attention. Instead, I think about what amnesty could mean in Ooola and about Ambrose and Robin and the red bird on Ms. Ullman's wall.

English is the last class of the day, and when the bell rings, I race out. Ambrose is waiting for me on the corner. "Mubbles," I say to him, which means hello in Ooola. "Mubbles, Rachel," he says.

I met Ambrose last year when my dad was giving a speech about a new technique in nose jobs. It was a whole afternoon of plastic surgeons speaking about cutting and pulling and bending. I went because it seemed like a way for me to act really interested in my dad's work. I was sitting by myself in the front row. I was the only kid in the whole auditorium. But then Ambrose came in. He sat down right next to me. He pointed towards the doctors sitting on stage waiting for their turns to speak. "That one's mine," he pointed to a roly-poly, red-headed man on the left side of the stage. "Which one's yours?"

Ambrose's father is really different than my dad. His father mostly works on people who've been burned in fires or injured in accidents. He tries to make them look the way they looked before they got hurt.

I fell in love with Ambrose the instant he sat down next to me. He says that he fell in love with me right then too. He says that unconsciously we'd already begun communicating with each other in Ooola. I was nervous about what Ambrose would say the first time I brought him home and introduced him to Robin, but he didn't blink an eye. He's very sensitive. He writes love poems to me in both English and Ooola. He's even asthmatic, which makes me love him more. Because I know he needs taking care of.

Ambrose takes my hand as we walk across the park. The Smythe-Durham School is on the east side of the park, and I live on the west side. I'm glad because that way we get to walk through the park every day and Ambrose can give quarters and dimes to the homeless people who live in the grass and trees. Sometimes he drops the money into their cups, sometimes right into the palms of their hands. Some of them say "God bless you." Some of them say, "Hey, Carrot Top." And some of them don't say anything. I wonder if the ones who don't say anything are really speaking to us in a language on another frequency.

When we get to my building, the doorman, Billy, who likes Ambrose, gives him a special handshake. "It's from the nineteen sixties," Billy says. "It's called a power-to-the-people shake." Ambrose and I give power-to-the-people shakes to each other in the elevator on the way upstairs. I wonder if Robin used to shake hands like that before she took too much LSD. In the elevator, Ambrose also gives me a little kiss right on the tip of my nose, which I'm sure he does because I told him that it's growing. "Swampy," I say to him, which means thank you in Ooola.

We walk inside the apartment. The first thing I always do is look around for Robin. When I was little I used to look around because I was worried that she'd flown away while I was gone, but now I do it just because I like to. But I don't see her, so I figure she's in her bedroom. Ambrose and I go into the kitchen and make tuna fish sandwiches. I like mine with more onions than he does and he likes his with more mayonnaise. What we both like is to make them thick, with lots of lettuce and tomatoes crammed in. And we both like them on hard rolls with seeds. My dad disapproves of the way I eat. He tells me I'm not too young to start counting calories. But since he won't be home until much later, I stuff my sandwich to the limit.

Then Ambrose and I pour ourselves some cherry seltzer, which is my favorite flavor, and we go into the living room and get ready to work on inventing words for colors. We sit on the rug, and we surround ourselves with all of my dad's dictionaries and thesauruses. We even take his medical dictionaries out and use words from them. For instance, in Ooola, Cortisone means dinnertime, and Tetracycline means helicopter. We have to be very careful not to get tuna fish on the white rug.

Robin wanders in. I'm happy to see her. I smile at her. She's wearing a baggy light blue dress. She takes tiny bird steps. She smiles back at us and wanders past us into the kitchen.

Ambrose says, "How about sponge for blue?"

I try it out. "Robin is dressed in sponge today."

"Now I'm not sure," Ambrose says. "Did that sound right to you?"

"Well, let's think about the meaning of blue." That's how we work. We think about what words mean to us. I once explained our method to Ms. Ullman and she told me that what we do is called free associating.

I begin. "The sky."

"The sea," Ambrose says.

I say, "My dad says that women with blue eyes get the most upset if their noses are big because they feel gypped, like since they got the blue eyes they should have also gotten the tiny noses."

"Bluefish," Ambrose says.

"My dad says that the blue in the black and blue marks that women get on their skin after face lifts is a unique shade of blue, not found anywhere else."

"Singin' the blues," Ambrose says.

Robin comes in from the kitchen and sits down with us. She tucks her legs under her dress. She's made herself a tuna fish sandwich too. She hardly uses any mayonnaise or onions at all, and her sandwich is much thinner than ours. Ambrose and I take big bites of our sandwiches. Robin takes tiny bird-sized bites. I want to say something to her but I don't know what to say. When I was little I used to say things like, "Pretty bird, fly." But now I'm usually just quiet around her. What I want to say most of all is that I hope it didn't hurt much when my dad gave her the mind job. I believe that my dad wouldn't hurt her deliberately. I believe that he loves her too. But he has this saying that he uses a lot, "The end justifies the means." Ms. Ullman says if I want to ask Robin about the mind job, maybe I should just come out and ask.

"Listen," I say to Ambrose instead, "I think I like sponge for blue."

Ambrose smiles. He has these wonderful crooked teeth that braces just don't seem to help. "I get the sponges most every night," he says.

Robin takes a sip from my glass of cherry seltzer. And then she clears her throat. It's a tiny sound. Ambrose and I both stare at her. I've never heard any noise come from her throat before. Robin turns away from us and looks over her shoulder. Then she turns back and takes another sip of seltzer. She clears her throat again. Ambrose takes my hand. I hold onto his hand for dear life. We keep staring at her.

"Children," Robin says.

I hear it clearly. It's the first word Robin has ever spoken to me. Her voice is soft and sad. It's the voice that birds really would speak in if they could, I'm sure.

"Children," Robin says again.

I can't say a word. I look at Ambrose. He's having trouble breathing. I'm afraid he's going to have an asthma attack and I won't be able to take care of him because I'm in a state of shock. But luckily Ambrose calms down. He takes deep breaths and counts to ten. He begins breathing normally again and color returns to his face. And he actually answers her, like he's just having a regular conversation with anyone. "Uh huh?" he asks.

Robin looks over her shoulder and then back at us. I'm sure she won't answer. Maybe someone put LSD into our tuna fish sand-wiches and Robin never spoke at all. Maybe we just imagined her voice. But I'm wrong. She answers. She speaks very slowly. She stops between words. She looks as though she's concentrating and working very hard on speaking. "Children. I know that . . . you are inventing . . . new words . . . A new . . . language."

"Mother," I say, finally, putting down my sandwich, "why haven't you spoken all these years?" My hand in Ambrose's is all sweaty. I feel like a very very little girl, much younger than eleven. I also feel like an old woman, maybe a hundred years old. I can't believe that I'm asking her this and that she's going to answer me.

Robin waits a minute before speaking. This time her words come more quickly. She's not stumbling so much. "I chose not to speak. It was my own choice. I'd grown very sad. But now . . . I speak because I'm so very pleased . . . that you care so much, Rachel . . . the way I did."

I don't say anything for a minute, I feel so surprised. All these years Robin could have talked, but she didn't want to because she was sad. I remember a word my dad used once. "Disillusioned," he said. "Your mother, Rachel, had grown disillusioned." I keep staring at Robin and I start to feel very sad, myself. I don't like the sound of the word disillusioned. I don't want to include it in Ooola.

Ambrose squeezes my hand and says, "It's spaghetti." Spaghetti means okay in Ooola. I squeeze his hand back. And then I take Robin's hand and I squeeze it, too. She squeezes back. She holds my hand tight.

And I think that maybe Ambrose and I don't need to keep Ooola a secret from everyone. Maybe it would be wonderful if one day

everyone in the whole world spoke only Ooola. And there wouldn't
be any words in Ooola for homelessness or crime or prisons or wars
or mind jobs and nobody would want a different skin color or a
smaller nose or larger breasts. Everyone would feel fine just the
way they were. And Robin would talk all the time, because she
wouldn't be disillusioned, and my dad would only do plastic surgery
on people who'd been injured. Even though Robin didn't know
about Ooola during the nineteen sixties, I guess that was the way
she wanted it too. But she failed. At least, she thought she failed.
But maybe what she's saying now is that, because of me, she hasn't
really failed.

I feel shy and I look at Ambrose. Ambrose says, "It's spaghetti."

JANICE EIDUS

Real Life

Then, I went to school to
get through, get a husband,
get on with real life.

Since then, I slapped my two-
year-old so hard, broke his arm.
He wouldn't eat eggs.

Watched white shoes wheel my mother
past me into the emergency room
her skin winter sky gray
drowned in her body's fluid

Laughed at my husband doing stretching
exercises on the green hall rug
Watched him jog on the grass by the river
until one day he didn't come back

Measured urine
Refused my father a glass of water
Watched him cry from thirst

Sold the bed I was conceived in
for twenty-five dollars

Now, at school again, I see the
sunset from my towered window
Apricot, mauve, violet, cerise. Nice.
We discuss language. Argue about words. Nice.

MARY ANN MANNINO

Jetties Were the Bridges I Crossed

for Solomon & Maria Mercado

I.

The Atlantic City Steeplechase Pier
Was the playground I ran in,
Scaled roller coasters as far as my eye could climb
Peered into deep mysterious seas

Sand mounds were the backyard
In which I dreamt,
Converted them to hills of snow
The ocean rolled up to meet

Jetties were the bridges I crossed
Dark-green and black
Majestic beyond their smoky veil of ocean mist

> *I was often afraid*
> *For my father who braved them in winter*
> *Sitting at their very edge*
> *Fishing for hours and for years*
> *His solitary tiny figure far off—*

The Boardwalk
Was the unfinished hardwood floors of my home
Where I strolled for hours with Mother
Amid giant giraffes and
Clouds of cotton candy overhead

II.

In Massachusetts Avenue school
My hours were spent
In daydreams of Puerto Rico
Of sparkling turquoise oceans

Waves rolling up
To my second floor window

In Massachusetts Avenue School
As I gazed at the
Snowy sidewalk below,
Mr. Grant my middle-aged white teacher
Bellowed into my ear
Smashing it to pieces
Fourth graders made easy targets
Little brown pegs hobbling
Around concrete school yards
Speaking Spanish to each other

I washed Mr. Grant's blackboards
Thinking this would buy my escape
But I could not wash away
My self
I could not wash away
My family

III.

*(En mi casa toman El Pico)**

The kitchen was the hub
From which all toil
And a splash of ignorance
Generated good memories
For the years to come

Spanish spilled over
Turkey preparations,
Chicarron & plantano stuffing
And adobo spices
Brought the Pilgrims' bird
Closer to the swine
Puerto Ricans preferred
On such occasions

* In my house we drink El Pico

My brother holed up in his room for hours
Played rock & roll
The lyrics danced inside my brain all night
Iron Butterfly,
Jimi Hendrix,
The Doors
Dance with me
'Til this day.

NANCY MERCADO

Rock'n'Roll

I've thought
About the many nights
Of rock'n'roll I've spent
In my youth—
Hard-core.

My grandmother taught me
How to rock.
She hummed Elvis
While she hemmed my pants.
She liked Elvis.
She liked him so much
That she bought me
A black leather jacket
With zippers and a motorcycle hat
Like Marlon Brando's.
That really pissed Mrs. Taylor off!
She kicked me out of first grade.
She said I would be a bad influence
On all the other kids.

I didn't like those snotty-nosed kids anyway.
They couldn't rock
Like Grandma.

M. L. LIEBLER

Sally

I was never much one for artificial trees, but my stepmother bought one once. It was aluminum and small enough to fit on her stereo. It had a snow-sprayed, cardboard color wheel with red, green, blue, and yellow cellophane and rotated when plugged in. She had her reasons for buying it: her apartment was too small and on the second floor; her two boys had moved out years ago; it was cheaper, no expensive decorations; easier to store for next year, and durable. Also, she did not have to struggle with putting it up, decorating it, and taking it down when January showed its new face. These were all sound reasons, and I could not begrudge her for them. My stepmother thought it was a beautiful tree. Secretly, though, I named the tree "Disco Tree" because of its rotating color wheel which cast spinning, colored lights on the ceiling, creating a disco-like effect.

Once while visiting my stepmother before the holidays, she fell asleep on the couch watching (for the twentieth time) the uncolorized, 1947 version of *Miracle on 34th Street*. I covered her with an afghan, turned off the TV, and stared at the aluminum tree. Its silvery strips were moving up and down in a current of warm air which rose from the heating vent. As the color wheel rotated, the whole room took on the lighting of a dance floor with baubles of light like planets circling ceiling and walls.

My stepmother loved to go to dances in starlit ballrooms, and even into her late sixties could outshine many twenty-year-olds. She was 5'1", quite busty and hippy—a body, it seemed, more suited to watching TV—but once out on the dance floor, smiling and singing along with the song, she was light and graceful. Her body energized transmitting that spirit to almost everyone she danced with, young and old.

Her father used to take her to weddings when she was four or five. She would dance for the bride and groom who would clear a table for her. The people would throw pennies, and her father would keep the pennies in a bag for her to buy Christmas gifts. She had five sisters and three brothers and loved children. She taught her brothers steps to different dances and how to lead a partner. Before her father came home from work, she would teach her younger sisters, who would beg, "Balla, balla con mia!" (Dance, dance with me!) In the twenties, she would Charleston, shimmy, flea hop, and Chicago. In the sixties, she would cha-cha, tango, lindy, and twist. She would crash parties and weddings, mingle with the guests, pluck the wallflowers from their walls and have them dancing and enjoying it. "I had a ball," she would say, fanning herself. She would dance with men, other women, children, or even by herself to the music on a jukebox. "Dancing is my life," she would say.

Once when my father was making his eggs, a song she liked played on the radio. She turned up the volume, turned off the burner, grabbed my father and said, "Let's cut a rug, kid."

He muttered, "Cheeze, Sally, you're crazy!" but a minute later, he was smiling and dancing the lindy as the pans on the kitchen shelf rattled.

My stepmother has arthritis now and doesn't dance much anymore at seventy-nine years old. Over the years, she and I have had our differences—what to eat, whom to marry, where to live, among others. I looked at her sleeping under the wheeling lights of her small, aluminum tree. I thought of her dancing through all those years, and the differences seemed to melt into a warm spot.

That night I dreamed of a small, dancing tree with lights and of a circle of smiling children gathered around the tree. They had their arms stretched out in front of them and were calling out in various tongues, "Dance, dance with me!"

FRANK FINALE

Painting the Christmas Trees

In my Odyssey of dead-end jobs,
cursed by whatever gods
do not console,
I end up
at a place that makes
fake Christmas trees:
thousands!
some pink, some blue,
one that revolves ever so slowly
to the strains of silent night.

Sometimes, out of sheer despair,
I rev up its rpms
and send it spinning
wildly through space—

Dorothy Hamill
disguised as a balsam fir!
I run a machine
that spits paint
onto wire boughs,
each length of bough a different shade—
color coded—so that America will know
which end fits where.

This is spray paint of which I speak—
no ventilation, no safety masks,
Lots of poor folk speaking
various broken tongues,
a guy from Poland with a ruptured disk
lifting fifty-pound boxes of
defective parts,
A Haitian
so damaged by police "interrogation"
he flinches when you
raise your arm too suddenly near

and all of us hating the job
knowing it's meaningless
Yet singing, cursing, telling jokes
unentitled to anything but joy—
the lurid, unreasonable joy
that sometimes overwhelms you
even in a hole like this.

It's a joy rulers
mistake for proof of "The Human Spirit."
I tell you it is Kali
the great destroyer,
her voice singing amidst butchery and hate.
It is Rachel the inconsolable
weeping for her children.

It goes both over and under
"The Human Spirit."
It is my father
crying in his sleep
because he works

twelve-hour shifts six days a week
and can't make rent.

It is one hundred and ten degrees
in the land of fake Christmas trees.
It is Blanca Ramirez keeling over pregnant
sans green card.
It is a nation that has
spiritualized shopping
not knowing how many lost
to the greater good of retail.
It is Marta the packer
rubbing her crippled hands with
Lourdes water and hot chiles.
It is bad pay and worse diet and
the minds of our children
turned on the wheel of sorrow—

no language to leech it from the blood,
no words to draw it out—
a fake Christmas tree
spinning wildly in the brain,
and who can stop it
who
unless grief grows a hand
and writes the poem.

JOE E. WEIL

City Lights

Going there for the first time 1961:
it was so much smaller then
that crowded downstairs full of poetry
racks of tattered little mags against the wall
those small white tables where folks sat reading/writing
Vesuvio's was like an adjunct office

Arriving again a year later, two kids in tow
Lawrence gave me a huge stack of his publications
"I've got books" he said "like other people have mice"

And North Beach never stopped being mysterious
when I moved out here in 1968
that publishing office on Filbert & Grant was a mecca
place to rejoin the kids if we got separated
during one of those innumerable demonstrations
(tho Lawrence worried, thought I shd keep them
out of harm's way, at home) *I* thought they shd learn
whatever it was we were learning—
It was right around the corner from the bead store
where I found myself day after day, picking up supplies

How many late nights did we haunt that place
buy scads of new poems from all corners of the earth
then head to the all-night Tower Records full of drag queens
& revolutionaries, pick up a few songs

And dig it, City Lights still there, like some old lighthouse
though most of that scene is gone,
the poetry's moved upstairs, the publishing office
right there too now   & crowds
one third my age still haunt the stacks
hunting for voices from all quarters
of the globe

DIANE DI PRIMA

There I Was One Day

There I was one day
in the parking lot of the First Brothers' Church
on one foot, a giant whooping crane
with my left index finger against my temple
trying to remember what my theory of corruption was
and why I got so angry years ago
at my poor mother and father, immigrant cranes
from Polish Russia and German and Jewish Ukraine—
the good days then, hopping both ways like a frog,
and croaking, and trying to remember why it was
I soothed myself with words
at that flimsy secretary, not meant for knees,
not meant for a soul, not least a human one,

and trying to remember how I pieced together
the great puzzle, and how delighted I was
I would never again be bitten twice,
on either hand, the left one or the other.
I stopped between the telephone pole and the ivy
and sang to myself. I do it now for pleasure.
I thought I'd trace the line of pure decadence
to either Frank Sinatra or Jackie Gleason,
and thence to either the desert or the swamp,
Greater Nevada or Miami Beach;
or I would smile with Stalin or frown with Frick,
Stalin and Frick, both from Pittsburgh; Mellon,
Ehrlichman, Paul the Fortieth, Paul the Fiftieth.
I learned my bitterness at the dining room table
and used it everywhere. One time I yanked
the tablecloth off with everything on top of it.
It was the kind of strength that lets you lift
the back end of a car, it was the rush
of anger and righteousness you shake from later.
My Polish mother and my Ukrainian father
sat there white-faced. They had to be under fifty,
maybe closer to forty. I had hit them
between the eyes, I had screamed in their ears
and spit in their faces. Forty years later I stutter
when I think about it; it is the stuttering
of violent justice. I turned left on Third—
it was called Pomfret in 1776—
and made my way to the square—I think I did that—
past the Plaza II and the old Huntington,
and did an Egyptian turn. There were some other birds
sitting there on the benches, eating egg salad
and smoking autumn leaves. They didn't seem to care
or even notice. We sat there for the humming
and later we left, one at a time, and limped
away at different speeds, in different directions.
I ended up doing a circle, east on one street,
north on another, past the round oak table
in the glass window, past the swimming pool
at the YW. Just a walk for me
is full of exhaustion; nobody does it my way,
shaking the left foot, holding the right foot up,

a stork from Broadway, a heron from Mexico,
a pink flamingo from Greece.

GERALD STERN

An American in Trapani

In far off Sicily I sing
Like an American
Though lost in the whirl of events
I still see wet pavements glistening

Under the corner lamp lights,
The endless corners of New York City
And I hear the syncopated jazz of Gershwin
Throbbing in my ears.

All part of me
The upbeat, the step ahead
To sweet tunes.
I left it all

Because of crazed composers
Beating their political tomtoms
To the tune of war,
Beats that crashed into me

That grogged me
That punchdrunked me
And made me flee
Like a whipped dog

Dragging my secret dreams along
Because no ears could hear
Other than the great hurrahs for war.
But oh! The pulse of street cars

And afternoon rushes,
Of the big town.
That still lives in me

Like a gigantic echo
Splitting into all the Brooklyn slangs

And multicolored accents
Of the biggest crowd I know.

This all reminds me
I am an American.

NAT SCAMMACCA

Made You Mine, America

America
in the poems of Walt Whitman
Langston Hughes
Allen Ginsberg
the songs of Woody Guthrie and Joan Baez
I made you mine

rushing to you
at night and daybreak
by air and water—
on the land
getting a social security number
in the year nineteen-hundred-seventy
working the graveyard shift for ITT
a teen ager four levels below the ground
a cashier in a three by eight booth
under the Denver Hotel Hilton
sheltering derelicts
who slept on beds
of cardboard and newspaper
pillows of shoes
my young body luring
late night prostitutes and transvestites
hip to my accent
the midnight thief
pouring mace into my eyes
escaping
up the long ramp

passing through barbed wire
and waiting for hours in the INS lobbies
facing grouchy secretaries

overwhelmed by the languages
they can't speak and accents
they can't enjoy
becoming naturalized
in the year of bicentennial celebration

the migration of my parents
to your welfare state
of millions living
in tenement housing
reeking with the smell of urine
and cheap liquor

traveling
the US of A
as large as Whitman's green mind
white beard and red heart
from the Deadman's Pass rest area
on the old Oregon Trail
to the Scenic Overlook at Dixie line, Maryland
from Mountain Home—Idaho
to Rockford—Illinois
as large as Mark Twain's laughter and irony
from YMCA's casket-size single rooms
in Brooklyn
Chicago
San Francisco
to Denver's Republic Hotel
the home of broken old men
and women subsisting on
three hundred sixty four dollar
social security checks

waiting on
Denver oilmen in the Petroleum Club
Nights of Jazz at El Chapultepec
the Larimer of the past
where Arapahoes lived in their
tepees and now sleep
on the sidewalks
with battered lips
and broken heads

going door to door on Madison Ave., Seattle
selling death insurance
for American National
servicing houses of bare minimum—
a TV and a couch
drunken men and women
lonely ailing old African
women making quilts
selling each
for fifty dollars

marrying a teacher
a third generation auto worker
whose parents shared crops
in Caraway, Arkansas

fathering two tender boys
born in America
with their blue and brown eyes

substituting
for teachers
babysitting bored middle school children
driving them
home in a school bus
teaching your youth
to write English
and speak Persian

loving
your children
daughters
sons
mothers
fathers
grandmothers
grandfathers
hating your aggression
you aligned yourself with the worst
of my kind
exiled my George Washington—

Dr. Mohammad Mosaddeq
helped Saddam bomb my birthplace
destroy the school of my childhood
his soldiers swarming the hills of Charzebar
where as a child I hunted
with my grandfather
sold arms to warmongers
who waged battles on grounds
that my great-grandfather made
fifteen pilgrimages on foot
to Karbala

now I lay claim
to your Bill of Rights
and Declaration of Independence

I came to you
not a prince
who had lost his future throne
not a thief finding
a cover in the multitude
of your metropolis
hiding behind your volumes of law
not a merchant dreaming of exploiting
your open markets
not a smuggler
seeking riches overnight
but a greenhorn seventeen-year-old
with four hundred dollars
after dad sold his prized Bretta rifle
and mom some of her wedding jewelry
with a suitcase of clothes
and books—
Hafez
Rumi
Shakespeare
Nima
Forugh
and a small Koran—
my grandmother's gift
not to conquer

Wall Street
Broadway
or Hollywood

I came to you to study
to learn
and I learned
you can't deny me parenthood
I lost my grandparents
while roaming your streets
traveling across your vastness
you can't turn me down
I gave you my youth
walking and driving Colfax nights long
I came with hate
but now
I love you
America

                                        ALI ZARRIN

Ode to Elizabeth

"Grimy Elizabeth," *Time* magazine intones.
This city escaped the race riots
Never quite sank and, consequently, never rose.
It's not a town for poets.
You live here, you work the factory or a trade.
Down the burg, in Peterstown,
Italian bricklayers sit
on stoops, boxes, chairs, playing poker
into one A.M.
Drive up Elizabeth Avenue
and you'll hear the salsa music blast from every window.
Even the potted geraniums dance.
In La Palmita, old Cuban guys sip coffee
from little plastic cups.
They talk politics, prizefights, Castro,
soccer, soccer, soccer.

Our Mayor looks like a lesser Mayor Daley:
smokes cigars, wears loud plaid suits,

the penultimate used-car salesman.
He's been in since '64, a Mick with a machine.
He's re-elected because he's a consistent evil
and, here in Elizabeth, we appreciate consistency.

Half the law of life is hanging out, hanging on
to frame houses, pensions.
Every Sunday, ethnic radio: Irish hour, Polish hour,
Lithuanian hour. My father sits in the kitchen
listening to Kevin Barry.
He wishes he could still sing.
Two years ago, they cut his voice box out:
Cigarettes, factory, thirty years' worth of
double shifts. My father's as grimy as Elizabeth,
as sentimental, crude.
He boxed in the Navy, bantamweight.
As a kid I'd beg him to pop a muscle
And show off his tattoo.

We are not the salt of the earth.
I've got no John Steinbeck illusions.
I know the people I love have bad taste
In furniture. They are likely to buy
Crushed-velvet portraits of Elvis Presley
And hang them next to the Pope.
They fill their lives with consumer goods,
Leave the plastic covering on sofas
And watch *Let's Make a Deal*.
They are always dreaming the lottery number
That almost wins.
They are staunch Democrats who voted for Reagan.
They are working class, laid off when
Singer's closed, stuck between chemical dumps and oil
refineries in a city where Alexander Hamilton
once went to school.
In the graveyard by the courthouse,
lie Caldwells, Ogdens, Boudinots.
Milton is quoted on their graves.
Winos sleep there on summer afternoons
under hundred-year-old elms.
They sleep on the slabs of our Founding Fathers

and snore for History.
I have no illusions.

The Irish of Kerry Head have vanished,
but up in Elmora, you still can see
the Jewish families walking home from synagogue.
They are devout, they are well-dressed,
They read the Talmud.
Twelve years ago, I used to go to the Elmora Theater
with twenty other kids.
It was a run-down movie house that never
got the features till they'd been out a year.
Because the Elmora was poor, it showed
foreign films; art films we didn't know were art:
Fellini, Wertmuller, Bergman. It cost a dollar to get in.

We'd sit there, factory workers' kids, half hoods,
watching *Amarcord*,
When the grandfather climbed the tree
In *Amarcord* and screamed, "I want a woman!,"
we all agreed.
For weeks, Anthony Bravo went around school
screaming, "I want a woman!" every chance he got.
I copped my first feel there,
saw *Hester Street, The Seduction of Mimi*.
Once they had a double feature:
Bruce Lee's *Fists of Fury* with Ingmar Bergman's
The Seventh Seal.
I remember two hundred kids exploding
when Jack Nicholson choked the nurse in *Cuckoo's Nest*.
Sal Rotolo stood up, tears streaming down his face,
screaming, "Kill the bitch! Kill that fuckin' nurse!"
and when they took Jack's soul away,
we all sat there silent.
It lingered with us all the way home,
empty-eyed and sad.
Here in Elizabeth, the tasteless city,
where *Amarcord* was allowed to be just another flick,
where no one looked for symbols,
or sat politely through the credits.
If Art moved us at all, it was with real amazement;
we had no frame of reference.

And so I still live here,
because I need a place where poets are not expected.
I would go nuts in a town where everyone read Pound,
where old ladies never swept their stoops
or poured hot water on the ants.
I am happiest in a motley scene,
stuck between Exxon and the Arthur Kill . . .
I don't think Manhattan needs another poet.
I don't think Maine could use me.
I'm short, I'm ugly, I prefer Mrs. Paul's Fish Sticks
to blackened redfish.
I don't like to travel because I've noticed
no matter where you go, you take yourself with you,
and that's the only thing I care to leave behind.
So I stay here.
At night, I can still hear mothers yelling,
"Michael, supper! Get your ass in gear!"
Where nothing is sacred, everything is sacred;
where no one writes, the air seems strangely
charged with metaphor.
In short, I like a grimy city.
I suspect "Culture" because it has been given over
to grants, credentials, and people with cute haircuts.
I suspect Poetry because it talks to itself
too much, tells an inside joke.
It has forgotten how to pray.
It has forgotten how to praise.
Tonight, I write no poem. I write to praise.
I praise the motley city of my birth.
I write to be a citizen of Elizabeth, New Jersey.
like a goddamned ancient Greek, I stand for this smallest
bit of ground, my turf, this squalid city.
Here, in the armpit of the beast.
Tonight, the ghosts of Ogdens, Caldwells, Boudinots
walk among the winos.
They exist in the salsa music blaring on Elizabeth Avenue.
They rise up and kiss the gargoyles of Cherry Street.
They are like King David dancing naked
unashamed before the covenant.
Tonight, even the stones can praise.
The Irish dead of Kerry Head are singing in their sleep,
and I swear, the next time someone makes a face,

gives me that bite the lemon look, as if to say,
"My Gawd . . . How can you be a poet and live
In that stinking town?" My answer will be swift:
I'll kick him in the balls.

JOE E. WEIL

from Krik? Krak!

You remember thinking while braiding your hair that you look a
lot like your mother. Your mother who looked like your grandmother and her grandmother before her. Your mother had two
rules for living. *Always use your ten fingers,* which in her parlance
meant that you should be the best little cook and housekeeper who
ever lived.

Your mother's second rule went along with the first. Never have
sex before marriage, and even after you marry, you shouldn't say
you enjoy it, or your husband won't respect you.

And writing? Writing was as forbidden as dark rouge on the
cheeks or a first date before eighteen. It was an act of indolence,
something to be done in a corner when you could have been learning to cook.

Are there women who both cook and write? Kitchen poets, they
call them. They slip phrases into their stew and wrap meaning
around their pork before frying it. They make narrative dumplings
and stuff their daughters' mouths so they say nothing more.

"What will she do? What will be her passion?" your aunts would
ask when they came over to cook on great holidays, which called
for cannon salutes back home but meant nothing at all here.

"Her passion is being quiet," your mother would say. "But then
she's not being quiet. You hear this scraping from her. Krik? Krak!
Pencil, paper. It sounds like someone crying."

Someone was crying. You and the writing demons in your head.
You have nobody, nothing but this piece of paper, they told you.
Only a notebook made out of discarded fish wrappers, panty-hose
cardboard. They were the best confidantes for a lonely little girl.

When you write, it's like braiding your hair. Taking a handful
of coarse unruly strands and attempting to bring them unity. Your
fingers have still not perfected the task. Some of the braids are long,
others are short. Some are thick, others are thin. Some are heavy.
Others are light. Like the diverse women in your family. Those
whose fables and metaphors, whose similes, and soliloquies, whose

diction and *je ne sais quoi* daily slip into your survival soup, by way of their fingers.

You have always had your ten fingers. They curse you each time you force them around the contours of a pen. No, women like you don't write. They carve onion sculptures and potato statues. They sit in dark corners and braid their hair in new shapes and twists in order to control the stiffness, the unruliness, the rebelliousness.

❦

You remember thinking while braiding your hair that you look a lot like your mother. You remember her silence when you laid your first notebook in front of her. Her disappointment when you told her that words would be your life's work, like the kitchen had always been hers. She was angry at you for not understanding. *And with what do you repay me? With scribbles on paper that are not worth the scratch of a pig's snout.* The sacrifices had been too great.

Writers don't leave any mark in the world. Not the world where we are from. In our world, writers are tortured and killed if they are men. Called lying whores, then raped and killed, if they are women. In our world, if you write, you are a politician, and we know what happens to politicians. They end up in a prison dungeon where their bodies are covered in scalding tar before they're forced to eat their own waste.

The family needs a nurse, not a prisoner. We need to forge ahead with our heads raised, not buried in scraps of throwaway paper. We do not want to bend over a dusty grave, wearing black hats, grieving for you. There are nine hundred and ninety-nine women who went before you and worked their fingers to coconut rind so you can stand here before me holding that torn old notebook that you cradle against your breast like your prettiest Sunday braids. I would rather you had spit in my face.

You remember thinking while braiding your hair that you look a lot like your mother and her mother before her. It was their whispers that pushed you, their murmurs over pots sizzling in your head. A thousand women urging you to speak through the blunt tip of your pencil. Kitchen poets, you call them. Ghosts like burnished branches on a flame tree. These women, they asked for your voice so that they could tell your mother in your place that yes, women like you do speak, even if they speak in a tongue that is hard to understand. Even if it's patois, dialect, Creole.

❦

The women in your family have never lost touch with one another. Death is a path we take to meet on the other side. What goddesses have joined, let no one cast asunder. With every step you take, there is an army of women watching over you. We are never any farther than the sweat on your brows or the dust on your toes. Though you walk through the valley of the shadow of death, fear no evil for we are always with you.

When you were a little girl, you used to dream that you were lying among the dead and all the spirits were begging you to scream. And even now, you are still afraid to dream because you know that you will never be able to do what they say, as they say it, the old spirits that live in your blood.

Most of the women in your life had their heads down. They would wake up one morning to find their panties gone. It is not shame, however, that kept their heads down. They were singing, searching for meaning in the dust. And sometimes, they were talking to faces across the ages, faces like yours and mine.

You thought that if you didn't tell the stories, the sky would fall on your head. You often thought that without the trees, the sky would fall on your head. You learned in school that you have pencils and paper only because the trees gave themselves in unconditional sacrifice. There have been days when the sky was as close as your hair to falling on your head.

This fragile sky has terrified you your whole life. Silence terrifies you more than the pounding of a million pieces of steel chopping away at your flesh. Sometimes, you dream of hearing only the beating of your own heart, but this has never been the case. You have never been able to escape the pounding of a thousand other hearts that have outlived yours by thousands of years. And over the years when you have needed us, you have always cried "Krik?" and we have answered "Krak!" and it has shown us that you have not forgotten us.

You remember thinking while braiding your hair that you look a lot like your mother. Your mother, who looked like your grandmother and her grandmother before her. Your mother, she introduced you to the first echoes of the tongue that you now speak when at the end of the day she would braid your hair while you sat between her legs, scrubbing the kitchen pots. While your fingers worked away at the last shadows of her day's work, she would make your braids Sunday-pretty, even during the week.

When she was done she would ask you to name each braid after those nine hundred and ninety-nine women who were boiling in your blood, and since you had written them down and memorized them, the names would come rolling off your tongue. And this was your testament to the way that these women lived and died and lived again.

EDWIDGE DANTICAT

from This Past Decade and the Next

I inherited the tempestuous
         energy
   of fighting
            against the fascist encampment
added a pinch
    of elegiac feelings american
& minstreled
         my interplanetary songs
   up & down the Raritan
to help radical
         democratic Poetry's
   spirit
             & body
      swim
        in this modern concrete city.

The town changed
        though not
              as I'd intended.
Joyce Kilmer's tree
            grew upside
       down.
Teachers skipped
       over the sex ed chapters
    in their Johnson & Johnson
                history books.
The Environmental Protection Agency's

Unidentified Flying Watchdog Copter
flew backwards
& its razorblades
broke thru
New Brunswick Cultural Center's
painstakingly stainglass'd
exit door.

. . . .

I flipped my mirror'd
sunglasses around—
no help.

I started pulling out my gray
hairs every morning
before work—
no help.

I dunked my designer sneakers
into the dirty riverbank—
only left waterlogged-
footprint puddles
over all where I'd been.

. . . .

I thought to give up
lay down
go right to sleep
wait for sexy utopian dream
to get me through
next day's nightmare,
but mom's concentration
camp inheritance
kept me awake
like unbreakable toothpick guardians
keeping watch
over my lids.
So I kept at it
getting up & falling
up & falling,
and getting up again

if for no other reason

        than the ethical question

    of knowing

        no other way

     to live.

I vowed to keep

    test firing new

        & experimental

   rocket pages

        one right after another

    till I hit upon the one

        to take off

from this real world

    I have worked like my scientist

        father

     to understand

  & fly

    in a billion different

        poetic directions

   like a heat-seeking daisy

        wheel

     searching for the next.

        ELIOT KATZ

Second-Grade Angel

Each choir had 6,666 legions,
with 6,666 angels in each of these
and I knew as sure as the fluorescent
   light
in that second-grade class kept blinking
that I had been one of them, still was,
   but sent
to Earth because of some unforgivable sin,
that all I had to do was lift the window
and I could soar out onto Ontario Street,
   wings
erupting from my shoulders, the white
   shirt
tearing off, the school's striped tie

and gray trousers floating away, and I knew
    I had fire
in my tongue, my right hand filled with
    lightning,
that Sister Maria must have seen it
    but decided
to keep quiet so the others wouldn't bow
    down to me and lose their places
as we Pledged Allegiance and recited
    the Commandments, the Mysteries,
the invisible wings on my either side telling me
    again
my true father was not a road man for the Golden
    Eagle bread company,
my mother not a textile stitcher who danced
    nights with drunks at Boney's,
knowing I could soar above the blue Earth, up
    into the darkness
where my brother did not walk alleys calling
    for rags,
that dogs howled when I walked by because
    they sensed
the fire in my body, that the dates of my birth,
    3/13/50
added up to the magical number of 66
and gave me power over seasons and planets, able
    to make
Margaret Blake throw up because she tripped me,
giving Ronny Michaels the hiccups for shoving
    me down the stairs,
sure even then I would ascend again some day,
despite my heavy body, the warts on my hands,
and I would become who I was, and I would know
    my real name.

LEN ROBERTS

Miz Rosa Rides the Bus

That day in December I sat down
by Miss Muffet of Montgomery.
I was myriad-weary. Feet swole

from sewing seams on a filthy fabric;
tired-sore a-pedalin' the rusty Singer;

dingy cotton thread jammed in the eye.
All lifelong I'd slide through century-reams
loathsome with tears. Dreaming my own
silk-self.

It was not like they all say. Miss Liberty Muffet
she didn't
jump at the sight of me.
Not exactly.
They hauled me
away—a thousand kicking legs pinned down.

The rest of me I tell you—a cloud
Beautiful trouble on the dead December
horizon. Come to sit in judgment.

How many miles as the Jim Crow flies?
Over oceans and some. I rumbled.
They couldn't hold me down. Long.
No.

My feet were tired. My eyes were
sore. My heart was raw from hemming
dirty edges of Miss L. Muffet's garment.
I rode again.

A thousand bloody miles after the Crow flies
that day in December long remembered when I
   sat down
beside Miss Muffet of Montgomery.
I said—like the joke say—What's in the bowl,
   Thief?
I said—That's your curse.
I said—This my way.
She slipped her frock, disembarked,
settled in the suburbs, deaf, mute, lewd and blind.
The bowl she left behind. The empy bowl mine.
The spoiled dress.

Jim Crow dies and ravens come with crumbs.
They say—Eat and be satisfied.
I fast and pray and ride.

ANGELA JACKSON

The Summer of Black Widows

The spiders appeared suddenly
after that summer rainstorm.

Some people still insist the spiders fell with the rain
while others believe the spiders grew from the damp soil like weeds
     with eight thin roots.

The elders knew the spiders
carried stories in their stomachs.

We tucked our pants into our boots when we walked through fields
     of fallow stories.
An Indian girl opened the closet door and a story fell into her hair.
We lived in the shadow of a story trapped in the ceiling lamp.
The husk of a story museumed on the windowsill.
Before sleep, we shook our blankets and stories fell to the floor.
A story floated in a glass of water left on the kitchen table.
We opened doors slowly and listened for stories.
The stories rose on hind legs and offered their red bellies to the
    most beautiful Indians.
Stories in our cereal boxes.
Stories in our firewood.
Stories in the pockets of our coats.
We captured stories and offered them to the ants, who carried the
     stories back to their queen.
A dozen stories per acre.
We poisoned the stories and gathered their remains with broom
    and pan.

The spiders disappeared suddenly
after that summer lightning storm.

Some people still insist the spiders were burned to ash
while others believe the spiders climbed the lightning bolts and
        became a new constellation.

The elders knew the spiders
had left behind bundles of stories.

Up in the corners of our old houses
we still find those small, white bundles
and nothing, neither fire
not water, neither rock nor wind,
can bring them down.

SHERMAN ALEXIE

Tourists

1. JAMES DEAN
walks everywhere now. He's afraid of fast cars
and has walked this far, arriving
suddenly on the reservation, in search
of the Indian woman of his dreams.
He wants an Indian woman who could pass
for Natalie Wood. He wants an Indian woman
who looks like the Natalie Wood
who was kidnapped by Indians
in John Ford's classic movie *The Searchers.*
James Dean wants to rescue somebody beautiful.
He still wears that red jacket,
you know the one. It's the color of a powwow fire.
James Dean has never seen
a powwow, but he joins right in, dancing
like a crazy man, like a profane clown.
James Dean cannot contain himself.
He dances in the wrong direction. He tears
at his hair. He sings in wild syllables
and does not care. The Indian dancers stop
and stare like James Dean was lightning
or thunder, like he was bad weather.
But he keeps dancing, bumps into a man
and knocks loose an eagle feather.

The feather falls, drums stop.
This is the kind of silence
that frightens white men. James Dean
looks down at the feather
and knows that something has gone wrong.
He looks into the faces of the Indians.
He wants them to finish the song.

2. JANIS JOPLIN

sits by the jukebox in the Powwow Tavern,
talking with a few drunk Indians
about redemption. She promises each of them
she can punch in the numbers
for the song that will save their lives.
All she needs is a few quarters, a beer,
and their own true stories. The Indians
are as traditional as drunk Indians can be
and don't believe in autobiography,
so they lie to Janis Joplin about their lives.
One Indian is an astronaut, another killed JFK,
while the third played first base
for the New York Yankees. Janis Joplin knows
the Indians are lying. She's a smart woman
but she listens anyway, plays them each a song,
and sings along off key.

3. MARILYN MONROE

drives herself to the reservation. Tired and cold,
she asks the Indian women for help.
Marilyn cannot explain what she needs
but the Indian women notice the needle tracks
on her arms and lead her to the sweat lodge
where every woman, young and old, disrobes
and leaves her clothes behind
when she enters the dark of the lodge.
Marilyn's prayers may or may not be answered here
but they are kept sacred by Indian women.
Cold water is splashed on hot rocks
and steam fills the lodge. There is no place like this.
At first, Marilyn is self-conscious, aware
of her body and face, the tremendous heat, her thirst,
and the brown bodies circled around her.

But the Indian women do not stare. It is dark
inside the lodge. The hot rocks glow red
and the songs begin. Marilyn has never heard
these songs before, but she soon sings along.
Marilyn is not Indian, Marilyn will never be Indian
but the Indian women sing about her courage.
The Indian women sing for her health.
The Indian women sing for Marilyn.
Finally, she is no more naked than anyone else.

SHERMAN ALEXIE

Like Mexicans

My grandmother gave me bad advice and good advice when I was
in my early teens. For the bad advice, she said that I should become
a barber because they made good money and listened to the radio
all day. "Honey, they don't work como burros,"[1] she would say
every time I visited her. She made the sound of donkeys braying.
"Like that, honey!" For the good advice, she said that I should
marry a Mexican girl. "No Okies, hijo"[2]—she would say—"Look,
my son. He marry one and they fight every day about I don't know
what and I don't know what." For her, everyone who wasn't Mexican, black, or Asian were Okies. The French were Okies, the Italians in suits were Okies. When I asked about Jews, whom I had
read about, she asked for a picture. I rode home on my bicycle and
returned with a calendar depicting the important races of the world.
"Pues si, son Okies tambien!"[3] she said, nodding her head. She
waved the calendar away and we went to the living room where
she lectured me on the virtues of the Mexican girl: first, she could
cook and, second, she acted like a woman, not a man, in her husband's home. She said she would tell me about a third when I got
a little older.

I asked my mother about it—becoming a barber and marrying
Mexican. She was in the kitchen. Steam curled from a pot of boiling
beans, the radio was on, looking as squat as a loaf of bread. "Well,
if you want to be a barber—they say they make good money." She

1 like burros
2 son
3 Well, yes, they're Okies too.

slapped a round steak with a knife, her glasses slipping down with each strike. She stopped and looked up. "If you find a good Mexican girl, marry her of course." She returned to slapping the meat and I went to the backyard where my brother and David King were sitting on the lawn feeling the inside of their cheeks.

"This is what girls feel like," my brother said, rubbing the inside of his cheek. David put three fingers inside his mouth and scratched. I ignored them and climbed the back fence to see my best friend, Scott, a second-generation Okie. I called him and his mother pointed to the side of the house where his bedroom was, a small aluminum trailer, the kind you gawk at when they're flipped over on the freeway, wheels spinning in the air. I went around to find Scott pitching horseshoes.

I picked up a set of rusty ones and joined him. While we played, we talked about school and friends and record albums. The horseshoes scuffed up dirt, sometimes ringing the iron that threw out a meager shadow like a sundial. After three argued-over games, we pulled two oranges apiece from his tree and started down the alley still talking school and friends and record albums. We pulled more oranges from the alley and talked about who we would marry. "No offense, Scott," I said with an orange slice in my mouth, "but I would never marry an Okie." We walked in step, almost touching, with a sled of shadows dragging behind us. "No offense, Gary," Scott said, "but I would *never* marry a Mexican." I looked at him: a fang of orange slice showed from his munching mouth. I didn't think anything of it. He had his girl and I had mine. But our seventh-grade vision was the same: to marry, get jobs, buy cars and maybe a house if we had money left over.

We talked about our future lives until, to our surprise, we were on the downtown mall, two miles from home. We bought a bag of popcorn at Penneys and sat on a bench near the fountain watching Mexican and Okie girls pass. "That one's mine," I pointed with my chin when a girl with eyebrows arched into black rainbows ambled by. "She's cute," Scott said about a girl with yellow hair and a mouthful of gum. We dreamed aloud, our chins busy pointing out girls. We agreed that we couldn't wait to become men and lift them onto our laps.

But the woman I married was not Mexican but Japanese. It was a surprise to me. For years, I went about wide-eyed in my search for the brown girl in a white dress at a dance. I searched the playground at the baseball diamond. When the girls raced for grounders, their hair bounced like something that couldn't be caught. When they sat together in the lunchroom, heads pressed together, I knew they were talking about us Mexican guys. I saw them and dreamed them. I threw my face into my pillow, making up sentences that were good as in the movies.

But when I was twenty, I fell in love with this other girl who worried my mother, who had my grandmother asking once again to see the calendar of the Important Races of the World. I told her I had thrown it away years before. I took a much-glanced-at snapshot from my wallet. We looked at it together, in silence. Then grandma reclined in her chair, lit a cigarette, and said, "Es pretty." She blew and asked with all her worry pushed up to her forehead: "Chinese?"

I was in love and there was no looking back. She was the one. I told my mother who was slapping hamburger into patties. "Well, sure if you want to marry her," she said. But the more I talked, the more concerned she became. Later I began to worry. Was it all a mistake? "Marry a Mexican girl," I heard my mother say in my mind. I heard it at breakfast. I heard it over math problems, between Western Civilization and cultural geography. But then one afternoon while I was hitchhiking home from school, it struck me like a baseball in the back: my mother wanted me to marry someone of my own social class—a poor girl. I considered my fiancee, Carolyn, and she didn't look poor, though I knew she came from a family of farm workers and pull-yourself-up-by-your-bootstraps ranchers. I asked my brother, who was marrying Mexican poor that fall, if I should marry a poor girl. He screamed "Yeah" above his terrible guitar playing in his bedroom. I considered my sister who had married Mexican. Cousins were dating Mexican. Uncles were remarrying poor women. I asked Scott, who was still my best friend, and he said, "She's too good for you, so you better not."

I worried about it until Carolyn took me home to meet her parents. We drove in her Plymouth until the houses gave way to farms and ranches and finally her house fifty feet from the highway. When we pulled into the drive, I panicked and begged Carolyn to make a U-turn and go back so we could talk about it over a soda. She pinched my cheek, calling me a "silly boy." I felt better, though, when I got out of the car and saw the house: the chipped paint, a cracked window, boards for a walk to the back door. There were rusting cars near the barn. A tractor with a net of spiderwebs under a mulberry. A field. A bale of barbed wire like children's scribbling leaning against an empty chicken coop. Carolyn took my hand and pulled me to my future mother-in-law who was coming out to greet us.

We had lunch: sandwiches, potato chips, and iced tea. Carolyn and her mother talked mostly about neighbors and the congregation at the Japanese Methodist Church in West Fresno. Her father, who was in khaki work clothes, excused himself with a wave that was almost a salute and went outside. I heard a truck start, a dog bark, and then the truck rattle away.

Carolyn's mother offered another sandwich, but I declined with a shake of my head and a smile. I looked around when I could, when I was not saying over and over that I was a college student, hinting that I could take care of her daughter. I shifted my chair. I saw newspapers piled in corners, dusty cereal boxes and vinegar bottles in corners. The wallpaper was bubbled from rain that had come in from a bad roof. Dust. Dust lay on lamp shades and window sills. These people are just like Mexicans, I thought. Poor people.

Carolyn's mother asked me through Carolyn if I would like a *sushi*. A plate of black and white things was held in front of me. I took one, wide-eyed, and turned it over like a foreign coin. I was biting into one when I saw a kitten crawl up the window screen over the sink. I chewed and the kitten opened its mouth of terror as she crawled higher, wanting in to paw the leftovers from our plates. I looked at Carolyn who said that the cat was just showing off. I looked up in time to see it fall. It crawled up, then fell again.

We talked for an hour and had apple pie and coffee, slowly. Finally, we got up with Carolyn taking my hand. Slightly embarrassed, I tried to pull away but her grip held me. I let her have her way as she led me down the hallway with her mother right behind me. When I opened the door, I was startled by a kitten clinging to the screen door, its mouth screaming "cat food, dog biscuits, *sushi*. . . ." I opened the door and the kitten, still holding on, whined in the language of hungry animals. When I got into Carolyn's car, I looked back: the cat was still clinging. I asked Carolyn if it were possibly hungry, but she said the cat was being silly. She started the car, waved to her mother, and bounced us over the rain-poked drive, patting my thigh for being her lover baby. Carolyn waved again. I looked back, waving, then gawking at a window screen where there were now three kittens clawing and screaming to get in. Like Mexicans, I thought. I remembered the Molinas and how the cats clung to their screens—cats they shot

down with squirt guns. On the highway, I felt happy, pleased by
it all. I patted Carolyn's thigh. Her people were like Mexicans, only
different.

GARY SOTO

American Milk

Then the butter we put on our white bread
was colored with butter yellow, a cancerous dye,
and all the fourth grades were taken by streetcar
to the Dunky Company to see milk processed; milk bottles
riding on narrow metal cogs through little doors that flapped.
The sour damp smell of milky-wet cement floors:
we looked through great glass windows at the milk.
Before we were herded back to the streetcar line,
we were each given a half pint of milk in tiny
milk bottles with straws to suck it up. In this way
we gradually learned about our country.

RUTH STONE

Contributors ~

Francisco X. Alarcón, Chicano educator and poet, is the author of several books of poetry, including *Tattoos* and *Snake Poems*. His latest collection, *Laughing Tomatoes*, is for children.

Elizabeth Alexander is a visiting poet-in-residence at Smith College. She is the author of two books of poetry, *The Venus Hottentot* and *Body of Life*, and a verse play, *Diva Studies*.

Sherman Alexie, an enrolled Spokane and Coeur d'Alene, is the author of several collections of poetry and fiction, including *Reservation Blues*, *Indian Killer*, and *Old Shirts & New Skins*.

Agha Shahid Ali has been writing poetry exclusively in English since the age of ten. He is the author of *The Half-Inch Himalayas*.

Tony Ardizzone is the author of *Larabi's Ox: Stories of Morocco*, winner of the Milkweed National Fiction Prize and a Pushcart Prize. His other books include *The Evening News* and *Taking It Home*.

Amiri Baraka's recent collections include *Transbluesency: The Selected Poetry of Amiri Baraka/Leroi Jones 1961–1995*, *Funk Lore: New Poems 1984–1995*, *Eulogies*, and *Wise/Why's*.

Stanley H. Barkan, whose latest book is *O Jerusalem*, was named NYC Poetry Teacher of the Year, and as publisher of Cross-Cultural Communications was the recipient of the 1996 Poor Richard's Award.

Laura Boss, founder and editor of *LIPS*, was a first-place winner of the Poetry Society of America's Gordon Barber Award. Her books include the Alta Award–winning *On the Edge of the Hudson* and *Reports from the Front*.

Joseph Bruchac, winner of the Paterson Prize for Children's Literature, is a writer and storyteller whose work often draws on his Abenaki Indian ancestry.

Anthony F. Bruno teaches at the University of Pennsylvania and is a recipient of the Lindback Award for Distinguished Teaching at Community College of Philadelphia.

Rafael Campo is a practicing physician and the winner of the National Poetry Series 1993 Open Competition. His two collections are *What the Body Told* and *The Other Man Was Me*.

Hayden Carruth, former editor of *Harper's* and *Poetry*, has published more than twenty volumes of poetry and has been awarded the National Book Critics Circle Award and the Shelley Memorial Award.

Grace Cavalieri is the author of eight books of poetry. For twenty years she produced and hosted *The Poet and the Poem* on public radio for the Pacifica network.

Tina Chang, born in Stillwater, Oklahoma, is a graduate of the creative writing program at SUNY Binghamton. Her work has appeared in the *Asian Pacific American Journal* and *Black Bough*.

David Chin teaches creative writing at Penn State. He is the author of a chapbook, *Chalked in Orange*, and seeks a publisher for his new collection, *Sky Frames*.

Renny Christopher teaches at California State, Stanislaus, and works as a horse wrangler in the summer. She is the author of a chapbook, *My Name Is Medea*, and a collection of poetry, *Viet Nam and California*.

Arthur L. Clements teaches literature and creative writing at SUNY Binghamton. His most recent books are *Dream of Flying* (poetry), *The Norton Critical Edition of John Donne's Poetry*, and *Poetry of Contemplation*.

Susan Deer Cloud Clements is the author of *The Broken Hoop* and *In the Moon When the Deer Lose Their Horns*. Her words try to keep the Sacred Hoop of Life whole.

Lucille Clifton, Distinguished Professor of Humanities at St. Mary's College of Maryland, has published over thirty-two books of poetry and children's stories. She was twice nominated for the Pulitzer Prize, and won the Juniper Prize and an Emmy Award.

Wanda Coleman is the author of more than seven books of poetry, including *Heavy Daughter Blues*. She is the recipient of fellowships from the California Arts Council and the Guggenheim Foundation.

Peter Cooley is a professor of creative writing at Tulane University. He has published six books of poems, the most recent being *Sacred Conversations*.

Robert Creeley, a recipient of the Shelley Memorial Award and the Poetry Society of America's Robert Frost Medal, is the author of numerous collections of poetry, short stories, novels, and essays.

Antonio D'Alfonso has published more than a dozen books, including *In Italics: In Defense of Ethnicity*. The publisher and an editor for Guernica Editions, he is also a filmmaker and a musician.

Edwidge Danticat is the author of *Breath, Eyes, Memory* and *Krik? Krak!*, a 1995 National Book Award finalist. She won the Pushcart Prize in 1995 and fiction awards from *Seventeen* and *Essence*.

Diana Der-Hovanessian, a New England–born poet, is the author of over ten books of poetry, including *Songs of Bread, Songs of Salt* and *Selected Poems*, and translations.

Toi Derricotte is the author of several collections of poetry, including *Natural Birth*, *The Empress of the Death House*, and *Captivity*. She is associate professor of English at the University of Pittsburgh.

Rachel Guido deVries is a poet and novelist who lives in Cazenovia, New York. Her books include *Tender Warriors*, a novel, and *How to Sing to a Dago*, poems.

Diane di Prima, whose work has been translated into thirteen languages, is the author of thirty-four books of poetry and prose. She lives in California, where she is writing her memoir for Viking.

Gregory Djanikian is the author of *The Man in the Middle* and *Falling Deeply Into America*. His poems have appeared in *The Nation*, *The American Scholar*, and other journals.

Sean Thomas Dougherty, a former high school dropout who grew up in a multiracial household, is editor of *Red Brick Review*. His latest book is *The Body's Precarious Balance*.

Denise Duhamel's books of poetry include *Exquisite Politics* (with Maureen Seaton), *Kinky*, *Girl Soldier*, *The Woman with Two Vaginas*, and *Smile!*

Stephen Dunn is the author of ten collections of poetry, most recently *Loosestrife*, a finalist for the 1996 National Book Critics Circle Award. He teaches at Richard Stockton College.

Janice Eidus, twice the winner of the O. Henry Prize and a Push-cart Prize, is the author of *The Celibacy Club* and *Vito Loves Geraldine* (stories), and *Urban Bliss* and *Faithful Rebecca* (novels).

Alfred Encarnacion's forthcoming collection is *Threading the Miles.* His work has appeared in the anthologies *The Open Boat* and *Unsettling America*, as well as in *LIPS* and *Indiana Review.*

Maria Fama is the author of three books of poetry. She is a co-founder of Allegro, Inc., a video production company.

Frank Finale, now poetry editor for *the new renaissance*, served as editor in chief of *Without Haloes* for a decade. He is co-editor of *Under a Gull's Wing: Poems and Photographs of the Jersey Shore.*

Carolyn Forché's award-winning books include *Gathering the Tribes* (Yale Younger Poets Award) and *The Country Between Us* (Lamont Poetry Selection).

Daniel Gabriel's stories and articles have appeared in over one hundred publications in the United States, Canada, England, Wales, Australia, New Zealand, Belgium, and Italy. He is the recipient of the Loft-McKnight Award for Fiction.

Maria Mazziotti Gillan, director of the Poetry Center at Passaic County Community College in Paterson, New Jersey, and editor of the Paterson Literary Review, is the author of seven books, including *Where I Come From: Selected Poems, The Weather of Old Seasons*, and, most recently, *Things My Mother Told Me.*

Allen Ginsberg was a tireless chronicler and integral part of the Beat Generation until his death in 1997. His recent books include *Selected Poems*, a fortieth anniversary edition of *Howl*, and *Cosmopolitan Greetings: Poems 1986–1992.*

Diane Glancy is an associate professor at Macalester College in St. Paul, Minnesota. Her historical novel, *Pushing the Bear*, was published in 1996.

Michael S. Glaser is the author of *A Lover's Eye* and *In the Men's Room and Other Poems*, which won the *Painted Bride Quarterly* chapbook competition.

Suheir Hammad is the author of *Drops of This Story* and *Born Palestinian, Born Black*, both published in 1996.

James P. Handlin is a widely published poet who has received three New Jersey State Council on the Arts grants. He is the headmaster of Brooklyn Friends School.

Terrance Hayes's poems have appeared in journals such as *Red Brick Review, Cream City Review*, and *Poet Lore*. He received an MFA in poetry from the University of Pittsburgh in 1997.

David Haynes grew up in St. Louis, where his novel *Somebody Else's Mama* is partially set. He is also the author of the novels *Right by My Side* and *All American Dream Dolls*.

Marie Howe is a co-editor of *In the Company of My Solitude*, an anthology of writing about AIDS; and the author of *The Good Thief*, a National Poetry Series selection, and *What the Living Do*.

Angela Jackson, an award-winning poet and fictionist, was a twenty-year member of the OBAC Writer's Workshop. Her latest book is *And All These Roads Be Luminous: Poems Selected and New*.

Bruce A. Jacobs's first book of poems, *Speaking Through My Skin*, won the Naomi Long Madgett Poetry Award. His poems and prose have appeared in *African American Review* and *American Writing*.

Honorée (Honi) Jeffers was born in Kokomo, Indiana, and reared in Durham, North Carolina. She received an MFA in creative writing from the University of Alabama in 1996.

Edward P. Jones is the author of *Lost in the City: Stories*. His work has appeared in journals including *Callaloo, Ploughshares*, and the *Paris Review*.

Allison Joseph's books include *What Keeps Us Here, Soul Train*, and *In Every Seam*. She lives in Carbondale, Illinois.

Beena Kamlani has just completed a novel, *Carry-On Luggage*, a Connecticut Commission on the Arts fiction grant winner, and is at work on *Desertion*, a new novel.

Eliot Katz, co-founder of *Long Shot* literary magazine, is the author of *Space and Other Poems for Love, Laughs, and Social Transformation* and *Liberation Recalled*.

Shirley Kaufman is a poet, translator, and winner of prizes, including the Poetry Society of America's Shelley Memorial Award. Her latest book is *Roots in the Air: New and Selected Poems*.

Chris Kennedy's poems have appeared in *Ploughshares*, *The Three-penny Review*, and *The Quarterly*. His manuscript *Fire in the Match Factory* was twice a finalist for the Yale Younger Poets Prize.

Yusef Komunyakaa won the Pulitzer Prize in 1994 for *Neon Vernacular: New and Selected Poems*. His poetry collection *Thieves of Paradise* was published in 1997.

Maxine Kumin won the Pulitzer Prize for *Up Country*, the Academy of American Poets Fellowship, and the Levinson Award. Her most recent collection is *Connecting the Dots*.

Stanley Kunitz received the Pulitzer and Bollingen prizes, a National Medal of Arts award, and the Shelley Memorial Award. His collection of poetry *Passing Through* won the 1995 National Book Critics Circle Award.

Michael Lally is the author of twenty-two books, including *Catch My Breath*, a Josephine Miles Award winner. He has acted in *NYPD Blue* and other TV shows, and his poetry was featured in the films *Pump Up the Volume* and *Drugstore Cowboy*.

Lê Thi Diem Thúy has been touring her show, *Mua He Do Lua/ Read Fiery Summer*, since 1995. Her memoir, *The Gangster We Are All Looking For*, is forthcoming from Knopf.

Philip Levine was born in Detroit, held a succession of industrial jobs, and taught at California State, Fresno, for many years. His award-winning collections include *What Work Is* (National Book Award), *The Simple Truth* (Pulitzer Prize), and *Ashes* (American Book Award).

Toni Libro, a professor of creative writing at Rowan University, is a produced playwright and a published poet and short-story writer who has read from her works at the Geraldine R. Dodge Poetry Festival.

M. L. Liebler is the author of ten books. Much of his performance poetry with the Magis Poetry Band has been recorded on CD. He is the Detroit director of the YMCA National Writer's Voice Project.

Lyn Lifshin is the author of *Marilyn Monroe* and *Blue Tattoo*. She has edited four books of women's work and is the subject of the documentary *Not Made of Glass*.

Shirley Geok-lin Lim, chair of the Women's Studies department at the University of California, Santa Barbara, is the author of several books of literary criticism, poetry, and prose, including *Another Country* and *Monsoon History*.

Adrian C. Louis is an enrolled member of the Lovelock Paiute tribe and had two books published in 1997, *Wild Indians and Other Creatures* (stories) and *Ceremonies of the Damned* (poems).

Mary Ann Mannino is the associate director of the First Year Writing Program at Temple University. She is the author of *Stategies of Empowerment in the Writing of Italian/American Women*.

Lee Martin's story collection, *The Least You Need to Know*, was the 1995 winner of the Mary McCarthy Prize in Short Fiction. He teaches creative writing at the University of North Texas.

Linda McCarriston, a professor at the University of Alaska, Anchorage, is the author of *Talking Soft Dutch* and *Eva-Mary*, a Terrence Des Pres Prize winner and finalist for the National Book Award.

Walt McDonald, a former air force pilot, has published sixteen books, including *Counting Survivors*, *After the Noise of Saigon*, and *Night Landings*.

Tony Medina, who teaches at Long Island University, Brooklyn, is the author of *Emerge & See*, *No Noose Is Good Noose*, *Haiku d'etat*, and *Cantos for the Comatose*, and is co-editor of *In Defense of Mumia*.

Nancy Mercado is an editor of *Long Shot* magazine. Her work has appeared in *In Defense of Mumia*, *ALOUD: Voices from the Nuyorican Poets Café*, and *Changer L'Amerique*.

Tiffany Midge, an enrolled member of the Standing Rock Sioux, is the author of *Outlaws, Renegades and Saints: Diary of a Mixed-Up Halfbreed*, the winner of the Diane Decorah Memorial Poetry Award.

E. Ethelbert Miller, the author of several collections of poems, was awarded the 1995 O. B. Hardison Jr. Poetry Prize and received an honorary doctorate of literature in 1996 from Emory and Henry College.

Lenard D. Moore, the author of *Forever Home*, is the founder and executive director of the Carolina African American Writer's Collective.

Lesléa Newman is a Jewish lesbian author whose twenty-five books include *Every Laugh a Tear* (a novel), *A Letter to Harvey Milk* (stories), and *Still Life With Buddy* (poems).

Kathryn Nocerino is a poet, short-story writer, and critic whose work has appeared in the United States and England. Her books of poetry include *Wax Lips* and *Death of the Plankton Bar & Grill*.

Margie Norris, author of *How Come You Don't Close Your Eyes Like the Other Girls Do?*, has been living in the Bay Area and forging California and lesbian identities along with her Irish-Catholic one.

Naomi Shihab Nye is a co-editor of *I Feel a Little Jumpy Around You* and the author of several collections of poetry, including *Hugging the Jukebox*, winner of the National Poetry Series Award.

Sharon Olds, recipient of the Lamont Poetry Prize and the National Book Critics Circle Award among others, teaches creative writing at New York University and the Goldwater Hospital, a public hospital for the physically challenged. Her books include *The Father* and *Satan Says*.

Simon J. Ortiz is the author of *Woven Stone*, *Fightin'* (stories), and *From Sand Creek*, among others. He wrote the narrative for *Surviving Columbus*, the PBS documentary about the Pueblo people.

Grace Paley is the author of many story and poetry collections. Awards for her work include a Guggenheim Fellowship and a National Institute of Arts and Letters Award.

Julie Parson-Nesbitt, author of *Finders* and recipient of the Gwendolyn Brooks Significant Illinois Poet Award, teaches creative-writing workshops in the Chicago public schools.

Molly Peacock has served as president of the Poetry Society of America and has been honored with a Creative Arts Public Service Award as well as an award from the Ingram Merrill Foundation.

Robert Phillips is a former director of the Creative Writing Program and professor of English at the University of Houston. He is the author of five books of poetry.

Marge Piercy has written eleven novels and more than twelve books of poetry, which include *Mars and Her Children*, *My Mother's Body*, and *Circles on the Water*.

Leroy V. Quintana is a native New Mexican. He is the author of six books of poetry, including *The History of Home*, *Sangre*, *Interrogations*, and *My Hair Turning Gray Among Strangers*.

Rochelle Ratner is the author of the novels *Bobby's Girl* and *The Lion's Share*, as well as more than ten collections of poetry. She is the executive editor of *American Book Review*.

David Ray's several books of poetry include *Wool Highways*, *Kangaroo Paws*, and *Sam's Book*. He has won many awards, traveled widely, and given many readings and workshops.

Vittoria repetto outs herself as a downtown Italian American lesbian poet. Her work has appeared in *Mudfish*, *LIPS*, and *Italian Americana*. Her chapbook is entitled *Head for the Van Wyck*.

Len Roberts is the author of seven books of poetry, including *Counting the Black Angels*, *The Trouble-Making Finch*, and *Black Wings*, which was selected by Sharon Olds for the 1988–89 National Poetry Series.

Abraham Rodriguez Jr. is the author of *The Boy Without a Flag*.

Luis J. Rodríguez is publisher of Tia Chucha Press in Chicago and a poet, journalist, and critic. His awards include a Lannan Fellowship and a Lila Wallace Reader's Digest Writers Award.

Tom Romano, author of *Clearing the Way: Working with Teenage Writers* and *Writing with Passion: Life Stories, Multiple Genres*, teaches at Miami University of Ohio.

Liz Rosenberg is the author of two books of poetry, several children's books, and a novel, *Heart and Soul*. She teaches English and creative writing at SUNY Binghamton.

Charles Rossiter is the author of *On Reading the 1,000-Year-Old Sorrows in a Book of Chinese Poems* and is the recipient of a 1997 NEA Fellowship. He is also a member of the performance poetry group 3 Guys from Albany.

Ralph Salisbury, a Cherokee author, has published nine books, the most recent of which is *The Last Rattlesnake and Other Stories*. His awards include the Rockefeller Bellagio Center Award for fiction.

Sonia Sanchez is the author of *Under a Soprano Sky* and *Homegirls and Handgrenades*, winner of the American Book Award. She is a contributing editor to *Black Scholar* and *Journal of African Studies*.

Cheryl Savageau's *Dirt Road Home* was a finalist for the Paterson Prize. Her poetry has been widely anthologized and has appeared in journals including *The Massachusetts Review* and *AGNI*.

Nat Scammacca, born in Brooklyn, lives in Sicily, where he helped found the Antigruppo poetry collective. He is the author of numerous poetry and essay collections and a memoir, *Bye Bye America*.

Lynne Sharon Schwartz is the author of two collections of stories and five novels, including *Disturbances in the Field*, *Leaving Brooklyn*, *The Fatigue Artist*, and, most recently, *Ruined by Reading*.

Maureen Seaton is the author of four books of poetry, including *Furious Cooking* and *Exquisite Politics* (with Denise Duhamel). She teaches in the MFA program at the School of the Art Institute, Chicago.

Vivian Shipley is a professor at Southern Connecticut State University and the editor of *The Connecticut Review*. Her most recent poetry collection is *Poems Out of Harlan County*.

Edgar Gabriel Silex, a member of the Pueblo Nation, is the author of *Even the Dead Have Memories* and *Through All the Displacements*. His poems have appeared in *Callaloo*, *Chiron Review*, and *Red Dirt Review*.

Hal Sirowitz is the author of two collections of poems, *Mother Said* and *My Therapist Said*. He has performed his work on MTV's *Spoken Word Unplugged*.

Mary McLaughlin Slechta is a poet and fiction writer who resides in upstate New York. Her work reflects her Jamaican-American background.

Gary Soto is a prize-winning poet and essayist as well as a children's-book author and producer of short films for Spanish-speaking children. He lives in Berkeley, California, with his family.

William Stafford was the author of numerous poetry collections, including *Stories That Could Be True*. He served as poetry consultant to the Library of Congress and as poet laureate of Oregon until his death in 1993.

Felix Stefanile is the first recipient of the Italian Americana $1000 Ciardi Award for Lifetime Contribution to Italian American Poetry, sponsored by the National Italian American Foundation (1998).

Dona Luongo Stein is the author of the poetry collections *Children of the Mafiosi* and *Heavenly Bodies*, and a contributor to *Coast Lines: Eight Santa Cruz Poets*. She teaches writing at the University of California, Santa Cruz.

Lamont B. Steptoe is a poet/photographer/publisher/father and Vietnam veteran who was born and raised in Pittsburgh. He is the author of eleven collections of poetry.

Gerald Stern is the author of several poetry collections, including *Odd Mercy* and *Lucky Life*, winner of the Lamont Poetry Prize. His most recent book is *This Time, New and Selected Poems*.

Ruth Stone's books include *Second-Hand Coat* and *Who Is the Widow's Muse?*, which won the Best American Poetry of 1991 Award. She has also received the Delmore Schwartz and the Whiting Foundation awards.

David Trinidad teaches poetry at Rutgers University and the New School for Social Research. His books of poetry include *Answer Song* and *Hand Over Heart*.

Quincy Troupe is the recipient of a Peabody Award for *The Miles Davis Radio Project*, co-author with Miles Davis of *Miles: The Autobiography*, and the author of ten books, including *Choruses*.

Anthony Valerio is the author of four books, including *Valentino and the Great Italians* and *Conversation with Johnny*. His short stories have appeared in the *Paris Review*.

Mark Vinz, born in North Dakota, is a professor at Moorhead State University. His books include *The Weird Kid* and *Minnesota Gothic*, and his poems have appeared in journals such as *Antioch Review*.

Justin Vitiello's poetry collections, *Vanzetti's Fish Cart* and *Subway Home*, were published in English and Italian. His third book, *Poppies and Thistles*, will soon appear in English and Spanish.

Diane Wakoski is the author of several collections of poetry, including *Emerald Ice: Selected Poems 1962–1987*. Her prose is collected in *Toward a New Poetry*.

T. H. S. Wallace is director of the Wildwood Poetry Festival at Harrisburg Area Community College, where he also teaches English and creative writing.

Afaa M. Weaver's forthcoming volume is *Talisman* and his new play is *Candy Lips & Hallelujah*. His other books include *Timber & Prayer*, *My Father's Geography*, and *Water Song*.

Joe E. Weil is a tool grinder and a shop steward in the Teamster's union, as well as a poetry activist and founder of the Can of Corn poetry series—a reading at which poets collect food for the homeless.

Tobias Wolff is the author of a novel, *The Barracks Thief*, which was a PEN/Faulkner Award winner, and two story collections, *Back in the World* and *In the Garden of the North American Martyrs*. His memoir, *This Boy's Life*, was adapted into a film.

Yictove, born in New Orleans, has produced a poetry series on cable television, worked in the Safe Haven Program in East Orange, New Jersey, and directed readings at the Knitting Factory in New York City.

Lisa Yun teaches literature at SUNY Binghamton. Her work has appeared in the *Asian Pacific American Journal*, *MELUS*, the *Seattle Review*, and the *Georgetown Review*.

Ali Zarrin, born in Iran, is the author of several books, including *Modern Marriage* and *Made You Mine America*. He teaches literature at the University of Colorado, Denver.

Index ∾

Grateful acknowledgment is made for permission to reprint the following copyrighted works:

Francisco X. Alcarcón: "Shame" from Snake Poems by Francisco X. Alcarcón. © 1992 Francisco X. Alcarcón. By permission of Chronicle Books, San Francisco.

Elizabeth Alexander: "Tending" from Body of Life by Elizabeth Alexander, Tia Chucha Press, 1996. By permission of the author.

Sherman Alexie: "The Summer of Black Widows" and "Tourists" from The Summer of Black Widows by Sherman Alexie. © 1996 by Sherman Alexie. Reprinted by permission of Hanging Loose Press.

Agha Shahid Ali: "Cracked Portraits" from The Half-Inch Himalayas by Agha Shahid Ali, Wesleyan University Press. © 1987 by Agha Shahid Ali. By permission of the University Press of New England.

Tony Ardizzone: "Ladies' Choice" from Taking It Home by Tony Ardizzone. Copyright 1996 by Tony Ardizzone. Used with the permission of the author and the University of Illinois Press.

Amiri Baraka: "Say What?" Copyright © 1969 by Amiri Baraka. Reprinted by permission of Sterling Lord Literistic, Inc.

Stanley H. Barkan: "For Sal Sanjamino: On His Retirement" appeared in Paterson Literary Review. Copyright © 1992 by Stanley H. Barkan. By permission of the author.

Laura Boss: "My Son Is Worried About Me" and "Aunt Rose" from Reports from the Front by Laura Boss, Cross-Cultural Communications, 1995. Copyright 1986, 1989 by Laura Boss. "Aunt Dorothy" appeared in Paterson Literary Review. Copyright 1997 by Laura Boss. By permission of the author.

Joseph Bruchac: "Baptisms" appeared in The Chariton Review. By permission of the author.

Rafael Campo: "Rice and Beans," "Defining Us," and "Imagining Drag" from What the Body Told by Rafael Campo. Copyright 1966, Duke University Press. Reprinted by permission of Duke University Press.

Hayden Carruth: "Words for My Daughter from the Asylum" from Collected Shorter Poems by Hayden Carruth. © 1992 by Hayden Carruth. Reprinted by permission of Copper Canyon Press, P.O. Box 271, Port Townsend, WA 98368.

Tina Chang: "My Rough Skinned Grandmother" appeared in Footwork: The Paterson Literary Review. By permission of the author.

David Chin: "Sterling Williams' Nosebleed" appeared in MSS/New Myths. By permission of the author.

Arthur L. Clements: "My Mad Son Helps Me Into Heaven" from Dream of Flying by Arthur L. Clements. Copyright 1994 by Arthur L. Clements. By permission of the author.

Susan Deer Cloud Clements: "Tangerine" appeared in Earth's Daughters. By permission of the author.

Lucille Clifton: "daughters" and "fury" from The Book of Light by Lucille Clifton. © 1993 by Lucille Clifton. Reprinted by permission of Copper Canyon Press, P.O. Box 271, Port Townsend, WA 98368.

Wanda Coleman: "Coffee" from African Sleeping Sickness: Stories & Poems by Wanda Coleman. Copyright © 1990 by Wanda Coleman. Reprinted with the permission of Black Sparrow Press.

Peter Cooley: "Poem on the First Day of School" from Sacred Conversations by Peter Cooley. © 1998 by Peter Cooley. Reprinted by permission of Carnegie Mellon University Press.

Robert Creeley: "Mother's Voice" from Selected Poems by Robert Creeley. Copyright © 1991 The Regents of the University of California. By permission of the University of California Press.

Antonio D'Alfonso: "The Loss of a Culture" from The Other Shore by Antonio D'Alfonso, Guernica Editions. By permission of the author.

Edwidge Danticat: "Epilogue: Women Like Us" from *Krik? Krak!* by Edwidge Danticat. By permission of Soho Press, Inc.

Diana Der-Hovanessian: "Company Outing" appeared in *Prairie Schooner*. © 1996 Diana Der-Hovanessian. By permission of the author.

Rachel Guido deVries: "The Accordion" appeared in *Sinister Wisdom*, Summer/Fall 1990. By permission of the author.

Diane di Prima: "The Children" and "City Lights." © 1998 by Diane di Prima. By permission of the author.

Gregory Djanikian: "In the Elementary School Choir" from *Falling Deeply into America* by Gregory Djanikian. © 1989 by Gregory Djanikian. Reprinted by permission of Carnegie Mellon University Press.

Sean Thomas Dougherty: "Poem for Anthony, Otherwise Known as Head" from *The Body's Precarious Balance* by Sean Thomas Dougherty, Red Dance Floor Press. Copyright Sean Thomas Dougherty, 1993, 1997. By permission of the author.

Denise Duhamel: "High School Reunion" from *Smile!* by Denise Duhamel, Warm Spring Press. Copyright 1993 by Denise Duhamel. By permission of the author.

Stephen Dunn: "The Substitute" from *Local Time* by Stephen Dunn, William Morrow, 1986. "Legacy" from *Not Dancing* by Stephen Dunn, Carnegie Mellon University Press, 1984. By permission of the author.

Janice Eidus: "Robin's Nest" from *Vito Loves Geraldine* by Janice Eidus, City Lights, 1990. Copyright 1990 Janice Eidus. By permission of the author.

Alfred Encarnacion: "Mestizo" appeared in *Paterson Literary Review*. By permission of the author.

Frank Finale: "Sally" appeared in *Footwork: The Paterson Literary Review*. By permission of the author.

Carolyn Forché: "As Children Together" from *The Country Between Us* by Carolyn Forché. Copyright © 1980 by Carolyn Forché. Reprinted by permission of HarperCollins Publishers, Inc.

Maria Mazziotti Gillan: "Daddy, We Called You" appeared in *Gifts of Our Fathers*, edited by Thomas R. Verny. "Learning Silence" appeared in *Vivace*. "Training Bra" appeared in *LIPS*, 20/21. By permission of the author.

Allen Ginsberg: " 'You know what I'm saying?' " By permission of the Allen Ginsberg Trust. "Garden State" from *Collected Poems 1947–1980* by Allen Ginsberg. Copyright © 1979 by Allen Ginsberg. Reprinted by permission of HarperCollins Publishers, Inc.

Diane Glancy: "Kemo Sabe" from *Lone Dog's Winter Count* by Diane Glancy, West End Press, 1991. By permission of the author.

Suheir Hammad: Excerpts from *Drops of This Story* by Suheir Hammad, Writers & Readers Publishing, 1996. By permission of the author.

James P. Handlin: "Saying Farewell to My Father." By permission of the author.

David Haynes: "Senior Will" appeared in *Gargoyle*. By permission of the author.

Marie Howe: "Sixth Grade," "The Boy," and "Practicing" from *What the Living Do* by Marie Howe. Copyright © 1997 by Marie Howe. Reprinted by permission of W. W. Norton & Company, Inc.

Angela Jackson: "Miz Rosa Rides the Bus" from *Dark Legs and Silk Kisses* by Angela Jackson, TriQuarterly Books/Northwestern University Press, 1993. By permission of the author.

Edward P. Jones: "The First Day" from *Lost in the City* by Edward P. Jones. By permission of the author.

Eliot Katz: Excerpts from "This Past Decade and the Next." "This Past Decade and the Next" appeared in *Long Shot*. By permission of the author.

Shirley Kaufman: "Apples" from *Roots in the Air* by Shirley Kaufman. © 1996 by Shirley Kaufman. Reprinted by permission of Copper Canyon Press, P.O. Box 271, Port Townsend, WA 98368.

Chris Kennedy: "Legacy" appeared in *Onthebus*. By permission of the author.

Yusef Komunyakaa: "My Father's Love Letters" from *Magic City* by Yusef Komunyakaa, Wesleyan University Press. © 1992 by Yusef Komunyakaa. By permission of University Press of New England.

Maxine Kumin: "The Riddle of Noah" from *Connecting the Dots* by Maxine Kumin. Copyright © 1996 by Maxine Kumin. Reprinted by permission of W. W. Norton & Company, Inc.

Stanley Kunitz: "The Portrait" from *Passing Through: The Later Poems New and Selected* by Stanley Kunitz. Copyright © 1971 by Stanley Kunitz. Reprinted by permission of W. W. Norton & Company, Inc.

Michael Lally: "Sports Heroes, Cops, and Lace" from *Can't Be Wrong* by Michael Lally. Copyright © 1996 by Michael Lally. Used by permission of Coffee House Press.

Philip Levine: "Those Were the Days" from *New Selected Poems* by Philip Levine, Green House Review Press, 1997. Copyright © 1997 by Philip Levine. By permission of the author. "Among

Children" from *What Work Is* by Philip Levine. Copyright © 1991 by Philip Levine. Reprinted by permission of Alfred A. Knopf, Inc.

Toni Libro: "The Last Lesson" from *The House at the Shore* by Toni Libro, Lincoln Springs Press, 1997. Copyright © A. Libro, 1997. By permission of the author.

M. L. Liebler: "Rock'n'Roll" from *Stripping the Adult Century Bare: New & Selected Works* by M. L. Liebler, Burning Cities & Viet Nam Generation, Inc. Copyright © 1995 by M. L. Liebler. By permission of the author.

Lyn Lifshin: "Yellow Roses" from *Cold Comfort* by Lyn Lifshin, Black Sparrow Press, 1997. By permission of the author.

Shirley Geok-lin Lim: "Chinese in Academia" from *Modern Secrets*, 1989. By permission of the author.

Adrian C. Louis: "Half-Breed's Song." © Copyright 1994 by Adrian C. Louis. By permission of the author.

Lee Martin: "The Welcome Table" from *The Least You Need to Know* by Lee Martin, Sarabande Books, Inc. Copyright © 1996 by Lee Martin. By permission of the author.

Linda McCarriston: "Hotel Nights with My Mother" from *Eva-Mary* by Linda McCarriston, Tri-Quarterly Books, 1991. By permission of the author.

Walt McDonald: "Uncle Earl and Guns" appeared in *Many Mountains Moving*. By permission of the author.

Nancy Mercado: "Jetties Were the Bridges I Crossed." Copyright 1997 Nancy Mercado. By permission of the author.

Tiffany Midge: "Beets" appeared in *Blue Dawn, Red Earth: New Native American Storytellers*, edited by Clifford Trafzer, Anchor Books. © 1996 by Tiffany Midge. By permission of the author.

Lenard D. Moore: "Working Class." © 1997 Lenard D. Moore. By permission of the author.

Lesléa Newman: "Right Off the Bat" from *Secrets* by Lesléa Newman, New Victoria Publishers. © 1990 Lesléa Newman. "The Politics of Buddy" from *Still Life with Buddy* by Lesléa Newman, Pride Publications. © 1997 Lesléa Newman. By permission of the author.

Margie Norris: "Graffiti" from *How Come You Don't Close Your Eyes Like the Other Girls Do?* by Margie Norris. By permission of the author.

Naomi Shihab Nye: "Linked" appeared in *English Journal*. By permission of the author.

Sharon Olds: "I Go Back to May 1937" and "On the Subway" from *The Gold Cell* by Sharon Olds. Copyright © 1987 by Sharon Olds. "The One Girl at the Boys' Party" from *The Dead and the Living* by Sharon Olds. Copyright © 1983 by Sharon Olds. Reprinted by permission of Alfred A. Knopf, Inc.

Simon J. Ortiz: "A New Story" appeared in *Fight Back: For the Sake of the People, For the Sake of the Land*. By permission of the author.

Grace Paley: "Family" from *New and Collected Poems* by Grace Paley. By permission of Tilbury House, Publishers.

Julie Parson-Nesbitt: "Strange Country" from *Finders* by Julie Parson-Nesbitt, West End Press. © Julie Parson-Nesbitt, 1996. By permission of the author.

Molly Peacock: "Our Room." By permission of the author.

Robert Phillips: "No Consolation" from *Break Down Lane* by Robert Phillips, The Johns Hopkins University Press. © 1994 Robert Phillips. By permission of the author.

Marge Piercy: "Roomers, rumors" appeared in *Verve*, Spring 1997. By permission of the author.

Leroy V. Quintana: "Sangre 24: A Legacy" and "Sangre 14: Sterling, Colorado." By permission of the author.

Rochelle Ratner: "Singing Lessons" from *Combing the Waves* by Rochelle Ratner, Hanging Loose Press. Copyright 1979 by Rochelle Ratner. By permission of the author.

Len Roberts: "The Way of the Cross" and "Acupuncture and Cleansing at Forty-eight" appeared in *The American Poetry Review*, issues of May/June 1994 and September/October 1996, respectively. "Second-Grade Angel" appeared in *The Hudson Review*, Summer 1993. By permission of the author.

Abraham Rodriguez, Jr.: "The Boy Without a Flag" from *The Boy Without a Flag: Tales of the South Bronx* by Abraham Rodriguez, Jr. Copyright © 1992 by Abraham Rodriguez, Jr. Reprinted by permission of Milkweed Editions.

Luis J. Rodríguez: "Always Running" from *The Concrete River* by Luis J. Rodríguez. Copyright 1991 by Luis J. Rodríguez. Reprinted by permission of Curbstone Press.

Tom Romano: "The Silence That Widened" from *Writing with Passion: Life Stories, Multiple Genres* by Tom Romano. Reprinted by permission of Boynton/Cook-Heinemann, a subsidiary of the Greenwood Publishing Group, Portsmouth, NH.

Liz Rosenberg: "The Story of My Life" from *The Fire Music* by Liz Rosenberg. © 1986 Liz Rosenberg. Reprinted by permission of the University of Pittsburgh Press.